BISHOP VON GALEN

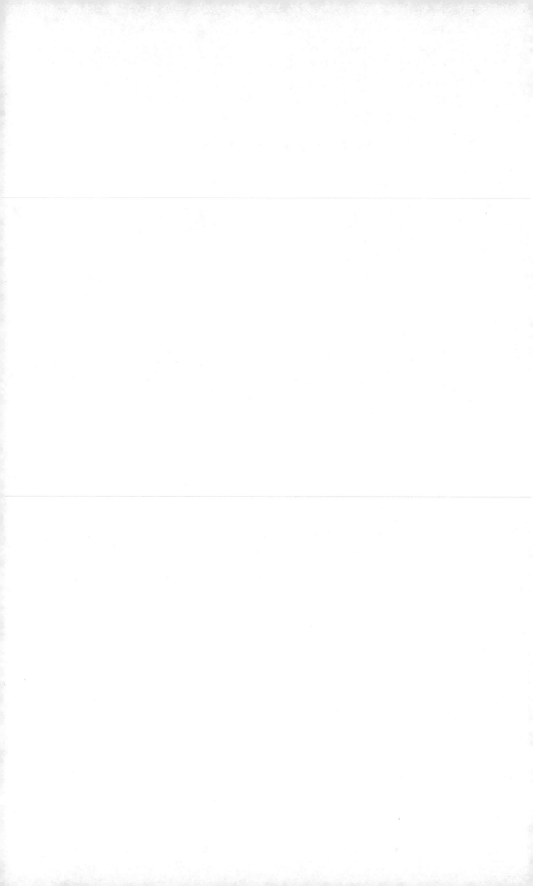

BISHOP

GERMAN CATHOLICISM AND

VON GALEN

NATIONAL SOCIALISM

✠ ✠ ✠ ✠ ✠ ✠ ✠ ✠ ✠ ✠ ✠ ✠ ✠ ✠ ✠

BETH A. GRIECH-POLELLE

Yale University Press   *New Haven & London*

Published with assistance from the foundation established in memory of Philip Hamilton McMillan of the Class of 1894, Yale College.

Designed by James J. Johnson and set in Stemple Garamond type by Tseng Information Systems, Inc.
Printed in the United States of America by Vail-Ballou Press.

Library of Congress Cataloging-in-Publication Data

Griech-Polelle, Beth A., 1964–
Bishop von Galen : German Catholicism and national socialism / Beth A. Griech-Polelle.
   p.   cm.
Includes bibliographical references and index.
ISBN 0-300-09223-7 (alk. paper)

1. Galen, Clemens August, Graf von, 1878–1946.   2. Cardinals—Germany—Biography.
I. Title.
BX4705.G12 G75   2002
282'.092—dc21   2002002410

A catalogue record for this book is available from the British Library.

The paper in this book meets the guidelines for permanence and durability of the Committee on Production Guidelines for Book Longevity of the Council on Library Resources.

10 9 8 7 6 5 4 3 2 1

These are three things that last: faith, hope, and love; and the greatest of these is love.

—1 CORINTHIANS 13:13

To my parents, my husband, and my son, who have shown me the unlimited living power of all three of these things.

Contents

Acknowledgments

I gratefully acknowledge the help, insight, and support of the following individuals, without whom this project might never have reached completion: Dorothy Amorosi, Alex Bachmann, Barbara E. Bender, Ann Callaway, Lois Crum, Belinda Davis, Ziva Galili, Susannah Heschel, Sirkka Kyle, Linda Lasko, Jay Marquart, Cynthia and Robert McCleery, G. Kurt Piehler, Barbara Pleva, Michael Polelle, Linda G. Schulze, Lynn Shanko, Carol Singer, Barbara Sirman, and Harvey Waterman.

I would also like to thank Professor John A. Lukacs, without whom I might never have even considered attending graduate school, and who instilled in all of his students a love of history.

Lastly, I would especially like to offer my gratitude to Professor Omer Bartov, who, I believe, embodies all of the best and finest qualities a mentor should have.

BISHOP VON GALEN

Introduction

Resist evil and conquer it with good.

—ROMANS 12:21

In January 1937 several German Catholic cardinals and bishops, including Bishop Clemens August Graf von Galen, traveled to Rome to ask Pope Pius XI to issue a public statement about the perils faced by Catholics in Nazi Germany. The German clergymen drafted what later came to be known as the papal encyclical *Mit brennender Sorge*. The encyclical, focusing primarily on the ideological errors of National Socialism, contained no outright condemnation of anti-Semitism, nor did it endorse Catholic participation in an open rebellion against the government. The advice given to Catholics, in general, was to shun unjust laws —advice essentially recommending passive disobedience on particular issues, leaving it up to each individual's conscience to decide which laws were unjust and how one should resist them.

When the German bishops and cardinals met at Fulda following the publication of *Mit brennender Sorge,* two factions emerged: Bishop von Galen favored public protests against some aspects of Nazi ideology, and Cardinal Adolf Bertram led a faction that feared any direct confrontation with the government.[1] Bertram, as leader of the Fulda Conference, claimed that direct opposition would result in another Kulturkampf (a struggle between Bismarck's government and the Catholic Church in Germany in the 1870s) and asked that the clergymen agree to present a united front to the public. As a result, the men agreed not to reveal any discord in public, and they "adopted a position that would be least offensive to them all."[2]

Von Galen has historically been portrayed as a staunch anti-Nazi resister, primarily because of three powerful sermons he delivered in the

summer of 1941. However, von Galen's "resistance" merits closer examination and debate. Why did von Galen choose to object to certain policies and not others? How does von Galen differ from the other church
leaders of the Nazi era, and where do their views coincide? How can we
place his choices in the broader context of church-state relations in the
1930s and 1940s? And where does von Galen fit in the debates over the
varied definitions of resistance?

In the aftermath of World War II, the Catholic Church made no declaration of guilt concerning its position toward the National Socialist
regime. When von Galen was raised to the purple in 1946, that drew attention once again to the various forms of resistance exercised by Catholic clergy during the Hitlerzeit.[3] Books covering the opposition of the
church had begun to appear even before the war was over; they portrayed the church as the natural and great opponent of the ideology of
National Socialism. Ecclesiastical historians such as Bishop Johann Neuhäusler and Nathaniel Micklem used evidence concerning Hitler's antichurch policy to integrate church figures into the pantheon of German
resisters. Neuhäusler and Micklem were representative of the immediate postwar trend of historians who sought to prove that there had indeed been resistance to National Socialism, even in Germany, and that
the theory of collective guilt could not be applied so handily against all
Germans. These early writers of the 1940s and 1950s tended to focus on
groups such as the July 20, 1944, conspirators, the activities of the bour-
geoisie, and other leading military and church figures who had been directly involved in political threats to the Nazi regime.[4] The majority of
these works tended to monumentalize the members of resistance groups,
leaving the impression that these figures were indeed larger than life.
Church historians of the 1960s and 1970s were encouraged to
examine the church's role under National Socialism because of such
pioneering articles as Hans Mommsen's "Gesellschaftsbild und Verfas-
sungspläne des deutschen Widerstandes" and Hermann Graml's "Die
aussenpolitischen Vorstellungen des deutschen Widerstandes." Both
men's studies questioned the motivations of the resistance fighters, connecting them with national-conservative ideals rather than with the
liberal-democratic leanings earlier attributed to them. Church historians began to write about a perceived lack of resistance on the part of the
Catholic hierarchy. Authors such as John S. Conway, Günther Lewy,
Hans Müller, and Gordon Zahn focused on the general failure of the

church leaders to exert moral or political leadership that might have inspired others to work to lessen the impact of National Socialism.[5]

Pathbreaking works such as Kurt Nowak's 1978 study of the relationship between the churches and euthanasia seriously questioned whether
resistance did exist in the churches of Germany.[6] Ernst Christian Helmreich's 1979 study extended beyond the confines of the euthanasia question, examined both the Protestant and Catholic churches in Germany,
and suggested that the Catholic Church hierarchy, in order to present a
united front to the public, mixed protests of certain Nazi policies with
continuous assertions of loyalty and obedience to the state, which resulted in confusion among their Catholic followers. He argued that most
of the bishops and cardinals in Germany decided to combine circumscribed opposition with assurances of patriotism, rationalizing their inaction by stating that they could criticize the specific government in authority while still supporting the idea of the German state. Their failure
to act decisively—coupled with their inability to perceive the impact of
Hitler's racial policy on the state—deprived the church of moral prestige
that it would have had if it had worked to mobilize the limited pockets
of resistance that did originally exist in Germany. Helmreich's argument, elaborated on in the 1980s by Donald J. Dietrich, questioned why
the Catholic bishops did not condemn Nazi policies more forcefully (if
at all), why resistance was not better mobilized, and whether German
Catholics would have given their support to bishops if the clergymen
had attacked what was seen by many to be a legitimate regime.[7]

The emphasis on social history since the 1970s has led to numerous works that range from studies of early Communist resistance to the
study of ordinary, nonpolitical citizens who refused to allow the total
penetration of National Socialism into their daily lives.[8] Throughout all
of these studies, what has come to be called the Bavaria Project highlights
the changing definitions of resistance.

Begun in 1973 by the Institute of Contemporary History in Munich,
the project originally focused on persecution and resistance specific to
Bavaria. The project's first director, Peter Hüttenberger, widened the
definition of resistance to include limited and partial acts of resistance.
Resistance was defined as behavior that threatened the aim of total control over individuals in society. Hüttenberger was soon replaced as director by Martin Broszat. Broszat's leadership over the Bavaria Project
brought with it the use of additional categories, in the attempt to further
refine the definition of resistance. Broszat had his share of detractors,

but he had broadened the notion of acts of resistance under a totalitarian system.[9]

In 1984 Ulrich von Hehl published a work, *Priester unter Hitlers Terror: Eine biographische und statistische Erhebung im Auftrage der Deutschen Bischofskonferenz,* which defined resistance fighters as those who had offered political resistance and who were subjected to persecution by the regime. Von Galen's name, noticeably, did not appear in Hehl's work. Joachim Kuropka, a noted scholar on Bishop von Galen, took issue with Hehl for his omission of von Galen's name from the roll call of resistance fighters. Kuropka took up the issue again in another essay, which appeared in *Clemens August Graf von Galen: Neue Forschungen zum Leben und Wirken des Bischofs von Münster,*[10] arguing that Hehl was incorrect in his assessment. Kuropka's articles supported Hüttenberger's definition of resistance, by claiming that von Galen was a resister because he was so viewed by the Nazi government. The edited volume in which Kuropka's work appeared, published in 1992, proved that von Galen's postwar image as a Resister with a capital *R* was still intact.

My research on von Galen and the question of resistance has been influenced by many of these learned scholars. However, I focus my assessment of von Galen as a resister according to the approaches developed by both Michael Geyer and Claudia Koonz. In Geyer's essay, "Resistance as Ongoing Project: Visions of Order, Obligations to Strangers, and Struggles for Civil Society, 1933–1990," he argued that historians should evaluate resisters in light of their ability to mobilize public opinion in such a way as to build solidarity where little or none had previously existed.[11] This idea seemed to add what was missing for me in many of the other concepts of resistance, because it had a moral imperative that struck me as particularly appropriate when assessing the role of a Catholic clergyman. Did von Galen recognize the urgent need to form a union with other persecuted minorities, or did he choose to oppose Nazi policies only when they collided with narrowly defined Catholic Church interests?

What began to emerge, as I thought more about the bishop's role under National Socialism, was something closer to what Claudia Koonz has referred to as "single-issue dissent," although in von Galen's case, I would alter the phrase slightly to "selective opposition."[12] As in the individual cases presented by Koonz, von Galen opposed certain Nazi policies vehemently, yet he remained in an overall sense loyal to the Nazi state. The ability to criticize selective topics eased the sense of oppression but did little to actually lessen the hold of National Socialism in a political sense. Unlike authors such as Joachim Kuropka, I do not believe that von Galen can be labeled a resister simply because other people subjectively believed him to be. It seems to me that such an application would lessen the sacrifices made by individuals who risked much more to defeat Nazism.

In this work von Galen emerges as an individual who practiced selective opposition within the rubric of overall support and accommodation to the Third Reich; that is, he supported anti-Bolshevism and German nationalist aims. His public speaking, which often combined patriotic exhortations with moments of rhetorical resistance, did not challenge the Catholics of Münster to meaningfully resist the regime; it merely tended to confuse them as he admonished them to limited instances of passive disobedience on specific issues. Von Galen's life can serve as an example not of the "Grand Churchman-Resister" but rather of an all-too-human individual of great public importance who represented the "typical" high-ranking Catholic cleric of the time, one who mixed some dissent with conformity, accommodation, and surrender to the regime in order to square the circle of loyalty to Germany under Nazi rule and loyalty to God.

This study explores aspects of von Galen's world that I believe have been neglected by or underplayed in other recent publications.[13] I briefly examine von Galen's early life to understand the variety of influences that later structured his responses to the Nazi regime. I also explore the Catholic background of theological justifications for revolution and resistance with which von Galen would have been familiar. Moreover, I connect von Galen's position in the Third Reich with the impact that the Kulturkampf of the 1870s had on German Catholics of the 1930s and 1940s. The lasting memory of the Kulturkampf, I argue, played a significant part in keeping von Galen from engaging in resistance against the state authorities. This connection has generally been omitted from current work appearing on von Galen. This is unfortunate, because we must understand resistance in Nazi Germany more generally based on the cultural resources and historical memories possessed by those we describe today as resisters. I also reexamine, in detail, the events of the summer of 1941 and the sermons that gave von Galen instant notoriety as an anti-Nazi resister. Unlike most scholars, who do not question the timing of von Galen's denunciations or his involvement with Protestants in the matter of euthanasia, I believe the three sermons of 1941 do not reveal an out-and-out proponent of anti-Nazi resistance. Instead, I argue that, as forthright as they were, they embraced passive disobedience to only select aspects of the Nazi state.

Furthermore, I examine von Galen's position on Judaism and Bolshevism. There have been studies that seek to evaluate von Galen's portrayal of Judaism, but the connection to Bolshevism and other "isms" are distinctly de-emphasized.[14] As von Galen was an ardent anti-Bolshevik until the day he died, I believe a reexamination of his views is appropriate. Finally, I address how I believe von Galen's image as churchman-resister was constructed after the war: I attempt to show how various events and historiography have frequently reinforced the notion that von Galen was a tireless fighter, not simply for the rights of German Catholics, but for all humanity.

For my primary sources on von Galen, I am chiefly indebted to the work of archivist Peter Löffler of the Bistumsarchiv in Münster, where I spent the majority of my time when I was in Germany. I also examined the resources of the Nordrhein-Westfälisches Staatsarchiv Münster and the Bundesarchiv Koblenz. A large portion of Bishop von Galen's sermons and correspondence was destroyed in fires following the heavy aerial bombardment of Münster, first in the fall of 1943 and then again in the fall of 1944. Löffler's two-volume collection, *Bischof Clemens August Graf von Galen: Akten, Briefe und Predigten* (Mainz, 1988) is part of the series Veröffentlichungen der Kommission für Zeitgeschichte; it is designated series A, volume 42. Although a few letters from the time period 1933–1946 have evaded Löffler's collection, the volumes represent the most comprehensive culling of still-extant correspondence to date. Therefore, I use Löffler's work as a major part of my primary source base.

For many Catholics in Germany, the memory of the Kulturkampf, the desire to prove that Catholics could be loyal (and not the *Reichsfeinde* that Bismarck had branded them as), combined with a longing to be accepted and no longer considered a minority in Germany, led many church leaders to emphasize that Catholics should be law-abiding citizens. Most did not question whether Hitler's war was a "just" one; rather they embraced nationalism, urging Catholics to prove that they too were German to the core. As for the anti-Semitic policies of Nazism, the bishops tended to call for a lessening of persecution of converted Jews. It was not until much later in the war that some individual clergymen protested the mistreatment of Jews; by then it was too late to effectively stop the process of the Final Solution.

There were, obviously, Catholic individuals such as Pastor Bernhard Lichtenberg and Father Alfred Delp, who recognized the evil inherent in Nazism. But as an entity, the church leadership chose to focus on maintaining or saving Catholic institutional structures on German soil while losing sight of the larger, ultimate, and more humane questions involved. Narrowing their protests to strictly "religious questions," they implied that governments rose and fell, but the church was to be eternal in its existence on German soil if not universal in its concerns. *Religious* came to mean not supporting the universal values of brotherly love and equality but rather keeping Catholic confessional schools, organizations, and associations alive. In the end it was this focus on the tactical, short-term needs of the church, rather than on the long-term moral legacy, that opens the church and von Galen to the severest critique. In short, the tragedy I focus on is how little of the immense cultural and spiritual capital of the church was risked in combating a fundamentally anti-Christian regime.

CHAPTER ONE

Von Galen's Early Life

You must all obey the governing authorities. Since all government comes from God, the civil authorities were appointed by God, and so anyone who resists authority is rebelling against God's decision, and such an act is bound to be punished. . . . The State is there to serve God for your benefit. . . . The authorities are there to serve God. . . . You must obey.

—ROMANS 13:1-5

In May 1941 Bishop Clemens August Graf von Galen was performing confirmations in Oldenburg. As he and his private chaplain approached the Castle Dinklage in their car, von Galen became very animated. Pointing to a window in the castle, he remarked, "That was the bedroom of my dear parents; there I was born on the 16th March 1878."[1]

Clemens August was the eleventh of thirteen children. His parents, known for their deep piety, were Count Ferdinand Heribert von Galen and Countess Elisabeth, née von Spee. The von Galen name had long been associated with the Oldenburg-Münsterland region; the von Galens had been there since 1667, when Christoph Bernhard von Galen was named the first bishop of Münster after putting down the Anabaptists, leaving the bodies of the "heretics" to rot in cages lining the city's gates.

"Clau," as the young count was affectionately called, led a lifestyle marked by spartan simplicity and rigorous Catholicism that was going to continue throughout his life. Castle Dinklage had no running water, no heat in the majority of its rooms, and no indoor bathrooms. The family lived, so to speak, close to nature. The family also made the practice of religion a daily presence in their lives. Years later, when von Galen wrote to his father saying how much he appreciated the Catholic values instilled in him as a child, he reflected, "As a child I never saw a bad

example or an occasion of sin in my beloved home, but rather only unshakably strong belief, true Catholic life and inner love of the Church."[2]

Each morning the von Galen family and their servants were required
by Ferdinand Heribert to attend chapel. Any child who missed mass received no breakfast. Arriving late to mass meant no butter on the morning bread.[3] Every evening ended with von Galen's father reciting the
rosary and saying a long evening prayer. Ferdinand, who encouraged his
sons to play with the other children of the region, go horseback riding,
and hunt, also played a significant role in influencing his sons' ideas concerning religion and its relationship to the state.

To more fully understand von Galen's attitude toward Hitler's regime, it is helpful to explore his conception of the ideal German state,
the ideal German citizen, and the church's relationship to both state and
citizen, all of which were heavily influenced by his father's beliefs.

Notions of State and Citizenship

When von Galen began to think about the role that morality could play
in politics, he could draw on a long family tradition. Ferdinand had been
deeply influenced by his uncle, Wilhelm Emmanuel von Ketteler, the
"working bishop" of Mainz, and Ferdinand transmitted his ideas to his
son. Ketteler (1811-1877), with whom Ferdinand had lived for a time, became one of the most influential Catholic authors on questions of German national identity. As bishop of Mainz, Ketteler used his position
to address the dominant social questions of the day. He argued that the
church must aid the working class in the fight against unchecked capitalism. Because of this, he established unions and cooperatives for workers;
he promoted legislation against child labor and for factory inspection.
Seeking an alternative to liberalism and socialism, Ketteler tried to shift
the church's focus from charity to social engagement.[4] He promoted
the freedom and rights of Catholics in particular and a "program for
all believing Christians . . . in Germany." Ketteler, like Johann Fichte
and Friedrich Jahn, believed that the newly unified German state should
be grounded in Christian principles. His conception of the ideal state
harked back to medieval times, when Germany ruled the Holy Roman
Empire (and when no Protestants existed in Germany).[5] In a pamphlet
in 1866, Ketteler reiterated his idea that freedom of conscience came only
through a society organized into feudal estates. He favored a paternalis-

tic, quasi-medieval universalism, but he argued that in order for Catholics to attain more power in Germany, they had to embrace the national and military objectives of Wilhelmine society.[6] He acknowledged that German society was dominated by Protestants and stated that behaving in an intolerant fashion toward them would only impede Catholic integration into the national community. He expressed the sentiment that Catholics could be just as loyal as Protestants: "We too are German in word and deed, we are true to Kaiser and Reich, we think and feel German. . . . We do not have to betray our religion in order to be patriots." Underlying this notion that Catholics and Protestants were equals in German citizenship was the idea that others, such as Jews and liberals, were not equal in status. "The German Catholic vision of a Christian state could be conceived as marginalizing Jews or Social Democrats but not Württemberg Pietists or Silesian Lutherans." In Ketteler's conception of the state, Christians would rule together against the forces of liberalism, socialism, capitalism, and, behind these forces of modernism, the Jews.

Ketteler's program of "social Catholicism" had been embraced by von Galen's father, Ferdinand. The elder von Galen attempted to translate the sociopolitical ideas of Ketteler into practical legislation while serving in the Prussian Parliament. He passed on his ideas of the "Christian social" program to his son Clemens August. Part of this ideological inheritance included the belief that Germany must be, above all, a Christian state.

So how did Clemens August envision his society? The best indication is his 1932 writing, *Die Pest des Laizismus und ihre Erscheinungsformen*, which was based on many of the ideas contained in Pope Pius XI's 1925 encyclical *Königtum Christi*. Von Galen denounced the secularization of a society that had divorced itself from God and the Commandments. He lamented the unraveling of religion and life and, like Ketteler, recalled medieval times when religion and life were intertwined. In von Galen's opinion, the modern world was fighting an epidemic in which public life was being corrupted by original sin and a love of materialism. He cited 1 John 2:16: "What does the world offer? Only gratification of corrupt nature, gratification of the eyes; the empty pomp of living; these things take their being from the world, and not from the Father." He ended with the warning that Catholics must be vigilant and not yield to secularization, or else the very foundation of Christianity would be destroyed.[7]

Von Galen feared the loss of Catholic Christian values in an increasingly modern world. He was against liberalism, individualism, socialism, and democracy. He thought these "isms" were destroying belief in the Christian God. He wanted hierarchy, ritual, and a foundation firmly rooted in Catholic Christianity.[8] Unfortunately, as we shall see, the Nazis seemed to offer a version of this.[9] Von Galen relied on the teachings of his father and his father's uncle as well as the education he received at various Jesuit institutions, all of which reinforced the notion that Catholics could survive best if they were obedient to the state. Reinforcing this reliance on obedience was the belief that "every human authority is a reflection of divine rule and is a participation in the eternal authority of God."[10] Thus the religious *Führerprinzip* coincided with the Nazis' secular *Führerprinzip*. Von Galen remembered that, from his earliest days, his father was concerned with the structure of the modern world. From Ferdinand, "Clau" learned that owing to original sin there was no such thing as a "Paradise on earth."[11] Living such a strict life with no "amenities" such as heat would certainly have highlighted that view.

Denying the modern, liberal world, Ferdinand pursued a "Christian social" program, which included legislation to restrict work for women and children and improve working conditions for factory workers. In the early days of his marriage, he visited the poor, bringing relief, until he realized that his presence made the recipients of his aid uncomfortable. After that, he passed his visitation duties to his wife, Elisabeth. She and her daughters made and delivered clothing for the needy.[12]

Elisabeth also played a central role in the young Clau's religious development. It was her obligation to instruct her children in their catechism and to prepare them for their first confession. She, like Ferdinand, tried to show the children that religious beliefs could be incorporated into daily living. She visited the poor and the ill, she made clothing for the less fortunate, and she heard petitions daily from the suffering of the community. Most of their petitions for aid were answered. For Clemens August, his mother's religious instruction never ended. She and he corresponded until her death in 1920.

Both Elisabeth and Ferdinand tried to instill in all of their children a sense of duty, self-discipline, punctuality, order, and diligence. Punishments were rare, but a severe reproof from Count Ferdinand was enough. No entreaties on the children's part were accepted. They had been taught that the family was a microcosm of God's universe and that to maintain the proper order of things meant to obey and honor their parents the same way they would be expected to obey and honor God. At the same time, throughout their upbringing, the von Galen children were taught to maintain their own convictions and inner strength. Unquestioning submission, particularly when it violated one's conscience, was not a von Galen characteristic. As an adult, Clemens August remembered the painful surprise in his parents' home when Pope Leo XIII, in 1885, bestowed the Order of Christ on Otto von Bismarck. This event was especially shocking because average German Catholics, along with many of their spiritual leaders, believed that Bismarck had been the instigator of the Kulturkampf. After that incident, the children were told that although obedience was a principle of order, no one should comply with false instructions. One's conscience set the boundaries.[13]

Despite the rigors of living in a stern, spartan atmosphere, von Galen remembered his childhood quite fondly. Years later, when reminiscing, he continually remarked about how ideal his parents' home had been.[14]

Education

Until 1890 Clemens August and his brother Franz (nicknamed "Strick") were tutored together at home. After making their first communion in Oldenburg, the two brothers were sent to a Jesuit Latin School, Stella Matutina, in Feldkirch in the Vorarlberg. Not much has been reported about the Jesuits at this school, but the lasting impact of the Kulturkampf in Prussian territory is evident, for Jesuits were not permitted in Münster at this time. Anti-Jesuit legislation made it necessary for the boys to leave their family and their state in order to receive a Jesuit education.

Likewise, in 1894, because of state regulations, the two boys returned home to attend a public school in Vechta, approximately ten kilometers outside of Oldenburg. The Stella Matutina academy was not recognized by the Prussian government because it was a Jesuit school. Two years after their return to the Oldenburg region, both von Galen boys passed the examinations that qualified them to attend a university.

By 1896 Clau and Strick went to Switzerland to study at the Catholic University of Freiburg, which had been established in 1886 by the order of the Dominicans. At the time of its founding, it was known for its young professors and its militant Catholicism. But by 1896, as the Kulturkampf was winding down, the faculty preferred to assume a more defensive position of simply holding firmly to their faith.[15] This defensive posture held its lessons for von Galen under the Nazi regime.

At Freiburg von Galen was exposed to the writings of Saint Thomas

Aquinas. The teachings of the university served to reinforce the earlier education he had received from his father, namely, that all power comes from God and that no society deriving its power from human authority alone can be tolerated.

Following the first winter semester at Freiburg, Clemens August and Franz went on an extended visit to Rome. An elder brother, Friedrich, guided his siblings around the city for three months.[16] At the end of this visit, Clemens August confided to Franz that he had decided to become a priest. The only remaining question in his mind was whether to become a Benedictine, leading the life of a contemplative priest, or a Jesuit, playing a more active role in society.

After completing a year of studies at Freiburg, Clemens August acted on his earlier decision and transferred to the Theological Faculty and Convent at Innsbruck. The school at Innsbruck was founded in 1669 by the Jesuits. Its program stressed support and understanding of different nations and various cultures. The rule of the university commanded community life, understanding, and tolerance. All levels of society were present at the school, from conservative aristocrats to middle- and lower-level scholarship students. Students were told that they would and must learn from one another because that was the only way to understand current social problems.[17]

At Innsbruck von Galen stood out among his peers—and not only because he had grown to the imperious height of six feet seven inches. His constant striving to fulfill Christian ideals inspired people and led him to become a mediator between the college teachers and the student body. As for studies, von Galen was not interested and did not excel in areas of abstract theories. Referring to his studies, he once remarked, "Thank God that I will never become a professor!" Instead, von Galen preferred to focus on practical things such as church-state relations: the state and the family, the state and science, the state and education. As his studies in social problems, moral theology, and sociology progressed, he reinforced his earlier training from his father and from his Stella Matutina days, resolving that "nothing but a society resting on God can produce tolerable social conditions: there can be no Paradise on earth."[18]

Von Galen's concern for the dangers Catholics faced when trying to live out their ideals in everyday public life appeared in an article he wrote for the school newsletter. The newsletter, which appeared quarterly, had originally been used by the seminarians during the Kulturkampf as a way of reporting state persecution, ill treatment, and arrests of priests. Von

Galen's contribution was an article about what he perceived to be a two-pronged threat to Catholicism. On the one hand, Catholics had to deal with the outer threat of the Kulturkampf. On the other hand, Galen contended, Catholics had to deal with modernism as a threat to their individual souls.[19] His viewpoint comes as no surprise, because Innsbruck emphasized scholastic philosophy and avoidance of new concepts and new ideas. Aquinas's theory of natural law was taught at Innsbruck as the only possible foundation for a truly modern Christian society. As democratic societies placed increased emphasis on power coming from the people, Aquinas's notion that all power comes from God seemed to weaken.

Two faculty members at Innsbruck, Hieronymus Noldin and Michael Hofmann, greatly influenced von Galen's outlook. Noldin's famous three-volume work *Summa theologiae moralis* was a handbook for ministers and father confessors based on the Ten Commandments and the Seven Sacraments. Von Galen praised his teacher's book because it dealt with practical issues and not simply theory. Hofmann likewise received praise in von Galen's letters to Franz for being practical when teaching and in his relationship with his students. In one letter Clemens August wrote to Franz of Hofmann, "He is an uncommonly superb man, a 'saint,' and at the same time he is very practical and sensible, suitably strict but fair."[20]

Letters to his parents confirmed that von Galen preferred solid, concrete topics rather than theoretical matters. When he wrote home to Dinklage, he revealed interests in such political issues of the day as Center Party politics and the question of Jesuits returning to Prussia, as well as church politics in general. In 1903 von Galen left Innsbruck to enter the seminary in Münster. On May 28, 1904, he was ordained a priest.

Throughout his formal educational instruction, von Galen was deeply influenced by his parents and his Jesuit instructors and their experiences with the Kulturkampf: "From now on, the experience of the Kulturkampf imprinted von Galen's political outlook because it implanted in him a foundation of mistrust towards state regulations. Galen combined his political leanings with his pastoral activities and continued as a priest to look after the 'other worldly' and secular welfare of his fellow human beings. Also as a priest he regarded it as part of his duty to continue to keep Catholic principles in public life."[21]

The principles of Aquinas and natural law, taught to von Galen by his father and the Jesuits, combined with their experiences with Kultur-

kampf legislation, colored the young priest's perception of the relationship between citizen and state, particularly in the area of religious freedom. The system of natural law obviously put von Galen at odds with
many principles of National Socialism, but it also made him question the
modernism and secularization of Germany at the turn of the century.

The Berlin Years

After serving for two years in Münster under his uncle, Suffragan-bishop
Max Gereon, von Galen was sent to Germany's capital. He arrived in
Berlin on April 23, 1906, and stayed there until April 16, 1929. It was the
longest time that von Galen spent in one place in his entire life. After
receiving word of his transfer to Berlin in 1906, von Galen noted the biblical phrase "I send you as a lamb among wolves." The newly transferred
priest was not unusual in his appraisal of the religious atmosphere of Berlin. One parish helper, after visiting more than three hundred people in
his parish, remarked: "One has the feeling . . . of working among a people
who know nothing of Christianity, and it has been suggested that a 'Society for Missions to the Heathen' is needed in the national capital."[22]

For the next twenty-three years, von Galen continually expressed
homesickness for the rural landscape of Münster and its outlying regions. The Berlin that von Galen saw had become a booming commercial
and cultural metropolis.[23] It had experienced a population explosion, increasing from 900,000 in 1871 to slightly less than 4 million by 1920. By
the end of the nineteenth century, Berlin was ranked fourth in size in
the world and was continuing to expand. It contained districts of Protestant elites, a Catholic community composed of primarily working-class
people, and a Jewish community of both middle-class and poorer immi-
grants.[24]

In a city this endlessly complex, religion did not bring the community together. In fact, religion and fears of a loss of religious belief came
to be a major source of internal division.[25] Contributing to the distinctive diversity of the city, religion became associated with the identity of
the various social classes in the metropolis. For the aristocracy, the army,
and the civil service, Protestantism reigned supreme. For the business
and professional classes, a hoped-for liberalism was a source of strength.
For the working class, Catholicism and Social Democracy vied for their
allegiance, with the latter more successful than the former.[26]

In this Berlin, von Galen tried to be an energetic and idealistic leader of his parish. He was placed as Curatus of Clemens-Hofbauer Church, where he attempted to live according to Catholic Christian principles. Remembering the foundations of his family life at Dinklage, von Galen wanted to be an example for his community. He preferred the traditional roles of the priest, so he made daily visits to the sick and poor, gave his own money to families in need, contributed to the parish newsletter, became president of the Catholic Young Men's Association, gave religious instruction in the schools, and raised money to build a proper structure for the young men's union meetings and activities. He also organized an aid society in which community members listed how they could help others in need with money or by providing goods and services. Then von Galen coordinated the list and put community members into service.

These types of services and unions were important, because the problem most frequently voiced by Catholics in Berlin at this time was "that of maintaining Catholic identity in an environment dominated by Protestantism and Social Democracy." By maintaining a wide range of facilities—hospitals, orphanages, and hostels—Catholics thought of themselves as a socially cohesive group despite the diversity of the city. The Catholic youth clubs, the associations for workers, the friendly societies, and the schools all contributed to the establishment of a Catholic subculture in which clergymen were generally recognized as leaders.[27]

Accounts of von Galen at this time describe him as a commanding presence because of the lifestyle he led. His rooms were furnished simply, he wore unpretentious clothing, and he spoke plainly so that his parishioners could understand him. He did not like the theater, secular music (except for military marches), or literature. He never read novels, preferring historical works. He never invited nobles to his table; he restricted his company to other priests or to the poor of his community, "and so he became the father of the poor." His only reported vice, which he refused to give up, was smoking his pipes. In his community of approximately thirty thousand, von Galen tried to re-create the close-knit family atmosphere of Castle Dinklage. For his efforts, he was named "Papa Galen" by the parishioners he served.[28]

Throughout his time in Berlin, von Galen wrote articles on various questions of the day. One of the most important issues at that time had to do with the outbreak of the First World War. Von Galen's position seems to be typical of many Catholics in Germany; they wished to serve in order to prove that they could be just as loyal as German Protestants.

As parish priest, von Galen encouraged his parishioners to serve their country willingly. He himself volunteered to serve in order to demonstrate his loyalty to the Kaiser, but he also wanted to go because he was loath to ask his parishioners to do something that he would not do himself. "I encouraged them, each who was able, to serve the Fatherland.... I have done this [volunteered] because I believe I must be a good example for my community."[29] Von Galen's attempt at service on the front lines was denied, however, because there were already so many willing recruits.[30]

During the war, von Galen was in charge of his community house, which had a military hospital for two hundred wounded soldiers. He also kept in contact with his male parishioners by sending circular letters to the front, letting the men know about the activities of the association. In August 1917 von Galen made a visit to the front lines in France. After witnessing the situation there, he remarked that the experience had been terrible yet also uplifting in regard to the optimistic disposition of the troops.[31] Feelings of German nationalism, apparently, could triumph over concern for the violations of the sanctity of human life in war.

Nowhere is von Galen's nationalism more apparent at this time period than when, in 1916 and 1917, he reacted to two reports concerning the German military's planned colonization of Eastern Europe. After reading the reports, he welcomed the plan of occupation and then went on to expand on this theme. In his article he stated that placing troops in Eastern Europe would not be enough. Rather, he wrote, German Catholics should be moved into the area, especially in Lithuania, in order to colonize there. He continued to hold his belief that Germans should expand into Eastern Europe even after the Second World War had ended. In 1946 he complained bitterly about the fate of ethnic Germans, expelled from the "newly-created" territories in Poland.[32]

His goal was not to expel or eradicate the Letts and the Lithuanians entirely, but rather to educate them to "think" and "feel" as Germans. He believed that German Catholic nobles should go to these conquered territories in order to teach their new countrymen what it meant to be German. In von Galen's plan, German Catholic families would settle in Lithuania, do the "creative" work, put down roots of their own, and give allocations to the neighboring Lithuanian families.[33]

He had, to put it generously, an overly idealized concept of the Catholic nobility—inherited from his father and mother—that was founded on the anachronistic belief that nobles had a sacred duty to behave without self-interest, that they should act out of consideration for the good of the community, that they should be honest and use the Ten Commandments as their guiding principles. Von Galen's idea of how a Catholic nobleman should behave is embodied in a nine-page letter he wrote to his nephew Bernhard, on the young man's twenty-first birthday. In it he described the difficulties rich men have in getting into heaven. He then exhorted his nephew to perform good works, such as helping the poor, looking for the best interests of the community over individual concerns, and so forth. He urged him to keep Dinklage traditions alive and to live as a true Catholic nobleman in genuine fellowship with the people of Dinklage. He also believed that one had the right to fend off infringements of one's own rights, particularly in matters of conscience.[34] The tension between individual rights and the interests of the community naturally rose again for von Galen with the Nazi Machtergreifung.

Following the German surrender in November 1918, von Galen, still in Berlin, stood amid a great storm of political upheaval. He dreaded the loss of the monarchy. He worried about the poor: he not only believed them to be destitute and uprooted by the war experience, but he also feared that they would embrace radicalism and anarchy. To deal with the immediate problems of homelessness, hunger, and poverty, he worked unceasingly to create soup kitchens, aid societies, and clothing drives.[35]

For the destitute of spirit, von Galen tried to enforce "old" moral values, as he firmly believed that declining authority was intimately tied to the decline in morals.[36] Von Galen was not alone in his opinions. "In particular, the apparent irreligion or religious apathy of large sections of the working class was a matter of concern to the churches, and there were suggestions that a more general decline of the churches . . . was underway."[37] Von Galen, for his part, would tolerate no criticism of the Catholic Church or of its leadership. Once while he was out on a walk, a companion criticized the popes of the Middle Ages. The critical remarks spurred von Galen into a rage. Heinrich Portmann noted that von Galen "was a true son of the Church" because he would permit no criticism of the Holy Father.[38] This was true for the rest of von Galen's life. It also had tremendous implications for him once Eugenio Pacelli became pope in 1939.

As old values continued to decline, von Galen perceived a similar decline in belief in God and the church. When he enforced a bishop's decree concerning women's clothing, he offended two "good" families by refusing their daughters communion because of the way they were dressed.[39] Small incidents such as this were symbolic to von Galen of the larger loss of century-old values.

He remained suspicious of the new Weimar democracy of post–World War I Germany. In his opinion, "the revolutionary ideas of 1918 had caused considerable damage to Catholic Christianity."[40] He believed this in part because of his Jesuit training in the teachings of Thomas Aquinas, which had left him with the firm conviction that no state could survive without the benefit of divine authority. He also believed that the upheavals following the war set the stage for further godlessness in society.

In 1945 von Galen submitted a notice to the occupying authorities listing topics to be explored in a discussion. On the list he made it clear that he believed the British were again attempting to force democracy on Germany. He also argued, "Democracy brought us misfortune before 1933. Democracy brought Hitler to power. Democracy will now bring Communism." To von Galen, if a government rested on purely human foundations, it would be fragile. It is odd that von Galen believed he could not fully support the Weimar Republic because of its democratic basis, yet he believed he owed obedience to the Nazi state, even taking the oath of loyalty to it as a bishop.[41]

Throughout the Weimar years, von Galen remained on the extreme right of German politics. He often criticized the Catholic Center Party for being oriented too far to the left. He believed the Dolchstosslegende explained the German Army's defeat in 1918—that Germany had been destroyed by "defeatist" elements on the home front. In an article published on the "war guilt question," von Galen defended Germany and laid the blame of guilt on home-front weakness.[42] He deplored the disappearance of the monarchy and "was opposed to all revolution."[43]

Between 1918 and 1933 von Galen became increasingly involved in the antirepublican disputes taking place among the Catholic nobles of the Rhenish-Westphalian region. Traditionally, Catholic nobles from this region had lent their support to the Catholic Center Party. However, after the war ended, many of the Catholic aristocrats distanced themselves from the Center Party and its involvement with the Weimar Republic. In particular, some members of the Catholic ruling class became so distressed over the liberal-democratic leanings of the post–World War I Center Party that they argued for the need to create a second Catholic political party. The most vocal proponents of this idea in the Rhenish-Westphalian region were brothers, Barons Hermann and Ferdinand von

Lüninck, both of whom said this second political party was necessary to represent conservative cultural and Catholic religious values.[44]

The question of a second Catholic political party's existence dominated the debates of the Rhenish-Westphalian Association of Catholic Nobility throughout the 1920s and early 1930s. This bitter struggle directly involved Clemens August and his closest brother, Franz. At precisely the same moment that the Lüninck faction was arguing against any type of accommodation with the Weimar "system," Franz von Galen was elected chairman of the association. Hoping to steer a middle course, the new chairman offered to reaffirm traditional, conservative Catholic values while simultaneously revealing his "antipathy towards Germany's new republican order." Franz's position as leader of the Rhenish-Westphalian Association of Catholic Nobility was continuously challenged by other Catholic nobles, who were being urged on by the Lüninck brothers. Franz von Galen resigned his position as chairman and terminated his association membership in 1928.[45]

By the early 1930s the Lüninck faction had become so troublesome that the bishop of Trier asserted that the Catholic nobility was "an object of great concern for the episcopate." In an attempt to defuse the situation, Clemens August asked the association to reassure the church of its loyalty to the existing Catholic Center Party. The leadership of the association was in the hands of the Lüninck faction, and they unanimously refused to have Clemens August's resolution brought before the general assembly of the association.[46]

By the summer of 1932, Catholic Center Party member Franz von Papen was serving as chancellor of the Weimar Republic; Clemens August, desperate to effect reconciliation between the Catholic nobility and the episcopacy of the church, once again petitioned the association, asking that they bring his resolution, already once denied, before the general assembly. He was fighting an uphill battle at this point, for his suggested resolution provoked this response from one of the association's barons: "Gentlemen, what is really at stake today? The real enemy that we have to fight together are the Masonic-Jewish powers that lead the struggle against the throne and altar and under whose domination the nobility would surely perish. . . . The essence of the National Socialist movement is the struggle against these powers. I therefore welcome this movement, for the enemy of my enemy is my friend."[47]

The baron's statement was immediately endorsed by Ferdinand von Lüninck, and the von Galen resolution was not passed.[48] This entire episode is useful in revealing von Galen's political position in the late 1920s and early 1930s. He, like his brother Franz, abhorred the liberal values of the Weimar Republic, yet one can see him struggling to keep his opinions within the confines of the church-affiliated Catholic Center Party. Von Galen was not willing to become a maverick, leaving behind the accepted vehicle for Catholic political interests, the Center Party.

One of the keys to understanding von Galen's thought concerning the relationship of church and state involves his "measuring stick." He judged political systems according to the degree to which the systems were founded on Christian principles. He applied this measuring stick to the Weimar Republic, searching for the degree of incorporation and adoption of Catholic teachings (natural law, moral law).[49] As we shall see, von Galen did not use the same measuring stick when evaluating Hitler's government.

The main problem von Galen had with the liberalism of the Weimar Republic was that it had moved away from the concept that all power ultimately comes from God, not the ballot box. He also objected to absolutist systems because they deny the individual free will. Of course, one would think that opposition to Nazism would flow immediately out of this position. However, for von Galen it was more complex. Nazism, in his view, fought against godless Communism and socialism; it harked back to a traditional, orderly society that von Galen admired, and Nazism was ultranationalistic. What we find is a man who eventually selected elements of National Socialism to oppose, such as the euthanasia project, while he remained silent on the equally important issues of roundups, deportations, and mass murder of Jews. Von Galen's post–World War II biographers emphasize his "staunch resistance" to Nazism.[50] What they omit from their accounts is the question of Jews in Germany and what their place would be in a state based on "Christian" concepts. Opposition to selected Nazi policies did not always translate into solidarity with excluded groups such as the Jews.

CHAPTER TWO

The Legacy of the Kulturkampf

For the sake of the Lord, accept the authority of every social institution.

—I PETER 2:13

"Memories fade—and the health of nations as of individuals depends on some measure of release from the wounds of the past." The memory of the Kulturkampf persecution instilled in many Catholics the desire to prove their worth to the German nation. The legacy of the mentality of being discriminated against by the state led many to fight to keep Catholic identity and community alive in a Protestant-dominated atmosphere.[1]

Although many historians view the Kulturkampf as a dismal failure under Bismarck's administration, I would argue that the effect of the Kulturkampf was the successful internalization of fears that the state would once again designate Catholics as "outsiders," thus making Catholics wary of separating themselves from the protection of an alliance with the national government. The implications of these fears meant that in the search for "Ein Volk! Ein Reich! Ein Führer!" Catholics sought a way of achieving tolerable coexistence with the Nazis rather than run the risk of being branded outsiders and having to fight yet another Kulturkampf.

The legacy of the Kulturkampf was a double-edged sword for Catholics under the Third Reich. Priests such as von Galen employed the language of another impending Kulturkampf to bind the Catholic community together; he revived tactics similar to those used during the Kulturkampf era in order to keep daily Catholicism alive (devotional cults, workers' associations, youth groups, outdoor celebrations, etc.), and he utilized similar techniques to register their protest. At the same time, however, the revival of Kulturkampf memories worked against Catholics because their desire not to be separated from the state kept them from engaging in an all-out, open battle with the government.

National Integration and Catholic Identity in the Second Reich

Religious, political, and social divisions within German society influenced the way both Catholics and Protestants viewed their national identity. Confessional animosities, drawing on a long history, resulted in conflict over the fundamental question of what it meant to be truly German. The German state found it difficult "to construct an imagined community of shared memory and sentiment across a torn confessional landscape."[2]

In the era of German nation-building, the Prussian drive to forge a new Reich under one unifying ideology exacerbated the already existing struggle between Catholics and Protestants and their often separate visions of what their nation should look like and whom it should include.[3] Each group tended to appeal to specific historical memories, experiences, and traditions when it imagined the "new" Germany. Each worldview, partially constructed against the other, resulted in a struggle over the question of integration into the national community.

By the end of the 1860s, Catholics were seeking to redefine their relationship to the new German state led by Protestant Prussia. "At first the relationship of Catholics to the new Germany was debated tranquilly." However, with the publication of Pope Pius IX's *Syllabus of Errors* in 1864, followed in 1870 by the *Doctrine of Papal Infallibility,* heated debates increased significantly in Germany between Catholic and Protestant leaders. In the *Syllabus,* Pius IX condemned the new intellectual attitudes toward modernized society. He attacked every type of liberalism as a threat to the church's existence. With the endorsement of this publication, German Catholics lost their former alliance with liberals and progressives who had previously fought for the inclusion of minorities in the German national culture.[4] With the publication of the *Doctrine of Papal Infallibility,* nationalists raised the question of dual loyalty for German Catholics. Catholics, despite the debates, continued to "develop their identity outside of the Protestant government."[5]

By the summer of 1871, Otto von Bismarck and his minister for education and cultural affairs, Adalbert Falk, had decided to move against political Catholicism. The opening salvo occurred in July 1871, when the Catholic division of the Ministry of Culture was dissolved and placed under a Protestant administration. Between 1871 and 1872 a series of legislation was enacted that sought to limit the influence clergy had over political and cultural life. Priests were outlawed from participating in political life, confessional schools were placed under state control, Catholic associations were disbanded, and all Jesuits were expelled from Prussian soil. By 1875 most religious orders had been dissolved or exiled, their institutions had been seized, remaining members of orders had been imprisoned, and the state had taken over the appointment of bishops.[6]

In 1874-1875 Bismarck's government sponsored the May Laws, which permitted the state to control all the training and assignments of priests. The May Laws also placed bishops under state control. Many priests of the Second Reich refused to submit to this legislation, and massive arrests and exiles followed. Some estimate that as many as eighteen hundred priests were either imprisoned or banished from the state. Pius IX, not willing to allow these events to continue, responded in 1875 with an encyclical that declared the May Laws null and void and warned that any priest who complied with these state policies would be excommunicated. Pius also encouraged German Catholics to practice passive resistance to unjust laws.[7]

This anti-Catholic legislation had a real effect on the daily lives of German Catholics in Prussian territory in particular. For the young von Galen, it meant that he had to leave his country as a young child in order to be educated by Jesuits. For others, something as important as a church wedding was no longer considered legal by the authorities; couples were forced to have civil ceremonies. Catholics saw their bishops disappearing into prison or exile. Some bishops administered their sees from exile. For Münster, Bishop Johann Bernard Brinkmann fled to Holland to escape arrest. Upon his return in 1884, he dedicated the city of Münster to the Sacred Heart of Jesus to remind his parishioners that Jesus was a symbol both of strength and of suffering.

In general, the Prussian bishops responded to state attacks as Pius IX had commanded—with passive resistance. Their main concern was to keep daily pastoral care alive. Throughout the Kulturkampf, there was an upsurge in Catholic involvement in organizations, associations, processionals, masses, and so forth. The Catholic Center Party used its political influence to forcibly protest Kulturkampf restrictions and fostered the growth of the German Catholic press. As devotion to Catholic institutions and ideals seemed to deepen, so did Catholics' mistrust of non-Catholics: "The *Kulturkampf* isolated German Catholics, and they re-acted, as groups forced into a ghetto usually do, by depending on their own powers and viewing the outside, all that was new, as hostile."[8]

The "Outsiders"

Alban Stolz, a prolific and popular Catholic writer, portrayed the German Catholic Church as an embattled entity. In his writings he called on his audience to sacrifice in order to win what he believed was a universal struggle. He suggested that Catholics could gain control of their world by fighting against the influence of modern science and Protestant professors.[9]

For all of his apocalyptic melodrama, Stolz was not completely incorrect in his observation that Protestant professors were arguing against Catholic inclusion in the definition of Germanness.[10] One of the most famous Protestant professors of the time, Heinrich von Treitschke, maintained not only "The Jews are our misfortune!" but also that Catholicism and German nationalism were incompatible. According to Treitschke, there could be only one Germany, and it could be nothing other than Protestant. In his view, a Catholic-dominated state would be intolerant, disunited, and spiritually and materially impoverished. Praising Martin Luther, Treitschke claimed that the destiny of German history was to complete the Reformation.[11]

Treitschke was certainly not alone in his depiction of Catholicism and its implications for state building. Writers such as Paul Bräunlich wrote pamphlets appealing to theories of social Darwinism. In *Germanic Faith*, Bräunlich claimed that history had proved that those races that had converted to Protestantism stood at the pinnacle. Roman Catholicism, to Bräunlich, was the religion chosen by nations in decline. Using nineteenth-century notions of gender differences, he likened Catholicism to "woman's" nature—effeminate, irrational, and weak—while Protestantism was portrayed as being robust, masculine, and dominating over all other nations.[12]

It was not only pamphleteers and professors who attacked the "harmful" influences of Catholicism on the life of a nation. Respected German poets referred to Catholics as "enemies within," waiting to hand over the nation to an international papacy. German nationalists claimed that

Catholics were tied to a feudal, medieval past, which threatened German identity by refusing to move with modern society. Heinrich von Sybel urged state intervention to loosen the influence of Catholic clerics on German society. Liberals portrayed Catholicism as fit only for absolutist systems.[13] The most common advice given to Catholics by Protestant professors, poets, and nationalists was a message similarly given to Jews in the Reich, "If Catholics were to be recognized as true Germans, they must rescind the weight of their dark, intolerant, and un-German past, a weight that bore down heavily . . . on the development of the German nation as a whole."[14]

It was apparently thought that assimilation to the Protestant ideal would bring about the moral improvement of the German nation. The expectation was that emancipation from the Catholic Church's influence would lead to conversion, which, in turn, would lead to a Christian state based on Protestant beliefs. A movement called Los von Rom had as its entire goal such freeing of Catholics.

To many it seemed that there could be only one church in the German nation and that church had to be Protestant. Catholicism was linked with descriptors such as *international, intolerant, illiberal, medieval, hierarchical,* and *effeminate.* Ironically, much of the same language, that is, of effeminacy, untrustworthiness, and internationalism was employed when describing the "problem" with Jews in the German nation. Some Catholics, feeling their outsider status, sympathized with Jews, also seen to be living on the margins of German society. Others, perhaps out of concern for their own standing in society, could not permit the persecution of another minority. Ernst Lieber, a leader of the Catholic Center Party, remarked, "As a minority in the Reich, we have not forgotten how we were treated, and for this reason . . . we will not lend a hand in the forging of weapons which will be used today against the Jews, tomorrow against the Poles, and on the following day against the Catholics. Do not expect us to support you so that you can toy with the idea—'we have rid ourselves of the Jews and now *bon voyage* to the Catholics.'"[15]

Although Center Party leaders Lieber and Ludwig Windthorst fought the trend of growing anti-Semitism in the early years of the Kulturkampf, several Catholic theologians and authors sought to prove that "crafty Jews" were masterminding the Catholic persecution.

Alban Stolz, in a writing of 1874, called upon Catholics to fight against the effects of liberalism and Judaism on the Christian German citizen.[16] A professor of Catholic theology, Canon August Rohling, explained to his audience that Jews had a corrupting influence on German culture. In the 1876 edition of Bishop Konrad Martin's book, Catholic theologian Joseph Rebbert urged the reexamination of the "Jewish Question." Rebbert stressed that Jews were cosmopolitan and because of this threatened to break apart the nation. He claimed that in a Jewish-dominated atmosphere, the Christian spirit would never be able to triumph.[17] Still other Catholic theologians, in an effort to distinguish themselves as part of the Christian majority, added to the attempts to further alienate Jews from German society. Men such as Albert M. Weiss and Constantin Frantz argued that Jews threatened the German nation because they were morally corrupt.[18] Others promoted the idea that it was the Jews, not the Catholics, who were involved in an international conspiracy bent on destroying Germany.

If there was one thing the majority of Catholics and conservative Protestants could agree on, it was the belief that the German nation had to be Christian.[19] "By defining themselves as the racial and spiritual opposites of the 'vile Jew,' true believers of all classes derived a feeling of worth and felt joined together in a mystical Volkish union."[20]

The Community

The quest to be fully integrated as an accepted member of the German nation had led many Jews and Catholics to set aside a variety of their own traditions. But accompanying the drive for greater assimilation, the question arose, "How much religious heritage was one to surrender, how many discriminations and indignities to accept in order not to call attention to the separateness of one's group?"[21]

For many individuals within each community, the answer was to pull closer together to maintain a distinctive identity. The history of shared traditions and collective memories created a certain type of cohesion.[22] For Catholics, the feeling of being second-class citizens, persecuted by their own government, led to an increase in religious involvement. "In fact . . . at the time of the *Kulturkampf*, Catholicism in Germany found itself at the crest of a religious revival." Membership in Catholic organizations increased and brought a sense of mutual support, reinforcing Catholic identity. "These organizations cut across state and diocesan boundaries, and Catholics were united into a German Catholic Church more than ever before."[23]

The scene of conflict over what the German nation would look like was being fought in churches, schoolrooms, monasteries, and charitable foundations. The Catholic population tended to ignore laws passed against them, and their organizations continued to meet. Public manifestations of Catholicism's strength included outdoor celebrations of the Mass, Corpus Christi Day processions, and public festivals and solemnities. In Münster, the Catholic population decorated the town with torches, banners, and garlands of flowers to celebrate the dedication to the very popular cult of the Sacred Heart. All of these open gatherings, organizations, and clubs helped to bind the Catholic community together, working to dispel minority-complex feelings: "[The] experience of persecution and resistance created the conditions for the formation of a Catholic community that transcended, at least in part, differences of class and status, a community that shared a common, emotive rhetoric, and that was bound by a dense, tightly woven network of Catholic organizations."[24]

As official state-sponsored Kulturkampf legislation gradually disappeared from Prussian territory, a popular Kulturkampf arose, led primarily by the Protestant League. The league's goal was to raise public awareness of the "danger" of the ultramontane influence in German life. Numbering half a million members by 1914, the association was determined to rid Germany of the "harmful" influences of Catholicism on German soil.

As the national government sought to unify the empire by mobilizing nationalist sentiment of both Catholics and Protestants, the Protestant League grew ever more fearful of Catholic acceptance into the German nation. Count Wilko Levin von Wintzingerode-Bodenstein, leader of the Protestant League in the early twentieth century, warned Chancellor Bernhard von Bülow that Jesuits would divide Germany into two nations. As proof he pointed to the growth in Catholic organizations and vocations and support by Catholics of minorities like the Poles. Bülow, however, seeking an end to the long history of discord, chose to ignore the count, claiming that the aristocrat was politically naive. The repeal of the anti-Jesuit law in 1904 was Bülow's attempt "through conciliation, to integrate German Catholics into the national state."[25] The attempt at integration was short-lived, because Bülow himself by 1906 called for an attack on ultramontane influence in German society.

Catholics responded to the new upsurge in attacks by making veiled appeals to conservative Protestants. For upper- and middle-class Catholics in northwestern Germany, the Union of German Catholics (established in 1900) saw no conflict between being "good" Catholics and "good" Germans. What they sought to do was to show the cultural bond between German Protestants and German Catholics as opposed to yet another minority group living in their midst—the Catholic Poles.[26] Increasingly conscious of their collective identity, German Catholics in Prussian territory tried to prove that "as Germans we are just as good as our countrymen of the other confession, and we do not just want to feel German but to actively support our German national community."[27] The struggle with Polish nationalism brought many Catholics and Protestants in this region closer together in a cultural mission to combat what they both considered to be an inferior culture.[28]

By the outbreak of World War I, the specter of being second-class citizens no longer haunted the Catholic Church as it had in the nineteenth century. In an ironic twist, movements like the Protestant League and Los von Rom pushed Catholics into a tighter alliance with the German national government rather than forcing them into opposition against the state (as Bismarck's attacks had done.) To many twentieth-century Catholics, the national government now offered protection against popular Kulturkämpfe fed by groups such as socialists, Old Catholics, Freemasons, and radical Protestants. Many Catholic leaders came to believe that an alliance with the state government translated into protection of Catholic rights and institutions. Political subservience ensured institutional survival, but the larger duty of the church, to address moral questions in a secular environment, was frequently quieted down in order to keep church-state relations harmonious.

In this way the long-term effects of the Kulturkampf can be interpreted as having crippled many Catholics. Certainly Bismarck's Kulturkampf did not succeed in eradicating Catholicism from Germany's political and cultural life. What it did, however, was to create for many Catholics the dread fear that they would one day again be branded as "enemies within" by their national government. Catholics had so internalized the portrayal of themselves as outsiders that many of them believed that they should constantly seek out and win the protection of the state government in order to be fully integrated into the German community. Church leaders, after the experience of the Kulturkampf, were reluctant to oppose the national government. "The *Kulturkampf* experience could not be forgotten."[29]

The New Era

The Kulturkampf experience impeded the ability of many German Catholics to take a strong stance against their national government. In an effort to avoid reclassification as "minorities," many Catholic leaders sought out accommodations in order to achieve a mutual understanding with whatever government was in office. When one examines the German Catholic hierarchy's position under the Nazis, and von Galen's relationship in particular, a pattern emerges. Certain aspects of the Nazi ideology are subject to criticism, but even the criticisms are overlaid with patriotic sentiments. Nothing was going to be done to jeopardize Catholic integration into the German community. Many Catholics believed that they were experiencing the same type of persecution that other minority groups in the Third Reich were undergoing. They failed to recognize that the unique nature of the persecution of the Jews set their suffering apart from that of other individuals. Because the church leadership (von Galen included) publicly denied any difference in the type of persecution being perpetrated, they resolved to fight only to protect Catholics from ostracism. Losing sight of larger moral issues, they defined the battle narrowly to take on only "Catholic" issues.

In 1933 the German Catholic hierarchy wanted to ensure acceptance as Germans in the new national community. Most of the leadership in the Catholic Church had been shaped by imperial, pre–World War I Germany. Many were monarchists. Almost all distrusted Weimar democracy, liberalism, and socialism, believing that these "isms" were destroying the moral foundation of German society. Cardinal Bertram, in seminary at the time of the Kulturkampf, disliked democracy. Von Galen believed the Weimar Constitution was "godless." Cardinal Michael Faulhaber thought the "liberal secularization of the state was blasphemy and the promises of Hitler to base the Nazi program on strong religious foundations could certainly be supported."[30]

Many Catholics wanted to believe that National Socialism would promote a Christian order. As threats to Catholicism's existence seemed to increase, the hierarchy used familiar strategies from Kulturkampf days to maintain the church on German soil. Resistance, as it appeared, was manifested primarily through sermons, pastoral letters, and formal complaints. Specific issues such as euthanasia were opposed, but no organized assault on the state was considered, nor could it be, because "no evidence has been uncovered which would point to their acceptance of revolution as a desirable and legitimate means to the end they hoped for." Catholics, taking lessons from Thomas Aquinas, were taught that they should uphold the government. "For revolution, even against a government which practices injustices and exemplifies a tyranny, is not permitted."[31] Hoping to outlast the Nazis, the church leadership focused on strictly, and narrowly defined, ecclesiastical matters.

The Concordat

With such a narrow focus, the Catholic Church organized its selective opposition around the only legal instrument it could fall back on—the Concordat. Ratified in July 1933, the Concordat served as a vehicle for protest and not a blueprint for resistance. The treaty actually brought weakness in that it attempted to limit the differences between church and state. The clergy were reluctant to "place their difficulties with the Nazis on the higher and broader plane of maintaining religious and humanitarian values."[32]

Relying on the parameters set down in the Concordat, many Catholics believed that belonging to openly Catholic organizations, mailing religious materials to soldiers at the front, sending priests to the wounded, and indoctrinating young people in youth groups were significant acts of protest. It was not only Catholics who interpreted these acts as resistance. Security Service (SD) reports reveal that the church by virtue of these acts was seen as a subversive threat to the regime. What the SD missed, however, was that virtually no member of the hierarchy "wanted to lay down the gauntlet to the regime and run the danger of losing a *Kulturkampf*. It seemed best to try to get along with the legally established authorities."[33]

Early in 1933 Cardinal Bertram noticed that Catholics, because of the ban on wearing uniforms in the church, were attending Protestant services in full uniform. The bishops then met and decided that they must lift the ban on attending Mass in uniform. Rather than openly confront the government and risk losing more of their congregation to Protestantism, the bishops decided to "fit in" and remove the ban.[34]

When the Concordat was signed, most Catholics thought they had achieved an understanding with the government. Despite increasing governmental violations of the agreement, the bishops continued to emphasize obedience to the established authority. In a sermon in September 1934, von Galen endorsed the "stab-in-the-back" legend and reminded his followers that no one wished to return to the Weimar system.[35]

Urging his congregation to follow and obey the authorities, he made constant references to the threat of another Kulturkampf and to the need to avoid such a situation again. He, like so many of the other bishops, struggled to "maintain a consistent non-resistance stance."[36] The fear of another Kulturkampf kept many Catholics in an uneasy alliance with the national government.

In August 1935, following the annual Bishops' Conference at Fulda, von Galen told his listeners that the bishops had reflected on the position of the Catholic Church in Germany. Seeing a series of ominous issues that appeared to be threatening Christian beliefs in the Fatherland, they prepared and mailed a detailed report to Hitler. The report made clear that they wished "to steer clear of the harm . . . of a *Kulturkampf*." Referring to the Concordat, von Galen said the bishops placed their faith in the agreement, thinking that it would restore "a hopeful understanding between State and Church."[37] Although von Galen was angry about the violations of the Concordat, he advised a course of passive resistance, quoting from 1 Corinthians 16:13: "Be awake to all the dangers; stay firm in the faith: be brave and be strong!"[38]

In December 1935 von Galen revealed to his congregation that the Fulda letter of August 1935 had so far gone unanswered. He again noted that the bishops had greeted the Concordat with hope, thinking that the treaty was a "sign of Church and State working together." Disappointed by the lack of response from the Führer, he explained that he decided to raise his voice publicly in order to "fend off the damages and the danger of a so-called *Kulturkampf*."[39]

Von Galen was not alone in believing that the church and state of Germany were about to face another Kulturkampf. Here we have an example of a Nazi official who believed that another battle was looming on the horizon. Ferdinand von Lüninck, writing to Reich Minister of the Interior Wilhelm Frick in the summer of 1935, offered the opinion that Catholics were looking for a "religious-philosophical settlement, and that a *Kulturkampf* threatens in full severity." Advising Frick, he wrote that it would be unwise for the state to wage a two-front war against both the Evangelical and the Catholic Churches. He suggested an appeasement of some type, although he also sent a reprimand to von Galen for his open opposition to the Landjahr (a year of compulsory service on the land) and for violations of the Concordat regarding the Schulgottesdienst (a struggle over the place of religious instruction in the school system).[40]

From yet another perspective, Nazi officials tried to convince Catholics that if there was an impending persecution of Catholics, it was because Catholic bishops were taking action against the state. In July 1933 the *Gauleiter* (district leader) of North Westphalia, Alfred Meyer, placed large red placards in Werne an der Lippe, which read, "German people, Listen Up! . . . Conscience-less agitators are at work, driving you into a *Kulturkampf!* They misuse religion for dirty political purposes!"[41]

These placards referred to an incident in which eight men, all members of the Catholic Kolping Union, distributed derogatory songs about Clemens August and the local cloister. At their interrogation, they admitted that they had hoped to damage the National Socialist movement by distributing these antichurch songs. Gauleiter Meyer stressed to the Catholic population that this was a fine example of the conspiratorial nature of ardent Catholics, branding them, once again, as enemies of the state: "Traitors of the nation, who want to push their dirty political deals under the mask of religion. . . . Trying to bring party and movement to a shameless end! You, German Volk, be watchful for the Devil who comes in sheep's clothing, but inside is purely wolf!"[42] The language used by Meyer drew a line between German *Volk* and traitors, that is, fanatical Catholics, implying that it was fanatics who brought about more trouble than there need be and that "true" Germans would not be against National Socialism.

In response to the red-poster incident, von Galen protested the closing of the Kolping Union in Werne by appealing to Article 31 of the Concordat.[43] He was unsuccessful in getting the union reopened. Despite the setback, von Galen continued to use the Concordat as a way of protesting specific governmental actions.

In October 1935 he prayed with a group of priests that the Concordat would be upheld and that Catholic schools and organizations would remain open. His fear was that young people, constantly exposed to neopagan ideals, would eventually become unaware of alternative beliefs. Referring to the recent Nuremberg party rally of September 1935, he said it was clear to him that Germany's future would be about race and nationalism. Comparing the current situation to the Kulturkampf of sixty years before, he explained to the men that there was a course of action that would fight anti-Christian propaganda as well as keep the church unconquered.[44] What was that course of action? Was it active, open rebellion against the heathen state? Von Galen recommended, instead, that the priests could renew Jesus' teaching, for "if we do that, the Church can withstand even the most brutal *Kulturkampf* and remain victorious."[45]

Victory, as von Galen envisioned it, could be achieved by maintaining Catholic school instruction, holding catechism classes, conducting pastoral house visits, giving sermons that spoke the Truth, and working with small groups of young people, addressing their practical, everyday questions. In essence, he wanted to keep daily sacramental life alive for Catholics in Germany. Ending with a quote from Mark 9:28-29, he told the priests that Christ had given them the power to cast out unclean spirits through prayer and fasting.[46]

Prayer and fasting, although not actively rebellious, were things von Galen could offer the individual, knowing that these were activities the individual could control. The individual could feel as though she or he were resisting the state's attempt at control, but the government would never know of the resistance. In this way the risk of further persecution by the state was decreased while the feeling of being actively opposed to the government was increased.

Pray and fast. Be patient and pray. These were constant themes that von Galen promoted in his sermons. In a January 1941 sermon, he revived the memory of Kulturkampf persecution when he once again dedicated Münster to the Sacred Heart of Jesus. Opening the ceremony with a direct reference to Bishop Brinkmann's original dedication to the cult, he remarked, "And truthfully, it was a dark time, when sorrow and danger existed for all German Catholics; it was the time of the so-called *Kulturkampf*." He then recalled legislation passed against Catholics and organizations persecuted because they were Catholic. He urged his parishioners to think of the importance of this dedication and advised them to think of what Jesus would say and then act accordingly.[47]

Despite the fact that this sermon does not urge open rebellion against the state, state representatives viewed the sermon as a threat. Ministerial Regent Joseph Roth wrote to Hans Heinrich Lammers, the chief of the Reich Chancellery, complaining that the sermon contained enemy content by reviving 1875 memories. Reinhard Heydrich, leader of the Reich Security Main Office, also wrote to Lammers following this incident and claimed that von Galen's parallels between 1875 and present-day circumstances were an attempt to destroy public calm and reduce the authority of the state. As punishment, Heydrich recommended a cessation of state donation payments to the diocese of Münster.[48]

Reviving the very popular cult of the Sacred Heart of Jesus was not the only way von Galen reminded his contemporaries that their suffering was similar to the suffering of Catholics of the Kulturkampf era. Using traditional Kulturkampf resistance tactics, von Galen revived the Great Procession, which commemorated Bishop Brinkmann's return to Münster following his exile in Holland. This procession occurred each July and celebrated the church's triumph over state-sponsored persecution.

In 1934 the Great Procession had almost 10,000 participants. One year later, in July 1935, the Nazis held a party rally in Münster. Alfred Rosenberg, author of *The Myth of the Twentieth Century,* was the guest speaker. In his speech, Rosenberg abused the bishop. The following Monday, approximately 19,000 Catholics appeared to march in the Great Procession, escorting the bishop back to his palace and giving him an ovation like never before. From the window of the bishop's palace, von Galen spoke with angry and invincible determination, assuring all who were present that he would never yield to the enemies of Christianity or to the persecutors of the church.[49]

Although the bishop's words were strong, he was not risking very much in that the neopagan ideology of Rosenberg was never officially incorporated into the platform of National Socialism; hence, criticism of it was not officially a violation of the Concordat. As a result of this incident, Kurt Klemm, *Regierungspräsident* (district president) in Münster (1934–1941), sent Frick Catholic newspaper clippings, claiming that von Galen had attacked the state and led followers to believe that the state was mistreating Catholics and depriving them of their freedom. Klemm also recommended that Catholic newspapers either stop printing political matter or submit to state censorship. Again, as in previous situations, red placards were put up in Münster, warning Catholics that if there was a Kulturkampf going on, it was not because the state wanted one: "German people, Listen up! Conscience-less agitators are at work. You are being driven into a *Kulturkampf!*"[50]

When the time for the 1936 Great Procession came around, the Nazis attempted to break down contact between von Galen and the Catholic participants by roping off sections of the cathedral square. Enraged, von Galen stormed to the pulpit and asked, "Can the shepherd be severed from his flock? Can the police divide Catholics from their own bishop by ropes and chains?" These are strong words indeed, but they were followed by only suggestions of passive resistance. "Sorrowful times, my dear people of Münster are at hand, but I know that steadfastness will prevail." When von Galen left the cathedral, the police could not contain the crowd. Young people in particular leaped over the barriers and ran to the bishop's window to give him an ovation.[51]

By 1937 the Nazis, apparently frustrated by their previous attempts to defeat popular enthusiasm for the bishop, decided to at least get something out of the event for themselves. Cameras were set up to film Catholics surrounding the bishop—propaganda proving that no Kulturkampf was occurring and that Catholics were free to celebrate their faith in Nazi Germany. The procession did take place, but at the location where the film was to be shot, no bishop appeared.[52]

Here it is necessary to stop and ask: if the bishop had so successfully thumbed his nose at the Nazis and done so repeatedly, why did he not try to raise his voice concerning the injustices and persecution of other minorities in the Reich? Limiting his scope to purely Catholic matters led him to willfully ignore the more radical nature of the persecution of the Jews.

The Unique Nature of the Persecution

We have seen in chapter 1 how von Galen envisioned German society as a state based on Catholic Christian values. He believed that secularism was undermining the foundations of the church and disrupting the moral order of society. He lamented the unraveling of the feudal-aristocratic structure and its replacement with technology, capitalism, and industrialization. He thought the Enlightenment legacy of rationality and scientific reasoning had fostered materialism, individualism, and liberalism, and he viewed this inheritance as a threat to the ecclesiastical hierarchy as well as to the foundations of Christianized Germany. Society was moving in a direction he disapproved of and was willing to speak out against.

Throughout this time, Jews were depicted as the main beneficiaries of the Enlightenment tradition. They were portrayed in popular writings as disseminators of the modern, liberal trends that von Galen so disliked. Feeling the strain of another attempt to mark Catholics as outsiders, von Galen focused on narrow ecclesiastical matters and refused to acknowledge that the racial definition of Jewishness had resulted in a much more dangerous wide-scale persecution of Jews, separating their misery from that of all other victims of discrimination and persecution.

If he could convince himself and others that all minorities were suffering equally under the Nazis, then it could reasonably be expected that each group would fend for itself. Refusing to see that remaining neutral in such an unequal battle added strength to Nazi persecution, von Galen continued to limit his attacks on the state to violations against Catholicism.

In a sermon to the Kolping Union in January 1935, von Galen expressed the feelings of upheaval and unease present in German society. Using the metaphor of building a new house, he asserted that in order for the new house of Germany to have a solid foundation, it must be built on "belief in the one and only God."[53] In this sermon he not only ostracized Jews from the "new house of Germany" by stating that Germany must be a Christian state, but he also reasserted his belief that a battle was being waged to destroy Catholicism on German soil. He claimed that they were living in a time of a new Kulturkampf, when once again a struggle between worldly and church authority was taking place. He believed that the very existence of the church in Germany was being threatened by attempts to destroy the Catholic community.

His sermon included references to bishops and priests who had been sent to court trials, deprived of their incomes, and damaged by smears to their reputations. He believed that individuals would question the authority of the church if they saw priests involved in the scandalous immorality and currency trials.[54] He believed these trials tended to make Catholics fearful of their place in German society. By focusing on Catholic problems and making no reference to similar and worse mistreatment of Jews, von Galen deflected attention from the government's more severe persecution of Jews.

Von Galen opened a July 1938 sermon with a quote from 1 Corinthians 12:26: "Body parts are all equally concerned for other parts." This could have been an opportunity to emphasize the need to care for all of one's neighbors regardless of their denomination, but the rest of the sermon focused only on Catholic matters. Ignoring the attacks and legislation passed against Jews, von Galen described the invasion of Bishop Johann Baptista Sproll's house in Rottenburg by a mob, how the mob vandalized Sproll's property, and how Catholics of Münster should pray for Sproll. After detailing Sproll's mistreatment, von Galen recalled the previous century's attempts to separate priest from parishioners, "Not since the time of the *Kulturkampf* . . . has one seen in Germany a high officeholder in the Catholic Church forcibly dismissed from his post for championing religious interest, without consideration if this hinders or makes impossible his daily duties." [55]

Ignoring the disruption of Jewish daily life in Germany, von Galen then proceeded to relate the story of the arrest of several men in Münster who had defended the right of Catholic schools to remain confessional. He beseeched his listeners to remember that they were all parts of one body and that if one body part was harmed, then all parts were affected. I would argue that in von Galen's definition, only Christians belong to the body, not Jews. Reminding his audience that the men arrested had done nothing illegal, he neglected to connect this to the persecution of innocent Jews. [56]

Again, in November 1938, after Kristallnacht (the night of broken glass), von Galen did not speak publicly in defense of the Jews for fear of endangering what he viewed as Catholics' precarious inclusion in the German state. He remained silent concerning the unjustified attacks against Jews living in his midst. In Telgte, a town in Münsterland, there had been four Jewish families. The synagogue that served as the place of worship for the fourteen Jews of Telgte was burned, and the homes and businesses of these families were set on fire. Von Galen certainly would have known what had happened in this small town of approximately ten thousand inhabitants, particularly because his favorite shrine was located in Telgte. Yet he chose to say nothing about this injustice. Heinrich Portmann, writing about the mood of the time, emphasizes "how easily the SA and SS could have attacked the Bishop's palace" as Germany's synagogues were set on fire that November night. [57]

In hindsight, it seems ludicrous to suggest that Catholics might suffer a similar fate as that of the Jews in 1938, but I argue that the powerful effect of the Kulturkampf and the subsequent "minority status" made many Catholics believe that they were close to being reclassified with Jews as being less than fully German. If they risked defending the Jewish community and appeared to be aligned with the Jews, they would be reconfirming their outsider status, and this was something most Catholics were not willing to confer on themselves a second time.

By 1941 no Jews remained in Telgte. In June 1941 von Galen gave two sermons in which he spoke of the Gestapo cellars and concentration camps, proving that he knew and understood what was taking place in these institutions of Nazi Germany. Again failing to seize the "moral moment" and describe what was happening to Jews, von Galen focused only on Catholics. In speaking of concentration camps, he described how "his priests were languishing. He was deeply affected on receiving the news of the deaths of his priests in Dachau."[58]

Although priests were dying in camps across Germany, the bishop failed to note the differences in the persecution. Individual priests might be rounded up, but their parents, siblings, and extended family were not being taken away. No mention is made of innocent Jewish men, women, and children being unfairly seized because of a "racial" designation. To maintain the precarious alliance between Catholics and Protestants, there apparently had to be an outsider; and that outsider would be the non-Christian.

The belief that the new Germany must be founded on Christian principles was shared by many others. Dr. Paulus van Husen, a member of the July 20 Resistance, wrote in an article in 1946 that "the general impression of all Christians in Germany . . . disposed them to set aside separating issues and to emphasize the common values, the common possession of the Good News and the Communion of Saints in Jesus."[59] Van Husen noted that men such as von Galen and Martin Niemöller influenced him because of their warnings of Nazi immorality and their beliefs in a Germany based on Christian values.[60] A state based on Christian principles would naturally align Catholics with Protestants and immediately define the Jews as outsiders. Just as Catholics of the 1870s–1880s had sought an alliance with conservative Protestants in order to be considered fully integrated into the German nation, Catholics of the Nazi era refused to part company with other Christians and relinquish their insider status. By arguing that all were suffering under the Nazis, they helped to create an atomized atmosphere. Even though members of the Catholic hierarchy did not necessarily endorse the anti-Jewish policies of the Third Reich, "they did nothing drastic for fear of heaping even more troubles on their own heads."[61]

In an oral history interview conducted by Franklin A. Oberländer, a Catholic priest, Father Heinz Fuchs revealed in a stunning way that many Catholics had divorced themselves from the unique nature of the persecution of Jews and that they were unwilling to be associated with such "outsiders." Father Fuchs, by birth part Jewish and part Catholic, identified more strongly with his mother's Catholic side of the family. Becoming a Catholic priest, he volunteered as an army chaplain in 1940 and served in France, Poland, and the Soviet Union. Throughout this time he never brought up his "racial heritage," although his church superiors were aware of his background. In 1943 Father Fuchs's father was arrested, deported to Auschwitz, and killed. At approximately the same time, Father Fuchs was arrested because of his "non-Aryan" background and sent to a labor camp until his release in early 1945.[62]

In the interview, Father Fuchs revealed that although he never experienced discrimination from the Catholic institutions he was a member of, neither did he or his family receive any aid during their persecution. Throughout his interview, Fuchs represented himself as a Catholic and as a German. Stating that Jewishness is a matter strictly of religious belief, he denied the racial claims of Nazism, thus defining himself as completely non-Jewish. He also attempted to show that other groups, such as Jesuits and Catholic aristocrats were being persecuted. He could not seem to bear the idea that he had been persecuted as a Jew. It was easier for him to be placed in a category with Catholic nobility. He "never addressed the uniqueness of the Nazi persecution of the Jews," despite the fact that his own father was murdered because of his Jewishness.[63]

Presenting the Jewish persecution as similar to that of Jesuit priests and Catholic nobility helped to fortify the idea that somehow all were suffering equally and hence each group must fend for itself. Ignoring the racial aspect of the persecution of the Jews, many Catholics chose to remain in an uneasy alliance with the Nazis in order to maintain their insider status and avoid another Kulturkampf. Von Galen, so hampered by the Kulturkampf memory, failed to seize the opportunity to use his moral authority to address issues beyond those affecting Catholicism.

CHAPTER THREE

Von Galen and Church-State Relations

Servants, be subject to your masters in all fear, not only to the good and moderate, but also to the severe.

—I PETER 2:18

Mother Mary Alice Gallin, in an excellent study of German resistance, examines four types of disobedience that appeared in theological writings of the time. The categories that she identified are (1) passive disobedience, (2) the use of legal means to have the laws changed, (3) armed self-defense against force used by the government to compel obedience, and (4) a rebellion in which the people take the offensive against the authority from which the law emanated.[1]

Gallin emphasizes that according to Catholic theology, the first three kinds of resistance are permissible, whereas the fourth is not.[2] Why was active, open rebellion against the state authority not permitted by theologians?

Theological Writings on the Question of Resistance

Catholic theology in Germany by the late 1800s was dominated by a neoscholastic movement that had embraced the teaching of Thomas Aquinas. In *Summa theologica,* Aquinas considered the possibilities of civil disobedience and discussed the differences between a leader who has seized power legitimately and one who has come to power through illegal or illegitimate means. In the case of a legitimate ruler, Aquinas condemned the idea of disobedience, including the extreme of tyrannicide. By the end of the nineteenth century, condemnation of tyrannicide had become accepted doctrine in Catholic teaching. It was reinforced when the pope issued the encyclical *Syllabus of Errors* in 1864. The *Syllabus* not only condemned tyrannicide; it also forbade revolution. "For revolution, even against a government which practices injustice and exemplifies a tyranny, is not permitted."[3] Similar themes were expressed by Pius IX's successor, Leo XIII, in the encyclical *Immortale Dei*, which prohibited revolution against the established government: "To cast aside obedience and by popular violence to incite revolt, is therefore treason, not against man only, but against God." Other encyclicals appearing at this time that examined the suffering of Catholics in Mexico, Spain, and Russia gave encouragement to citizens who refused to violate their consciences "but never encouraged the citizens to open revolt."[4] These teachings were reinforced to would-be professors and future bishops such as von Galen because the neoscholastic philosophy was vigorously taught by faculties in Mainz, in Münster, and in Freiburg, Switzerland.[5] Because von Galen attended schools in both Münster and Freiburg, we can assume that he was exposed to this tradition.

The embracing of neoscholasticism implies that an individual contemplating revolutionary activity would first have to ascertain that the state was using power arbitrarily; because of this, a citizen would have the right to actively resist the state authority. Second, the individual would have to consider the possibility of assassination of the authority if all other means of resistance had been ineffective.

If the average Catholic did not read the theological texts written in universities, what other sources might have been consulted? The two best-known Catholic texts dealing with moral theology that were in use in Nazi Germany were Reverend Antony Koch's *Handbook of Moral Theology* and Reverend Johann Pruner's *Lehrbuch der katholischen Moraltheologie*. If an individual consulted these sources seeking an answer to the question of resistance, he or she would have found that neither text makes a distinction between "self-defense" and "rebellion" against a tyrannical government. Koch states, "Laws which imperil higher rights or interests may be resisted by all legal means, such as remonstrances, appeals, petitions, agitation in the public press. To employ illegal means is tantamount to sedition. No matter what the provocation, revolution against a legitimate government is forbidden, because revolution by its very concept is an attack upon actually existing and divinely sanctioned rights."[6]

In a similar vein, Reverend Pruner, superior of the Eichstaett Seminary, stated that all power comes from God, and therefore no type of revolt is permitted. Still another common source that could have been consulted was the *Lexicon für Theologie und Kirche.* Under the subject entry "Tyrannenmord," the author, K. Hilgenreiner, stated that a tyrant who came to power via legitimate means but who ruled arbitrarily and despotically "may not be brought to death by 'private authority' in any case."[7]

From these general sources to the theologian's theology, it appears that German Catholics seeking clarification of issues of rebellion and assassination would have been confused at best. They were told to keep a pure conscience, but very little was done to encourage one to defend oneself against the government. There was practically nothing in the current literature that would have supported tyrannicide.

The history of the resistance in Germany reveals a remarkable group of individuals who concluded that resistance and even tyrannicide were morally justifiable. Dr. Paulus van Husen, a Catholic member of the Kreisau Circle, tried in 1946 to explain how he and some co-conspirators arrived at the conclusion that it would be justified to take action against Hitler. Distinguishing between *tyrannus ursurpationis* (a ruler who was illegitimate from the beginning) and *tyrannus regiminis* (a legitimate ruler using power unjustly and cruelly), van Husen, Count Claus Schenk von Stauffenberg, and many others of their circle agreed that although Hitler had come to power with the appearance of legitimacy, and despite the teaching of German academies, which were still against tyrannicide, it would be morally impossible to live under Hitler and his ideology.[8] Unfortunately, the Catholic leadership offered no active encouragement supporting revolutionary action that might have resulted in the removal of Hitler from power. Speaking of the German bishops' attitude, Gallin states, "Revolution was specifically rejected and denounced by them on several occasions."[9]

The Catholic Church in Germany desperately wanted to prove that it was German, and under such constraints active political revolutionary resistance was practically nonexistent. Most of the Catholic bishops chose to tolerate, accommodate, and collaborate with Nazis; this made it easier for Catholics swept up in the enthusiasm of National Socialism to remain within the church.[10] In March 1933 a common bishops' statement was issued: "Without revoking the judgment made in our previous declarations in respect to certain religious-ethical errors, the episcopate believes it can cherish the confidence that the designated general prohibitions and warnings need no longer be considered necessary. For Catholic Christians, to whom the voice of the Church is sacred, it is not necessary at the present moment, to make special admonition to be loyal to the lawful government and to fulfill conscientiously the duties of citizenship, rejecting on principle all illegal or subversive behavior."[11]

A statement such as this one only served to confuse Catholics and reconfirm in their minds that it would somehow be possible to reconcile the two conflicting value systems of National Socialism and Catholicism. Catholics were being told that they could be members of Nazism and Catholicism simultaneously. An example of the mixed message sent by the Catholic hierarchy has to do with von Galen's appointment as bishop of Münster.

Von Galen was the first clergyman to be appointed bishop after the signing of the Concordat. According to the treaty, von Galen had to appear before Prussian president Hermann Göring and swear an oath of loyalty to the state. Appearing before Göring in Berlin, von Galen made a point of producing his own crucifix and a copy of the New Testament, stating that he thought Göring might not have these items on hand (Göring did not).[12] Although von Galen drew attention to Göring's lack of religiosity, he attended the meal hosted by the Prussian president following the ceremony. He also left his card with Hitler and visited with President Paul von Hindenburg, observing all of the niceties and formalities of the situation.

Upon returning to Münster, Cardinal Karl Joseph Schulte, archbishop of Cologne, and the bishops of Osnabrück and Trier officiated at von Galen's consecration. The cathedral was the scene of columns of SA and SS men marching in procession with the swastika flags flying. The SA lined the roads leading to the cathedral, and in the evening they participated in a torch-lit procession in front of the bishop's palace.[13] As part of the ceremony, Nazi Party officeholders, from the Gauleiter to the lowest-ranking SA member, filed past von Galen, giving him the Nazi salute.

Eyewitness interpretations of the event vary widely. The bishop's would-be hagiographers, Heinrich Portmann and Max Bierbaum, emphasize Catholic Münster's support for their new bishop: "Ordinary folk . . . had limitless confidence in the new Bishop; a sound instinct led them in the confusion of the time to look for safety and rescue from the aggressive Catholicism of one of the race of von Galen." In contrast, Catholic scholar and philosopher Josef Pieper, who was a resident of

Münster, observed, "It is just not true that, in the summer of 1933, when the name 'Galen' was announced as the new Bishop, the whole diocese broke out in rejoicing. . . . Nor is it the case that Galen was immediately recognized as being a great opponent of the despotic regime. On the contrary, the pugnacious pastor of St. Lambert's was regarded, to put it bluntly, as a Nazi."[14]

Despite the varying opinions of eyewitnesses concerning the reaction of Catholic Münsterlanders, one thing emerges from both accounts. Men in SA and SS uniforms marched alongside the bishop, and the bishop gave the appearance of at least accepting National Socialism as legitimate. Von Galen, although he placed Göring in a slightly embarrassing situation at the swearing in, did not attempt to stress the differences that existed between the two ideologies, nor did he refuse to swear the oath of loyalty. By allowing the Nazis to participate in the consecration day ceremonies, von Galen made it easier for Catholics to think that they could be both Catholic and Nazi.

In the summer of 1934, von Galen once again allowed a similarly confusing message to be sent to Catholics. Since 1884, when Bishop Brinkmann (who served 1870-1889) returned from exile in Holland, a Great Procession was held throughout Münster to commemorate the event. Brinkmann had fled to Holland following arrest and harassment throughout the time of the Kulturkampf. In the July 1934 procession, von Galen did speak quite strongly to the participants, reminding them of the dark days of Kulturkampf persecution and the joy of Brinkmann's eventual return to German soil.[15] However, some of his stark message might have been lost when witnesses to the procession saw men in Nazi uniforms accompanying the bishop.

Processions, pilgrimages, and outdoor masses were typically used by German Catholics in the Second Reich to demonstrate their continued existence despite Bismarck's oppressive anti-Catholic legislation. If von Galen meant to convey a strong statement that Nazis were similar to anti-Catholics of the 1870s, his message would have been much more forceful if he had refrained from appearing with Nazis in uniform marching beside him. Josef Pieper, upon witnessing the procession, remarked, "And is it incomprehensible, therefore, that the ordinary man, watching the 'brownshirts' walking in the procession alongside Bishop von Galen, did not immediately regard them as mercenaries of the anti-Christ?"[16]

Most of the impact of the ceremony's message was lost on the audience when it confronted the strong visual symbol of Nazis participating in the event. As an audience member, one could walk away asking, Are Nazis persecuting Catholics, or are they Catholics themselves? Hitler also thought about possible comparisons between the Kulturkampf era and his regime. He was always quick to assert, "My desire is that no confessional conflict arise. I must act correctly to both confessions. I will not tolerate a *Kulturkampf.* . . . You need have no apprehensions concerning the freedom of the church."[17]

While Hitler was making assurances that no Kulturkampf would occur, and while Brownshirts marched in processions that were supposed to commemorate persecution of Catholics by state authorities, what were average Catholics told to believe concerning another possible Kulturkampf?

In a ceremony in 1941 rededicating Münster to the Sacred Heart of Jesus, von Galen, the current bishop, once again told the story of the persecuted, exiled, and finally triumphant Bishop Brinkmann. In an attempt to indirectly highlight similar "persecutions" of Catholics in 1941, he reminded the congregation of how Catholics in the 1870s had suffered under Bismarck. He told them about legislation that restricted Catholic clergy from ministering, how Catholic organizations and associations were closed down, how cloisters were taken over by the state, and how Catholics were accused of being "international" because their spiritual leader was in Rome. He reminded Catholics that the solution to these trials had been to rededicate themselves to Jesus' message and to maintain a religious atmosphere in their homes. This is not exactly an incitement to revolutionary activity against the state, although Nazi officials wrote letters to one another complaining that von Galen's sermon was full of enemy content. As punishment for reviving Kulturkampf memories, von Galen's diocese did not receive state donations. Reinhard Heydrich, at the Reich Security Main Office, was outraged that the bishop had drawn parallels between Kulturkampf times and present-day circumstances. He wrote to Lammers claiming that the bishop had tried to destroy public order and to reduce the authority of the state. Events did not escalate much further in this case because, as Lammers claimed, Hitler intervened and insisted that Heydrich refrain from further disciplinary measures.[18]

Although some Nazi officials interpreted von Galen's sermon as a threat to state security, the power of Kulturkampf memories was repeatedly diminished when bishops, such as von Galen, chose to attack the

Nazi state's actions indirectly without offering a clear indictment of the state's anti-Catholic actions. Most of the church authorities, von Galen included, had matured during the Kulturkampf era and chose to get along with the legally established authorities despite their reservations and misgivings. "To preserve as much as possible and to prevent even worse things, the church authorities often cooperated with the state." By cooperating, church authorities allowed Catholics to think "they could cooperate in the stirring events of the day without qualms and shout with all the rest, 'Heil Hitler.'"[19] Thus, the memory of the Kulturkampf actually was imagined in such a way as to limit the possibilities of resistance.

To more fully understand von Galen's attitude toward Hitler's regime, it is helpful to see whether his conception of the ideal German citizen and the church's relationship to both state and citizen altered under the Nazi regime. Throughout the Nazi years and despite increasing governmental violations of church rights, von Galen continued to preach obedience and duty to the state on the part of German Catholic citizens. For example, in a sermon delivered in September 1936, he said: "My dear listeners! I do not need to tell you, Christianity demands obedience, obedience to God, but also obedience to men. Already common sense tells us that only through obedience can order be maintained in the community."[20] Throughout the sermon, von Galen invoked numerous biblical citations, from 1 Peter 2:13–17, "For the sake of the Lord, accept the authority of every social institution. . . . God wants you to be good citizens. . . . Have respect for everyone and love of our community; fear God and honor the emperor," to Proverbs 8:15, "By me monarchs rule and princes issue just laws." He ended by telling the congregation that it was better to die than to sin.[21] It was left to the individual and his or her own conscience to decide which laws were just and which laws were unjust. Von Galen certainly never endorsed anything more than passive disobedience in his sermon.

Even as late as 1943, von Galen was still emphasizing the themes of obedience and duty to the Fatherland. When the philosopher Pieper was drafted into the German Army in 1943, he went to say farewell to the bishop. In Pieper's memoir he notes that as von Galen walked him to the door, he said, "And now go and serve your fatherland." Pieper remarked, "I was somewhat baffled; it was a long time since I had heard such words, but on his lips they were by no means a mere pathetic cliché; he meant them in all seriousness; they were to be taken literally."[22]

When priests who were serving at the front wrote or visited von

Galen and asked if they were fighting for an evil doctrine, the bishop reasoned that they were at war "not for the doctrine but for the sake of God and immortal souls. They hated the war but accepted and willed the sacrifice."[23] Much like the other German bishops, when war broke out, von Galen did not wonder whether the attack on Poland was part of the "just war" theory of Aquinas, as proper Catholic theologians would have instructed. Instead he rallied to the flag and called upon all Germans to do their duty for the Fatherland.[24] As the war continued, the Catholic hierarchy began to make distinctions between fighting for Germany and fighting for Hitler. By doing this, they hoped that they could show Catholics how to be good citizens, supporting their state but not necessarily a specific government.

Even the texts of von Galen's world-famous 1941 sermons—the sermons that bestowed the title of Resister on him—continued the established pattern of criticism watered down by conservative German patriotism. In each of the three sermons, he protested the evictions of religious orders, the scandalous immorality and currency trials, the closing of various Catholic organizations, and, finally, the euthanasia project. In powerful language, he starkly pointed out that institutionalized mentally ill persons were being murdered systematically. He charged the murderers with violating the Fifth Commandment, "Thou shalt not kill." However, in each one of the three sermons, von Galen still attempted to emphasize themes of duty and obedience. In his sermon of July 20, 1941, he stated, "We Christians, of course, are not aiming at revolution. We shall continue loyally to do our duty in obedience to God and in love of our people and fatherland. Our soldiers will fight and die for Germany. . . . We shall continue to fight against the external enemy; but against the enemy within, who strikes us and torments us, we cannot fight with arms. Against him we have one weapon: endurance—strong, tough, hard endurance."[25]

In the three sermons of 1941, von Galen generated a great deal of publicity, reinforced an already mobilized public opinion about euthanasia, and, more importantly, gave the church a seemingly renewed credibility that was sorely lacking. However, it is crucial to keep in mind that he only attacked portions of the National Socialist ideology and continued to urge overall loyalty to the Fatherland.[26]

Clearly, von Galen was expressing an opinion that was popular in German Catholic theological writings. Passive disobedience to laws that violated the church's teachings was permitted, but there was never an endorsement of active revolution, including tyrannicide. Here we see the limit of the resources of a theologically based notion of resistance. To the bishop, it was more important that Catholics maintain the institutional structures of the church than that they engage in active rebellions.

In a speech to clergy in Münster in October 1935, he explained to the clerics that priests, under the terms of the Concordat, could not be involved with political discussions. He did, however, emphasize that they could still be involved politically through work with the unemployed, youth groups, unions, and Catholic schools. He relied on Article 31 of the Concordat to protect the existence of confessional organizations that would fight against anti-Christian propaganda. In his address he suggested that the way to withstand a vigorous Kulturkampf and remain victorious would be to keep Jesus' message alive. The way to do that, he suggested, was through school instruction, catechisms, sermons that focused on the Gospel, pastoral house visits, and working with small groups of young people.[27]

Von Galen's thinking was representative of the thoughts of the Catholic hierarchy in general. They tended to focus on ecclesiastical-cultural goals: "Catholics were to make decisions on their political conduct within the state with an emphasis on religion, the Church, and schools as the building blocks of good political order."[28] The hierarchy placed its faith in the church's ability to outlast any secular government as long as it kept its structures intact.

The Concordat and Resistance

Von Galen, in his sermon, revealed that he believed the Concordat would assist the church hierarchy by protecting various Catholic organizations and structures from a Nazi seizure. When the Concordat was signed in 1933, Rome became the first legal partner to Hitler's regime. The leading church members had a legalistic mindset. Eugenio Pacelli (eventually Pope Pius XII) was a canon lawyer by training. Almost all of the church negotiators in this process, except Bishop Konrad von Preysing, who had studied secular law, were theologians trained in the neoscholastic tradition. They all tended to adhere to the belief that securing a legally defined place for the church would guarantee the church's continued existence in Nazi Germany. Hitler himself pushed for the Concordat because he shrewdly recognized that the Catholic Center Party's support would be needed in order for him to secure a two-thirds majority to pass the Enabling Act. He proposed the idea of an agreement with Rome over Easter weekend in the spring of 1933, the Center Party voted for the Enabling Act, and a Concordat was signed by July 1933.[29]

Once the negotiations were over, many celebrations were held throughout Germany to mark the occasion. The majority of the German hierarchy viewed the treaty as a symbol of peace between church and state, a guarantee that a second Kulturkampf had been avoided. In their enthusiasm for the occasion, some of the clergy voiced their support of National Socialism; Archbishop Gröber and Msgr. Franz Hartz were among the individuals who eagerly welcomed the two sides' drawing closer to each other. At the same time that Catholics were celebrating the success of the treaty, Heydrich was issuing orders to the Bavarian Political Police to step up activity aimed at eliminating Catholic organizations.[30] The German bishops, underestimating the regime's objection to the existence of Catholicism in Germany, reinforced the legitimacy of Hitler's government by signing the Concordat. Once the treaty was signed, the German bishops faced the question of how to criticize the National Socialists and still be considered "good Germans" legally. They met at Fulda in August 1933 to discuss this question.

At Fulda, Bishop Preysing pleaded with the other German clergymen present to issue a letter in which the errors of Nazism would be clearly delineated for Catholics. Cardinal Bertram, as leader of the Fulda gathering, once again refused any attempt at direct conflict with Hitler's government. One of the few realists was Pastor Bruckmaier of the Passau diocese, who stated, "There is a Concordat to be sure, but it exists only on paper."[31] By the end of the conference, the episcopacy had decided that the Concordat should be supported despite the growing tension over the existence of certain Catholic organizations. Essentially they decided to take up a defensive posture by protesting violations of the Concordat through written petitions, remonstrances, and formal sermons. To von Galen, the Concordat was a way for the state and church, working together, to avoid another Kulturkampf.[32]

The Concordat did provide a legal foundation on which the church could base its protests. Pacelli (later Pope Pius XII), even after the war, defended the Concordat: "Without the legal protection afforded by the Concordat, the subsequent persecution of the church might have taken even more violent forms. The basis of Catholic belief and enough of its institutions remained intact to permit their survival and resurgence after the war." If the Concordat did bring some strength to German Catholics, it also brought weakness in that the church, because of the restrictions of the Concordat, limited its focus to strictly church-related problems and failed to address the higher question of religious values.[33]

The Church Hierarchy and the Jewish Question

At the August 1933 Fulda Bishops' Conference, the clergy present agreed to ask the pope to add some words in the Concordat that would protect Christians who had converted from Judaism and who were suffering under recent "non-Aryan" legislation. This appeal went to Counselor Eugene Klee of the German Embassy, who dismissed their request, stating that the position of converts had nothing to do with the Concordat. Cardinal Pacelli, eager to keep the negotiations running smoothly, wrote a memorandum containing the request. Klee once again objected on the basis that the pope would not interfere in Germany's internal affairs. Pacelli, who never delivered his memo, later issued a statement: "The Holy See takes this occasion to add a word in behalf of those German Catholics who themselves have gone over from Judaism to the Christian religion . . . and who for reasons known to the Reich Government are likewise suffering from social and economic difficulties."[34] As this quotation reveals, the curia was concerned with converts, not Jews themselves. This position is also reflected in the attitude of the Catholic clergy: persecution of nonconverted Jews aroused little interest on the part of the Catholic leadership. We find virtually no protests by the papacy or members of the German Catholic hierarchy against the anti-Semitism of the regime. After the April 1, 1933, boycott of Jewish-owned and -operated stores, Cardinal Bertram wrote, "My scruples (against intervention) are first of all based on the consideration that this is an economic battle that does not have anything to do with our immediate church interests." Simultaneously, Cardinal Pacelli received a letter from Cardinal Faulhaber explaining why the church would not intervene to protect Jews. "This is not possible at this time because the struggle against the Jews would at the same time become a struggle against Catholics, and because the Jews can help themselves, as the sudden end of the boycott shows."[35] Archbishop Gröber, writing to a professor in Rome, justified his actions by saying, "I immediately intervened on behalf of the converted Jews, but so far have had no response to my action. . . . I am afraid the campaign against Judah will prove costly to us."[36]

These comments reveal the church's policy toward Jews. The church would concern itself with converts, but unconverted Jews could fend for themselves. Neither the pope in Rome nor the Catholic leaders in Germany pursued an aggressive policy of fighting to protect persecuted Jews, for fear that they would bring down greater troubles on their Catholic followers. The same policy of nonintervention was followed with the passage of the 1935 Nuremburg Laws. Churchmen sought to be impartial and neutral, falling back on the Concordat and legalistic procedures. In 1941, in response to announcements that Jews were to wear the Star of David on their clothing, the Catholic hierarchy protested, asking that Catholic non-Aryans be allowed to leave their Star of David at home when they were attending Mass. Cardinal Bertram advised his fellow leaders to remind their congregation of Saint Paul's teaching: "For those believing in Christ, there is neither Jew nor Greek, for all are one in Christ."[37]

Bertram, like so many of his fellow Catholics, thought that only Jews who had converted to Christianity were truly worthy of being saved. As for von Galen, he often stated in his sermons that he was violently opposed to the racism of the Nazis, but he rarely addressed the topic of anti-Semitism specifically. In 1934 he wrote the introduction to Professor Wilhelm Neuss's work that attacked the teachings of Alfred Rosenberg's *Myth of the Twentieth Century*. He supported Neuss's work not because it attacked the violent anti-Semitic rhetoric contained in *The Myth*, but rather because Rosenberg sought to exalt one race over all others.[38] Perhaps more revealing concerning von Galen's position on the Jewish Question is his behavior surrounding the events of the government-sponsored pogrom of November 1938, Kristallnacht.

The bishop was out in some of Münster's outlying regions performing confirmations when Kristallnacht occurred. Upon his return, he issued no public pronouncement condemning the violence. The events of Kristallnacht had presented a unique opportunity for the church leadership to regain some moral high ground, because the majority of the German population seems to have disapproved of the vicious pogrom. What is even more intriguing is that after the war Rabbi Fritz L. Steinthal, who had been the leader of the Jewish community in Münster, claimed that the bishop had sent a priest to his home to see if the rabbi needed assistance in getting out of the local jail. The priest, who also survived the war, claimed that the rabbi was mistaken. The clergyman asserted that he was not sent by von Galen but that he, upon witnessing the damage to the Jewish community in Münster, went of his own volition to the Steinthal home.[39] The priest's account contradicts Rabbi Steinthal's belief that von Galen cared about the fate of his family. It seems like a typical case in which a lower-level clergyman performed an individual act of courage without receiving support from the upper echelons of the church hierarchy.

Even in von Galen's 1941 sermon against euthanasia, he lists violations of the Ten Commandments but never directly admonishes the faithful, "Love thy neighbor as thyself." He often omits references to Jewishness when citing biblical passages. In a sermon in which he quotes from John 16, he omits the passage John 16:2–3, in which Jesus states, "They will expel you from the synagogues, and indeed the hour is coming when anyone who kills you will think he is doing a holy duty for God. They will do these things because they have never known either the Father or myself."[40] Perhaps the bishop thought this passage would strike his listeners a little too closely, making them feel uncomfortable about possible participation in violence perpetrated against Jews.

The occurrence of Catholic anti-Semitism or, at the very least, indifference to the fate of the Jews, should not be surprising in light of Catholics' desire to be integrated fully into the German nation and culture.[41] With the rise of Germany as a modern, industrialized liberal state, most Catholics felt that they could either oppose the new German state or attempt to be politically integrated by working within the system. Once the Catholic Center Party was created, most Catholics opted for inclusion in the Second Reich. When Bismarck attacked Catholics as Reichsfeinde, many responded by seeking to align themselves with Protestant conservatives. Both religious groups shared common ground in their opposition to liberalism and socialism.[42] They often shared anti-Semitic sentiments also. The Kulturkampf had forced Catholics to define their values and to establish a cultural identity. Anti-Semitism facilitated this process of self-definition.[43] A brief examination of why Catholics already accepted anti-Semitic thought helps us understand von Galen's idea of the perfect German state. The real enemy, in the view of many Christians, was not the heathen or the pagan, but the Jew.[44] In von Galen's pastoral of January 1934, he told Catholics that Jesus' blood redeems all people who accept his message. What he implied was that those who have rejected Jesus as the Messiah cannot be saved. It appears that both bishops and theologians could be classified as intellectual anti-Semites.[45]

Following the church's tradition from Saint Augustine on, Jews were not to be hated, but they did not need to be embraced either. Jews would always be open to being humiliated and persecuted, the tradition held, because they had rejected Jesus as the Messiah. But Jews were not supposed to be murdered, because there was always the possibility of conversion. Cardinal Schulte remarked in 1936 that the "greatest sin of the Jewish people was that it rejected the Savior and his teaching."[46] If one was not redeemed, then one could not be saved. Michael Schmaus, professor of dogmatic theology at Münster, believed and taught that persecution of Jews was part of God's justice. Pope Pius XII in *Mystici Corporis* (1943) instructed the faithful that only those who had been baptized were part of God's plan of salvation. The pope, the theologians, and the bishops failed to see that so-called "normal anti-Semitism," when uncorrected, would help contribute to the acceptance of Nazi racist anti-Semitic attacks.

Von Galen, although often critical of racist literature and remarks, was quick to point out to listeners that his blood was just as German as the next person's, if not more so because of his family's history. In a 1937 sermon at Vreden, he declared that he was descended from centuries of Westphalian Catholic nobility and added, "If anyone stands up and asserts that German blood speaks in him, I stand up here and assert the same myself."[47] In his effort to assert that Catholics were just as German as Protestants, he co-opted language similar to what the Nazis used when asserting that blood could establish one's credentials. The fears of blood purity were expressed by many Catholic theologians and bishops.

Bishop Ketteler (von Galen's great-uncle) attacked in the 1860s what he considered to be the corrupting influence of Jews on the German national economy, the family, and public morality. In the 1870s he claimed that "liberal Jewish dominance had reached a point where even 'German character' was being warped." By the early years of the twentieth century, Protestant racists were seeking alliances with the Catholic Center Party because they believed that the party was "safe from Jewish infiltration." Many came to believe that an alliance between Catholics and Protestants would be the only way to ensure that Germany was resting on a proper foundation. The Protestant League paper wrote, "The spiritual and moral development of all of Germany, including that of the

German Catholics, rests upon Christianity." In 1907 Wilhelm Hoens-broech established a union in an attempt to bring conservative Catholics and Protestants together. His organization proposed that "German Catholics bind together with German Protestants to support patriotic interests and assure the Christian national foundation of the state."[48] The religiously based criticisms from Catholics coexisted with the racist arguments, overlapping and reinforcing popular prejudices against the Jews.

Dr. G. K. A. Bell, Anglican bishop of Chicester, met von Galen in October 1945. Bell described how impressed he was with the Catholic bishop; he said that von Galen "believed firmly that Catholics and Protestants would work together. He said to me that it was clearly imperative that all who were at one in their belief in God, in their faithfulness to Christ and in their conviction of the soul's immortality should come forward on behalf of righteousness and peace."[49] The notion of an alliance between Catholics and Protestants in order to form a Christian state apparently was unaltered by the end of World War II and the full revelations of what racist anti-Semitism had wrought.

Theologians writing between 1918 and 1933 tended to offer Catholics a mixture of nationalism and "nonracial" anti-Semitism. Scholars developed what Werner Jeanrond terms *Volkstheologie* or *Reichstheologie.* Karl Adam, one of the foremost theologians of the time, stressed that the people and the church should work to support one another. He believed that it was the state's responsibility to maintain the purity of the Volk's blood. He also condemned what he called the Jewish mentality, which, he said, had pervaded German life. Erich Przywara, in a 1926 article, "Judentum und Christentum," argued that Judaism would be overcome by Christianity. Przywara urged the conversion of all Jews.[50] Jesuit father Gustav Gundlach approved of "moderate, political anti-Semitism" as long as it was restricted to combating "harmful Jewish influence." He argued that natural law proved the equality of all the redeemed. Those who had not been "redeemed" through Christianity were to be excluded from society.[51] By 1933 Gundlach was beginning to have his doubts about Nazism. Eventually Pope Pius XI called Gundlach to Rome to help draft an encyclical addressing the Jewish Question as a Christian, and not as a racial problem. Nothing ever materialized with this draft, because Pius XI died before it could be published and Pope Pius XII refused to endorse the document. Despite Gundlach's evolution in thinking, many theologians who rejected anti-Semitism on the social level nonetheless supported the theological underpinnings of religious anti-Semitism, thereby aiding the Nazis by making "anti-Jewishness" more acceptable. Repeatedly, Catholics were told by various theologians and clergymen that only those who had accepted Jesus as the Messiah could be saved. Theologian Friedrich Fuchs, although he rejected Nazism's claim that German blood redeemed an individual, stated in his writings that only Christians could be saved through Jesus' blood.[52] This type of thinking only served to reinforce notions of acceptable anti-Semitism.

Religious journals also contributed to the Nazis' success in that the journals frequently rejected articles that attempted to address the origins of Christianity and its connections with Judaism. Most articles that appeared emphasized commonalties between National Socialism and Catholicism, such as the antiliberalism, antisocialism, antidemocracy, and prohierarchy views found in both systems. By denying or avoiding the connections Christianity has with Judaism, these journals contributed to an acceptable form of "anti-Jewishness."[53]

By 1934 theologians had generally ceased to comment on the Jewish Question. They retreated into abstract moral treatises, which "certainly went unread by the average Catholic layman. . . . Early adaptation and later opposition could only confuse those who looked to the Church for guidance." Theologians failed to subject the National Socialist Weltanschauung to rigorous critique and failed to promote the basic premise that all individuals are created by God and have an inherent right to live unharmed. In the attempt to remain "good" Germans and "good" Catholics, theologians worked to reduce the conflict between Christian virtues and Nazi values. In the process, subtle distinctions were embedded in theological verbiage and were undetected by the faithful. The theologians contributed to the impression that "the Church was supporting the basic policies of the regime and only differing over minor issues."[54]

The German bishops and the pope had decided that the church, in order to fulfill its mission, had to be a viable institution and had to have proper relations with the state. Few theological writings existed for guiding opposition to the regime. The "resistance" offered was that of civil disobedience to specific laws; the "right to overthrow the government by force was not clearly delimited in the theology of the churches." Von Galen thought that preserving Catholic institutions and organizations on German soil would keep Catholic values alive; it was not a very ambitious or creative goal. By declaring the purity of von Galen family blood; refusing to offer outright, public condemnation of anti-Semitic policies; and recognizing Hitler's regime as a legitimate authority, von Galen contributed to the general impression that "despite superficial faults, National Socialism could not really be as evil as some had earlier suggested."[55]

Locked into following a policy that promised security, and blinded to suggestions of open rebellion, the German Catholic hierarchy, von Galen included, quite frequently failed to convey to the faithful that National Socialism and Catholicism were irreconcilable philosophies. In their desperate attempts to preserve Catholic organizations and associations while maintaining their loyalty to the German state, the bishops failed to defend the rights of all human beings. They had perhaps forgotten the words of Pope Pius XI, spoken to religious representatives from thirty-seven nations in July 1938; he stated that "because human reality is to be men and not beasts . . . human dignity is to be one single great family, the human type, the human race."[56]

CHAPTER FOUR

Von Galen, Eugenics, and the Nazis

We ought to obey God rather than men.

—ACTS 5:29

In the summer of 1941, Bishop von Galen delivered three powerful sermons that ranged from Gestapo seizures of ecclesiastical property to the Nazi euthanasia campaign to destroy the mentally ill and physically handicapped. Von Galen's third sermon, which protested euthanasia, was not the first public denunciation of "mercy killings," nor was it going to be the last. But the sermons did create an uproar both nationally and internationally. What made von Galen's sermons different from other denunciations was the distinctness and concreteness of details provided. The sermons were also effective because he was able to strike the right chord with listeners, alerting them to the possibility that they could all at one time or another become vulnerable under the Nazi state.

Von Galen's three sermons made such an impact that he became a kind of symbolic figure of resistance, particularly to northwestern Germans.[1] What should be pointed out, however, is that these sermons were not a plea for Catholics to use their imaginations and go beyond protecting the mentally ill and physically handicapped from Nazi aggression. None of the three sermons openly urged listeners to offer aid and protection to other persecuted minorities in the Third Reich. Most studies, when making reference to von Galen's historic speeches, fail to place the summer sermons in their appropriate context. The bishop's immediate outburst of 1941 had nothing whatsoever to do with information regarding euthanasia. What seemed to motivate the bishop to raise his voice to a new level of power and eloquence was not the murder of the incurably ill but the fear that Catholic institutions were about to be eradicated from German soil. The Gestapo seizures of Catholic properties and the subsequent displacement of Catholic religious men and women seemed to him to be a revival of the 1870s Kulturkampf. The first two famous sermons had nothing to do with protesting euthanasia. Most studies also neglect to integrate Protestant denunciations of euthanasia prior to von Galen's third, and most famous, sermon. Von Galen might not have ever spoken openly regarding euthanasia had he not been receiving concrete proof of the murders of innocents from Protestant pastors and Protestant directors of Germany's asylums.

Ever conscious of Catholics' seemingly precarious inclusion in the German state, von Galen waited to speak out against euthanasia until numerous public denunciations had been made by Protestant Germans. Maintaining the Catholic Church on German soil while fighting to keep Catholics from being categorized as enemies of the state, von Galen walked a delicate line between opposition and accommodation. He denounced certain specific government policies but never rejected the Nazi government in toto. Although von Galen has been remembered for his defiant 1941 sermons, it must be pointed out that he never once, in any of those sermons, encouraged Catholics to embrace activity against the state. Because of these sermons he became a figure of anti-Nazi resistance, although he never once incited Catholics to do more than remain selectively steadfast in their Catholic beliefs.

In the final analysis, von Galen did take a risk when he chose to voice his opinions so openly from the pulpit. However, even his forthright denunciations of Nazi policies did not by themselves cause Hitler to end the euthanasia project. The bishop seems to have been motivated by his desire to maintain the existence of Catholic institutions in Germany while protecting Catholics from the exile experienced during the Kulturkampf days. He was willing to fight for Catholic causes. He was not interested in aligning Catholics with those people who had been deemed enemies of the state.

Oath and Conscience

In a study of resistance, Mother Mary Alice Gallin declared, "Each man must act according to his conscience. . . . Ethics gives us the principles, but the application of the principle is usually a sensitive and difficult operation." At a meeting to discuss Nazi violations of the Concordat, von Galen expressed just this sentiment when he asserted that "each bishop must follow his own conscience. . . . The ultimate responsibility rested with bishops individually." Leaving each bishop to decide how he should apply ethical principles to the situation around him did not provide uniform guidance, nor did it offer a united stance against National Socialism. Many of the clergy became bogged down with the question of conscience versus the sanctification of an oath. All public officials, pastors included, had to swear the following under Hitler's government: "I swear I shall be loyal and obedient to Adolf Hitler, the Führer of the German Reich and people; respect the laws, and fulfill my official duties conscientiously, so help me God."[2] Von Galen became the first newly appointed Catholic bishop to take this oath in October 1933.

The application of ethical principles became enmeshed with the question of when it would be permissible to violate one's oath, if ever. In response, moral theologians in the Catholic tradition were fairly unified: most of them argued from Thomas Aquinas forward that no oath could be binding if it was contrary to God's commandments. However, because the Scriptures compel obedience to state authority and its laws, many of the German bishops took the position that Catholics owed obedience to the lawful authority because "every human activity is a reflection of divine rule and is a participation in the eternal authority of God."[3] Lost in a complex series of distinctions between conscience and obedience, party and state, the bishops preached an ambiguous, dual message to their parishioners. Catholics were generally advised to maintain their loyalty to the authorities but were simultaneously instructed to choose God's law over that of the state.

At the annual Fulda Bishops' Conference of 1934, the clergy present addressed the question of a binding civil oath. In the resulting pastoral, the bishops emphasized that citizens must take an oath of unconditional followership, carrying out their orders loyally. They undercut the state by adding, "Catholics will of course not be obligated to anything which is contrary to God or church law and thereby is contrary to their conscience." They stopped short of offering a clear delineation of what would be contrary to God's law. The confusion was furthered by a 1935 pastoral exhorting Catholics to follow their conscience while warning them that "they should neither listen to nor pass on wild rumors which were spread against authority. . . . Be patient and pray."[4]

In pastorals such as these, Catholics were reminded that God and conscience are the starting points regarding obedience toward earthly authority. The pivotal point arrived when temporal power demanded from the subject something that would violate natural law: "When the commands of the State are at variance with natural law and the commands of God, they are not to be obeyed."[5] This instruction did not mean that Catholics should embrace insurrection; it meant civil disobedience to unjust laws, or passive resistance. Catholics were still expected to conform to all other governmental legislation.

For some rare individuals, such as Count Stauffenberg or Peter Yorck von Wartenburg, the notion of the unconstitutional state meant that the state had abandoned "fundamental principles in so decisive a way that it had forfeited the obedience of its citizens."[6] Most ordinary German Catholics looking for guidance about obedience and possibilities of resistance would find a mixed message from the hierarchy. Each church statement coupled the theory of natural law (the right to practice one's faith unhindered) with such nationalistic pronouncements that individuals who resolved to act with determined resistance generally recognized that they would not receive official support from the church.[7]

The bishops, learning from the experiences of the Kulturkampf era, were determined to prevent any accusation that they were disloyal to the national government. Most of them, after examining their individual consciences, had decided to pursue a "campaign of defensive opposition."[8] Traditional means of protest—letters of complaint, petitions, and public protests—in order to maintain the practice of Catholic values in daily life were often successful in achieving their aim. For von Galen, legal weapons of protest led to the successful restoration of crucifixes in the Oldenburg schools. He used similar techniques of protest in the battle to expose the Nazi euthanasia campaign.

What must be remembered is that the Catholic Church never officially protested the anti-Jewish policies; it confined its objections to specific ecclesiastical interests, violations of the Concordat, and circumscribed clashes regarding one's "outlook on life."[9] The church might tell Catholics that following certain governmental laws was a matter of individual conscience, but it offered no support structure for or guide to Catholics who might consider revolt.

Despite the lack of guidance, there were numerous lower-level clergy who chose to obey their consciences rather than follow an immoral government.[10] August Wessing, a Roman Catholic priest in Münster, was arrested numerous times by the Gestapo in town. He was charged with repeatedly speaking to Polish and Russian "workers," speaking in Polish, and ordering nuns to mend the workers' clothing. Upon his ninth arrest, Wessing clarified his position to his interrogator: "I am a pastor and in this capacity I cannot be hostile to anyone, whether Polish, Russian or Jew." Later, in 1944, Wessing was punished for his "crimes against the state" by being sent to Dachau. He died there on March 4, 1945.[11]

It is unreasonable to expect that every opponent of Nazism would be willing, as Father Wessing was, to sacrifice his life for his conscience. Von Galen came face-to-face with such a choice in the summer of 1941. In three sermons, the bishop powerfully denounced Gestapo seizures of ecclesiastical institutions and then turned his focus to the realm of moral doctrine. After personally witnessing expulsions of priests and nuns by Gestapo agents in July 1941, von Galen returned to the Bishop's Palace, and "in that night he wrote the words which in the eyes of the world have indissolubly bound up his personality with the city of Münster. He was firmly convinced that the enemies of the church would soon put an end to his life here on earth. Looking death in the face, he trod the way of *conscience* and faithfulness, fully ready to receive at God's hands the grace of martyrdom."[12]

Was martyrdom a reasonable expectation for von Galen? Not many high-ranking Catholic clergymen were in concentration camps. Bishops Johann Sproll and Dr. Johann Neuhaüsler were imprisoned in Dachau. Eventually Bishops Dr. Michal Kozal of Poland and Gabriel Piquet of France were also placed there. Of the inmates of concentration camps, 9.78 percent were higher Catholic clergy.[13] Nonetheless, closer to home, von Galen knew of Protestant Pastor Martin Niemöller, who had resided in Münster from 1924 to 1930 and who had been imprisoned since 1937 for giving sermons about obeying one's conscience rather than the laws of men. Perhaps Niemöller's incarceration had left a mark on von Galen.

The bishop's sermons in the summer of 1941 were such forthright denunciations of certain Nazi policies that Göring wrote to von Galen, accusing him of violating his oath of loyalty by making agitational speeches and writings that sabotaged the German nation. He also warned the bishop to reconcile himself to his oath, because there was only one authority in Germany—the state. A few weeks later von Galen responded to Göring telling him that his oath must correspond to his conscience and that he was serving the German nation dutifully. Tweaking Göring further, he added that he would always obey just authority.[14]

Oath, conscience, obedience, authority—all of these terms seem to have coalesced in the summer of 1941 for von Galen. In order to examine the outburst in 1941, we must first turn our attention to the gathering clouds.

"The Duty to Be Healthy"

In early October 1939, despite the beginning of the war, the Nazi government declared 1939 the year of "the duty to be healthy."[15] This mandate included the idea of the destruction of "life unworthy of life." The discussion of euthanasia was by no means a creation of the Nazis. The novelty of the twentieth century was to turn the definition of euthanasia from death with dignity, or mercy-killing, to an economic tactic whereby "useless idiots" would be killed in order to save money and manpower for an already overburdened society.[16]

Following World War I, pressure increased to destroy the insane and the handicapped as a way of relieving other people from some of the financial strains and deprivations they were experiencing.[17] By 1920 men such as Alfred Hoche, professor of psychiatry at Freiburg University, and Karl Binding, a professor of law, could publish *Permission for the Destruction of Lives Unworthy of Life;* they argued that mental patients were taking resources that should be dedicated to national revival and that their destruction should actually be considered a humane act because those targeted could not appreciate the value of life anyway.

Binding, in his section of the book, asked, "Are there humans who have lost their human characteristics to such an extent that their continued existence has lost all value both for themselves and for society?" He answered the question by observing, "If . . . one thinks of a battlefield covered with thousands of young corpses . . . and one compares them with our institutions for idiots . . . one is shocked by the sharp discrepancy between on the one hand, the sacrifice of man's most precious resource and, on the other hand, the tremendous care devoted to creatures which are not only completely worthless but are of negative value."[18]

Professor Hoche emphasized the economic burden posed by the mentally ill and the handicapped, arguing, "The question of whether the resources of all kinds devoted to these living burdens is justified was not an urgent one in the prosperous days gone by; but now things are different." He concluded that Germany must move into a new era in which the killing of "living burdens" would be regarded as a higher moral duty. Ignoring the values of mercy and empathy, he said this new morality would "cease continually implementing the demands of an exaggerated concept of humanity and an exaggerated view of the value of human life at great cost."[19]

Ernst Mann published a novel in 1922 in which he advocated killing the poor as a way of eliminating poverty.[20] In 1936 Helmut Unger's novel *Mission and Conscience* portrayed a young woman's struggle with multiple sclerosis and the fatal injection of morphine that ended her life. In the novel the doctor who overdosed the young woman was tried and acquitted. This novel later formed the basis of a Nazi pro-euthanasia movie, *I Accuse.*[21]

Hitlerschnitt: The Buildup to Euthanasia

Even before the actual killing of patients was discussed, other "solutions" aimed at social control were put forward by many in the medical community. These discussions were directed at "breaking the defective links in the hereditary chain" while promoting relief from the increasing expenditures of caring for "undesirables" in the welfare system. What one can see emerging from the discussions of community well-being was a dual policy supported by various Nazi leaders. On the one hand, they would extol the virtues of family life and motherhood, and on the other hand, they could urge the sterilization and euthanasia of those individuals classified as unfit or of lesser value. The creation of such a hierarchy, ranging from those of "high value" to those of "lesser value" was partly the work of Reich Minister of the Interior Wilhelm Frick, who in June 1933 compiled a list of "experts" who could suitably address the interrelated topics of racial policy and population control. These individuals would be called upon to generate ideas and to help plan the course of German racial policies.[22]

Although many physicians supported the idea of sterilization for some people, it was not a legal reality for German doctors until the summer of 1933. Sterilization was, however, already legal by this time in Switzerland, in Denmark, and in twenty-eight states in America.[23] In fact, by 1933 many German doctors were worried that America's laws regarding the sterilization of the mentally ill and criminally insane would propel America ahead of other nations in its programs of racial hygiene and social progress. The German doctors not only wanted to catch up to the Americans; they desired to surpass them. What they needed was a law permitting such actions.

On July 14, 1933, the Law for the Prevention of Genetically Diseased Offspring (the Sterilization Law) was passed. According to this law, genetic health courts would be established to evaluate individuals and decide whether a particular person needed to undergo sterilization. In many respects the Sterilization Law can be seen as an outgrowth of the medical community's arguments that this process could solve pressing social problems. Sterilization promised, among other things, an end to "shiftlessness, ignorance, laziness in workers; deviant sexual behavior; increasing numbers of the ill and insane; poverty and the rising costs of social services." In the earlier twentieth century, men such as Dr. Erich Friedländer, the director of Lindenhaus in Lippe, argued that caring for chronically ill patients was a "luxury that Germany could not afford."[24] His arguments were picked up by the "Apostle of Sterilization," Heinrich Boeters, in the 1920s.

Boeters, a medical officer of Zwickau, pushed for legal changes that would allow "idiots, blind, deaf, dumb and illegitimate mothers of 'low eugenic value'" to be sterilized. Boeter's suggestions were lauded as "pioneering" and "modern" by Dr. Robert Gaupp. In Gaupp's presentation to a group of psychiatrists in 1925, he not only praised Boeter's work, but he also pointed to the American physicians and their advanced work with vasectomies and X-ray sterilization. Arguing that World War I and the Treaty of Versailles had left Germany with an expanding population and a diminishing economic base, Gaupp claimed that the German people now faced a veritable eugenics crisis. The doctor tried to convince his audience that German law needed to be changed, and quickly, because "the less valuable [were] reproducing more rapidly than the more valuable." To drive home his point, Gaupp ended his presentation with a quote from social Darwinist Herbert Spencer: "A people consisting of hereditarily valuable individuals is the first condition of the well-being of the nation."[25] Gaupp may not have succeeded on that day in 1925 in convincing doctors that the law should be changed in order to sterilize "less valuable" patients, but there were others who elaborated on his themes.

At the Twenty-Fifth Annual Conference of Bavarian Psychiatrists in July 1931, the topic of sterilization was discussed at great length. Not all of the medical officers present agreed with the idea of involuntarily sterilizing their patients. One such man, Oswald Bumke, a professor of psychiatry in Munich, argued: "If we can prevent the occurrence of mental illnesses with the aid of sterilization. . . . Then certainly we should do so—but not because the state is saving money, but because every mental illness signifies perpetual suffering for both the patient and his relatives. In this case, economic perspectives are not just inappropriate but dangerous. One only needs to take the idea to its logical conclusion—that one should do away with all those people who at the time seem dispensable for financial reasons. . . . That would certainly save money, but I suspect we would not do it." Bumke continued, noting how the current atmosphere was charged with scientific theories of race, and then he made a prediction: "If one were to drag the discussion of sterilization into today's arena of political struggle, then one would probably pretty soon hear less talk about the mentally ill, but more about Aryans and non-Aryans."[26]

Ignoring Bumke's observations about the dangers of combining a sterilization program with economic theory, Berthold Kihn from Erlangen presented a lecture in 1932 on how to raise the quality of the population. Specifically, Kihn offered four ways to address the expanding population and its decreasing quality. He first suggested eugenic marriage counseling and the prohibition of "unfit" unions, but he pointed out that this would be essentially useless because the great masses of people would ignore it. He presented the option of isolating people who were unfit to reproduce in asylums but then countered that this would become financially prohibitive. What was left to do, then? As Kihn saw it, there were only two remaining options: the destruction of "life unworthy of life" or castration or sterilization for those deemed less valuable. Kihn stated that because of the current financial crisis, these radical solutions were the only options that were still viable. He believed that of the two, eugenic sterilization was the preferred "humane" choice. Completely contradicting Bumke, Kihn stated, "Every measure is permissible which appears cheap and effective in the struggle against the less valuable."[27]

By July 26, 1933, the Law for the Prevention of Genetically Diseased Offspring had been published. Many proponents of eugenic sterilization were convinced that through effective propaganda, the German people could come to see the need for such measures. The Protestant chairman of the Inner Mission, Hans Harmsen, found the cost-cutting aspect of sterilization appealing. He argued that sterilization would permit the Inner Mission to "replace universal charity with biologically deter-

mined selective benefits." Because Harmsen was also in charge of the
Inner Mission's asylums, he pushed sterilization as a "moral duty." To
Harmsen, sterilization was not about God's individual creations living in
the present, but about the possibility of future creations.[28] This, in fact,
was exactly how the government hoped individuals would see the Sterilization Law: they were supposed to understand that it was not intended
to be punitive. Undergoing sterilization was an "individual's ultimate
sacrifice for the good of the community."[29]

German Protestant women who read the Protestant publication *Der
Bote* found these themes repeated in their journal's pages. In 1933 articles
in *Der Bote* focused on the divine "order of creation," arguing that some
races were simply inferior to others.[30] Other articles worried over the
possibility of diluting racial purity and agreed with governmental interference in the matter: "If our race is to be saved from downfall it is the
sacred obligation of our leaders to build a dam and put an end to any
additional, ominous dilution of Aryan blood, even when in the process
harsh measures cannot be avoided." Marriage and reproduction were
now to be considered a community matter, for "the genetically healthy,
racially valuable family will decide Germany's future." The readers of
Der Bote were treated to an entire issue dedicated to informing them
about the Sterilization Law, including whom the law would affect and
the reasons for the favorable disposition of the German Protestant
women's auxiliary toward the new law.[31]

Further attempts were made to convince the public of the dire need
for the law. To enhance public interest, newspaper articles portrayed asylum directors in their "ongoing struggle for 'race and nation'." The Nazi
newspaper *Völkischer Beobachter* gave reason upon reason for sterilizing patients. Tours of asylums were also given to the interested public.
Between 1933 and 1939, 21,000 people (6,000 of them members of the
SS) went through Elfging-Haar asylum alone. These tours were deemed
successful when, at the tour's conclusion, a visitor would ask aloud why
the patients were even kept alive. For those unable to go on a tour, the
Racial and Political Office produced several films, all of them intended
to portray the economic burdens of caring for the chronically ill and the
potentially harmful effect their reproduction could have on Germany's
culture.[32]

For most German Catholics, the issues relating to eugenics and
euthanasia were consigned to theological journals until July 14, 1933.
Once the Sterilization Law was passed, the Catholic bishops met to dis-

cuss the law and its conflict with Catholic moral doctrine. Frick had promised them that once the Concordat was ratified, the government would reconsider the proposed law on sterilization. The Concordat was ratified in July, and the Sterilization Law went into effect anyway. Meeting at Fulda, the bishops decided not to run the risk of ruining the new church-state relationship created by the Concordat. Many of those present feared that "flat rejection could jeopardize their newly-won civic equality."[33] Instead, resorting to classic anti-establishment methods, they prepared a detailed memorandum explaining the Catholic position on matters pertaining to sterilization. The document petitioned the government to redesign the law so that Catholics would not be subjected to a conflict of conscience. More specifically, the bishops urged exemptions for Catholic doctors; however, they never endorsed or fought for nuns or social workers' concerns regarding the sterilization program. Many Catholic women now found themselves required by the new law to prepare the patient and the instruments for sterilization. They began to ask their Catholic leaders for directions. Those present at the August 1933 Fulda bishops' meeting had received a letter from a woman begging them to issue "authoritative instructions" and not "subtle distinctions."[34]

At first thought, this request for authoritative instructions does not seem so bold. The Sterilization Law seemed to be completely in conflict with Catholic moral doctrine. Pope Pius XI had issued *Casti Connubi* (On Christian marriage) and had declared the body of man inviolable. Although Pius's position appeared to be very clear and straightforward, some Catholic theologians, such as Professor Joseph Mayer of the Paderborn Academy, continued to defend sterilization, abortion, and euthanasia. As the debates continued, more Catholic intellectuals emerged who argued the complexities of the question. Two Catholic theologians who endorsed the Sterilization Law were Karl Eschweiler and Hans Barion. Both men contended that sterilization was not in conflict with Catholicism. Others, such as Franz Walther, argued against the law, stating that such a stance arose from the moral collapse of society. Otto Schilling maintained that the state's ultimate aim should be to protect the lives of innocent children.[35]

Because there seemed to be no clear-cut agreement on the part of Catholic theologians, many bishops established a complex set of rules pertaining to the involvement of workers, nurses, and doctors in the process.[36] But after setting up the guidelines, they chose not to enforce them. The majority of German bishops, although they disagreed with the sterilization measures, seemed to recognize that average Catholics could lose their jobs over this issue, and so they adjusted their position to fit with the new set of circumstances they were confronting. They chose to accommodate themselves and their parishioners in order to avoid a possible conflict with the state. This was particularly important when individuals such as Minister Frick warned priests about violating the Sterilization Law. "The Church's condemnation of sterilization was labeled as sabotage of the national renewal and a malicious attack on the state and party. It was seen as an attack on the dynamic and legal foundations of the state. The bishops were uncomfortable whenever their loyalty was attacked and continued their retreat, camouflaged by patriotic speeches."[37]

In Frick's view, state interference in such a private realm would especially require the loyalty of German women. The "Volkmutter" would have to place the best interests of the nation over those of even her own children. Her job would be linked to that of Mother Nature, pruning the weak to ensure the future strength of her creations. The *Volkmutter* was required to set aside her feelings of Christian charity and empathy for individual suffering. She was to work scientifically and relieve herself of the obligation to aid those weaker than her. Like the doctor, the new German woman was told that her job as a mother included the duty to ensure the future success of the community by ridding society of its "unproductives." Her goal should no longer be universal charity to all those in need, but rather charity only to the racially fit and valuable members of society. According to Frick, in a 1935 speech, the need to sterilize "defectives" should be binding on all Germans, including Catholics.[38]

Originally the legislators who crafted the Sterilization Law envisioned the formation of almost 1,700 genetic health courts. The number of courts never reached that number, but by July 1934 the government had successfully created the State Health Offices, with departments for gene and race care. The departments established 181 genetic health courts, which would be presided over by one lawyer and two doctors per court. These agents handled proposals for sterilization and marriage approvals, and by 1943 they had centralized an "index of the hereditary value of all inhabitants of Germany."[39] The courts recognized that their very existence violated the principles of doctor-patient confidentiality, but they proceeded anyway. The new kind of doctor, *der Erbarzt* (the genetic doctor), was a man of vision; he cared for the future of the race just as the *Volkmutter* did. Dr. Otmar Freiherr von Verschuer's publication *Der Erbarzt* explained that doctors could no longer look at a patient as an individual, "but only as one part of a much larger whole—his family, his race, his Volk."[40] Population policy was now about quality, not quantity.

On March 15, 1934, the first genetic health court convened in Berlin. It heard 348 cases in two months, with the result that 325 individuals were ordered to be sterilized. People brought before the court did retain the right of appeal. In 1934, 4,000 appeals were made, only 377 of them successful. The rest were to be sterilized. People who refused to undergo the procedure were frequently imprisoned in concentration camps. The bulk of these victims had not applied to be voluntarily sterilized. Their private information was given to state medical officers by family physicians, directors of institutions, and mayors. The victims included unskilled workers, agricultural laborers, servants, prostitutes, unemployed housewives, and inmates and ex-inmates of psychiatric clinics. For a brief time, some individuals avoided sterilization if they agreed to recommit themselves, at their own expense, in single-sex institutions. In a cruel irony, many of these people were taken from those institutions, not to be sterilized but to be euthanasized, beginning in 1939.[41]

By 1939 the sterilization program was slowing down. Estimates of the number of individuals who had undergone sterilization range from 300,000 to 400,000.[42] Throughout 1938 there was a decline in the number of cases brought before the genetic health courts. This decline stemmed in part from an internal power struggle among various Nazi leaders over the implementation of the Sterilization Law. After much debate, there was a change in the composition of the health courts. One layman and one laywoman (both of whom had to be party members) were added to hear the court cases. Many German physicians stopped bringing patients before these altered courts, believing that there were now too many obstacles to clear. Finally, by 1939, the government had decided that more drastic measures were needed to "cleanse" Germany. From this point on, euthanasia, not sterilization, was the goal.[43]

The successful implementation of the 1933 Sterilization Law was a highly significant step in the radicalization of Nazi racial policies. Operating from 1933 through 1939, genetic health courts, working in league with German physicians, had been able to eliminate an entire generation of "defectives." Sterilization, the prohibition against bearing "unworthy" children, was expanded to the murder of at least five thousand children 16 years old or younger, between 1939 and 1944.[44] In addition, the sterilization program wanted directors of asylums to meet National

Socialist propaganda at least halfway; they did not necessarily accept the premise that there was "life unworthy of life," but they did come to accept "the view that there was 'naturally life of lesser value' and that [it] was in the nation's collective best interest to sterilize." Many had bought into the ideas that "hopeless cases had to be subordinated to racial considerations so that a material deprivation on the part of the genetically healthy [would] not result from supporting such cases excessively."[45] The implementation of the Sterilization Law also helped to prepare individuals for more dramatic measures to come.

A New Phase

With the advent of World War II, it was claimed that killing the insane and the crippled would create a larger food supply as well as free up more hospital beds for those who "deserved to live." As early as 1935, Hitler had told Dr. Gerhard Wagner, leader of the Doctors' Association, that in the event of war he would enact euthanasia. Because he recognized that he would have to work outside of the law, the euthanasia campaign was placed in Division 4, Health and Care of the Sick, part of the Ministry of the Interior.[46] The program's operational center was in a villa, Tiergartenstrasse 4, which gave the project the nickname Aktion T-4.

Moving quickly to eliminate the "unworthy," Dr. Victor Brandt notified other individuals, such as Hans Heinze, Helmut Unger, and Hans Hefelmann, in the spring of 1939 that he was forming a committee whose work would center on the elimination of deformed and retarded children. The committee had questionnaires ready by August 1939. The forms were to be filled out by doctors treating children age three and under. Simultaneously, Dr. Leonardo Conti was assembling a group to work on the adult euthanasia program.[47]

As the euthanasia campaign got under way, lawyers, judges, and prosecutors began to voice doubts regarding the legality of the process. Judge Lothar Kreyssig charged Reichsleiter Philipp Bouhler with murder and began criminal proceedings against him. As a result, Judge Kreyssig was prematurely retired. A meeting between T-4 personnel and members of the Ministry of Justice was called in April 1941 in Berlin as a partial response to the questionings. Viktor Brack addressed the audience, handing out photographs of severely ill patients and explaining that an actual law could not be passed at that time.[48] He made it clear that

Hitler insisted on secrecy even though most relatives of the ill would be in agreement with the procedures. Other speakers followed Brack, detailing the courage it required to kill and how causes of deaths could be forged. One prosecutor stated after the meeting, "I know . . . that these colleagues had misgivings about the measures envisaged. . . . In the view of the older lawyers an unpublished directive of Hitler's could never become law. However, according to the official view it was the case that the Führer's directives had the force of law. But the lawyers of the old school had misgivings 'in their heart of hearts.'" Despite their misgivings, "Germany's legal finest left in silence."[49]

If the guardians of law and justice remained silent, what about the guardians of the moral order? "Both accommodation and circumscribed resistance highlight the story of the German Catholic approach to such sensitive and related issues as euthanasia and anti-Semitism." Hitler's order authorizing the euthanasia campaign was backdated to September 1, 1939. This campaign gave the state the ultimate authority over the individual. In contrast to this, Pius XII issued his first papal encyclical, *Summi Pontificatus,* in October 1939. There he warned that the state could not be the final arbiter of the moral order and that the state should not try to replace God. Although this sounds like a harsh challenge to the Nazi view of the state, the Nazis considered Pius's statement so innocuous that they allowed it to be read in all Catholic Churches in Germany. As the killings continued, word began to spread about what was taking place in Germany's asylums. On July 28, 1940, von Galen wrote to Cardinal Bertram relaying information about the "happenings" at the institutions in his diocese, including one institute called Bethel in Bielefeld. Von Galen also included a sample questionnaire that doctors were being asked to fill out on patients and notified Bertram of the need to clarify the position of the Catholic Church on this moral question.[50]

The timing of von Galen's actions is significant. Already numerous individuals, primarily Protestants, had been challenging the Nazi government on the question of euthanasia. Von Galen's sermon against euthanasia in August 1941 certainly drew the most attention, but he was not the biblical "lone voice crying out in the wilderness." Precedents of opposition already existed, ones that he knew of personally. I argue that von Galen recognized that German Protestants were opposing the government and were still looked upon as "authentic Germans"; thus, he reasoned that German Catholics could join in the battle against euthanasia without the risk of losing their identity as German nationalists.

Von Galen's involvement with Protestants actually furnished him with concrete proof of Nazi euthanasia plans.

How had von Galen come across a copy of the questionnaire? A Protestant Pastor, Fritz von Bodelschwingh, director of Bethel Institution for epileptics, had personally contacted Bishop von Galen to tell him about the plans for a euthanasia campaign in Westphalia. In July 1939 von Galen wrote the minister a note of thanks for his personal involvement in the matter. By this time Bodelschwingh had already been to Berlin to meet with Reich Minister for Church Affairs Hans Kerrl to inform him of governmental plans for inmates.[51]

By June 1940 Bethel had received three thousand questionnaires to be completed by August 1. Bodelschwingh, recognizing that completed forms meant death for some patients, refused to complete them. The pastor contacted Dr. Conti and asked for a meeting. Conti refused. Bodelschwingh then reported the information to local officials. He also notified all the staff at Bethel, and they were unanimous in supporting his decision not to fill out the forms despite the order. Berlin officials were then told of his recalcitrance and arrived at Bethel, attempting to force the pastor to complete the forms. At about the same time, the Royal Air Force bombed the area, killing thirteen children at Bethel. Minister of Propaganda and Enlightenment Paul Joseph Goebbels made much of the British "Child Murder," and Bodelschwingh was able to use the Nazi propaganda for his own purposes. Still refusing to complete the forms, Bodelschwingh asked his Berlin visitors, "Shall I condemn the acts of the English and then extend my hand to child murder on a far larger scale?"[52]

Still pursuing safety for his patients, Bodelschwingh wrote to Göring in January 1941. He chose Göring because the brother of Göring's wife was a patient at Bethel. Göring replied to Bodelschwingh that the minister's information was inaccurate and referred Dr. Brandt to him. Brandt personally went to Bethel and in February 1941 forced the registration of all patients at the institution. Bethel's staff anxiously awaited the next move. They were still waiting when Bodelschwingh wrote to Brandt appealing to his conscience to end the program. By this time it was August 1941, and Hitler had just ended the program four days prior to Bodelschwingh's appeal.[53] The major problem for Bodelschwingh after August 1941 was that no one ever told him or his staff at Bethel that the euthanasia campaign had been halted. So Bethel lived on in a constant state of alert throughout the war.

Bodelschwingh's defiance saved all the patients at Bethel from euthanasia—with one large exception. According to a law passed August 30, 1940, Jews were no longer allowed to be housed in German institutions. In September 1940 Bethel staff members received word that a transport was coming for the Jewish patients. The staff worked quickly, sending three patients home, transferring another, and getting one person taken in by a family member at the last moment. This left seven Jewish patients, all of whom were moved to Poland and killed.[54]

Bodelschwingh was not the first Protestant pastor to protest the Nazi euthanasia campaign. The first documented action by representatives of either confession was taken by Pastor Paul Gerhard Braune, director of the Hoffnungstal Institution near Berlin (and vice president of the Central Committee for Innere Missions of the German Evangelical Church). Pastor Braune, seeing the questionnaires and guessing what the results would be, traveled to Hans von Dohnanyi (Dietrich Bonhoeffer's brother-in-law) in the German Army's Supreme Command. Dohnanyi told Braune to give concrete proof of murder in a written memorandum, which Braune did in the period May–June 1940.[55]

Braune continued his investigation by meeting with Pastor Bodelschwingh, warning him of the impending campaign against mentally ill and handicapped people in Westphalia. Both men went to Minister Kerrl, who claimed ignorance of the project. Braune persisted in his mission, alerting government officials and protesting the project. In a meeting with Minister of Justice Franz Gürtner, Braune was able to prove that hundreds of invalids had already been killed. Leaving a furious Gürtner behind, Braune submitted a copy of his findings to Göring. In August 1940 Braune was arrested by the Gestapo. He was held for three months, finally obtaining his release only with the promise to discontinue his actions against the state. After his release, Braune asserted, "The official Church remained completely silent, the official Innere Mission also did not dare do anything. . . . When I was released, the treasurer of the Innere Mission reproached me for having gone out on a limb over this matter. One mustn't do that."[56]

Overlapping with Braune's investigation was the mission of Protestant bishop Theophil Wurm. Wurm, in Württemberg, sent a letter in July 1940 to Minister of the Interior Frick. The letter did not mince words, claiming that euthanasia was contrary to all Christian beliefs. Frick received another letter in September 1940 from Wurm. The second letter ended with a series of queries, including "Does the Führer know?" Bishop Wurm's letter was widely circulated, establishing him as the spokesman for the Protestant churches. Later Wurm received a registered letter from Dr. Conti. The doctor assured Wurm that there was a legal basis for euthanasia but that it could not be revealed at the present time.[57]

At this point, Protestant pastors were making their opposition more widely known. It is also at this time that the Catholic episcopacy became involved in the protests. Most studies, when speaking of von Galen's involvement in the euthanasia question, portray his actions as if they were occurring in isolation. Many studies seem to imply that he had finally gathered enough proof and had decided that he could not face his conscience unless he spoke out.[58] I would suggest that von Galen and the rest of the Catholic hierarchy carefully chose the time to speak out. Worried lest they be classified as outsiders or internal enemies, they waited for Protestants, that is, the "true Germans," to risk a confrontation with the government first. If the Protestants were able to be critical of a Nazi policy, then Catholics could function as "good" Germans and yet be critical too.

Von Galen, for his part, had detailed information about the euthanasia program in July 1940 and relayed his information to Cardinal Bertram. Bertram then waited until August 11, 1940, to write a letter of protest to the Reich Chancellery Office, addressed to Lammers, another Catholic. In the letter Bertram asserted the eternal sanctity of human life, deriving some of his guidance from Pius's papal encyclical of October 1939. By addressing the letter to another Catholic, Bertram probably hoped that his arguments would appeal to Lammers's upbringing and that he would not risk being labeled an internal enemy for voicing opposition to state policy.

Shortly after Bertram wrote to Lammers, the bishops met again at Fulda. The euthanasia project was discussed, and the bishops decided to use traditional means of protest. They sent the government a long letter asking the officials to consider the wishes of parents and relatives and calling for an exemption of Catholic-run institutions.[59] They also nominated Bishop Heinrich Wienken, leader of the Caritas Association since 1937, as their spokesman.

Wienken took the task of representing the Catholic hierarchy very seriously. He was described as diligent, unobtrusive, a good bureaucrat, and one who believed that the church should refrain from "anything injurious or harmful to the political welfare of wartime Germany."[60] He was a safe choice on the part of the bishops. They knew Wienken would not shake the Nazi officials up by ranting or threatening them. He believed that he could use the Catholic Church to support the regime, thereby proving to skeptical Nazis that Catholics did have a true place in Nazi Germany.

Testifying at the euthanasia trials of the 1960s, the elderly Wienken suggested that the Catholic Church was slow to respond to the question of euthanasia because he had believed that a patriotic church would be able to alter radical Nazi policies. He came late to the conclusion that a patriotic church only aided the Nazis. One official later remarked, speaking of the trials, "If you give the devil your finger, he will take your hand."[61]

When Wienken first began to meet with the various representatives at the Ministry of the Interior, he found that all of them tried to justify the project to him. He remained firm and threatened public protests if the violations continued. By the next round of meetings, however, Wienken retreated and asked that the T-4 procedures be more thorough with longer periods of patient observation. He was also very concerned to earn the exemptions of sick priests from the scope of the euthanasia campaign. Indeed, Wienken's correspondence with von Galen at this time reveals that the bulk of Wienken's work had to do with his petitions to officials for the release of priests and teachers sent to Dachau. Most of his attempts were futile. Apparently some of the Catholic bishops were worried that Wienken had been corrupted by the very officials whom he had been sent to confront. Cardinal Faulhaber wrote to the church representative, castigating Wienken and charging that he was "beginning to sound like T-4 officials."[62] When the government representatives refused to put anything in writing for Wienken, talks broke down. As things continued to heat up for the Catholic Church, Cardinal Faulhaber wrote to both Minister of Justice Gürtner and Minister of Justice Hans Franz complaining about the conflict of conscience Catholics were facing with the policy of euthanasia. Faulhaber stressed to Gürtner that the individual had natural rights and that euthanasia upset the moral order of the nation. The situation further intensified from an official, dogmatic point of view when Pius XII was questioned by *L'Osservatore Romano,* December 6, 1940, on the concept of euthanasia. The pope's brief response said volumes: "This is contrary to both natural and the divine positive law." This terse statement unequivocally condemned "mercy killing," but what would the Catholic bishops do with this statement in

Germany? Von Galen decided to print the pope's answer in the *Münster Amtsblatt*, but not until March 9, 1941.[63] The Nazis responded by alerting Münster's police officers to be on their guard in the event of difficulties.[64] They also responded by calling a meeting of judges and lawyers in Berlin to assure them that Hitler had given legal sanction to euthanasia.

The summer of 1941 brought the invasion of the Soviet Union. The bishops met at Fulda just two days after the Soviet campaign had begun. Ignoring the expansion of war and welcoming the fight against Bolshevism and "godless atheism," they focused only on the perils facing the church in German society. Cardinal Bertram wrote a hard-hitting letter, listing specific grievances including the recent Gestapo seizures of church and monastic institutions.[65] A few days after the Fulda meeting, von Galen made world news by giving three sermons addressing essentially the same questions that had been discussed at Fulda.

What did von Galen say that caused such an uproar? These sermons have been described as "the most outspoken and forthright denunciation of government practices that issued from a Catholic leader throughout the war. But it should be noted that they were directed at issues (euthanasia and confiscation of property) that touched the Catholic Church directly."[66] The euthanasia protest did give the Catholic Church some renewed moral credibility, but the clergy involved in the protests did not challenge their listeners further when the killing machinery was sent to destroy innocents in the East.

"His Greatest Hour"

Throughout July 1941 large portions of Münster were destroyed by aerial bombardments. While these air raids were taking place, Gauleiter Alfred Meyer, along with other local party officials, decided that the time was right to move against the church. They did not randomly make this decision. Meyer had received a letter from Martin Bormann urging Gauleiters to confiscate church property. Bormann shrewdly noted that the population did not seem upset with the seizures as long as the properties were then utilized for such institutions as hospitals or special schools. Meyer, who believed it was very difficult to enforce party regulations in a Catholic-dominated atmosphere,[67] was nevertheless willing to attempt a move against the church.

On July 12, 1941, von Galen received news that Gestapo agents were seizing certain Jesuit institutions in Münster. Rushing to one of the scenes, the bishop caught the Gestapo in the act of driving priests out. Furious, von Galen called the Gestapo thieves and robbers to their faces. Looking at his chaplain, he said, "Now I can be silent no longer," and he stormed back to the Bishop's Palace and retreated to his private room. The house staff could hear his labored typing—one finger, one letter at a time. Throughout the night, in the summer heat of July, all they could hear was the peck of the typewriter keys, an occasional clearing of the throat, or a cough. With hindsight, von Galen's chaplain and later biographer, Heinrich Portmann, remarked that now the bishop was ready to become a martyr. "Priests of his diocese were suffering in the camps and dungeons of the Gestapo, or, driven from their homes, were pining in loneliness. For them he wrote in that night the words of righteousness."[68]

It was clear to von Galen's chaplain that the bishop intended to be a martyr, but only a martyr for a Catholic cause. Von Galen, outraged over the mistreatment suffered by priests, not Jews or other minorities, spoke his conscience. But what had his conscience prompted him to type that night?

The following Sunday morning arrived, warm, with an uncanny stillness.[69] At 10:15 A.M. the bishop told Portmann they should begin their walk to church. Portmann noted at the time that a strange unrest had possessed the bishop. As the two men walked to St. Lambert's, von Galen nervously spoke to passersby.

Von Galen went to the pulpit in the church. At first he faltered in his speech. However, after about ten sentences, "a wonderful strength and serenity came over him." His listeners sat in their pews, some tearful, some trembling; most of them were shocked by the eloquence and resoluteness of their bishop's sermon. Afterward, the exhausted bishop was met by a crowd of clergy in the sacristy. After drinking a glass of water, he left St. Lambert's.[70]

Back at the palace, von Galen gave Portmann one typescript of his sermon and informed him that he had hidden two additional copies in unlikely places. If the Gestapo arrived, which von Galen clearly expected them to do at any moment, Portmann was told to quietly hand over his one copy. But the Gestapo never came.

What made the bishop anticipate an arrest by Gestapo agents? The theme of von Galen's sermon was justice as the foundation of the state. Using the air raids and attacks made on innocent German citizens as his starting point, he argued that the Gestapo was attacking "loyal German citizens . . . thrown on to the street like outlawed helots and hunted out of the country, like vermin." Was he talking about the deportations of Jews, taken from their homes and sent to the East? No. Von Galen reminded his listeners that they had all heard about the arrests and internments of innocent Germans. He then gave them two concrete examples—of two priests, exiled from Münster. He made sure to remind them that they could all be affected by these actions: "None of us is safe—and may he know that he is the most loyal and conscientious of citizens and may he be conscious of his complete innocence—he cannot be sure that he will not some day be deported from his home, deprived of his freedom and locked up in the cellars and concentration camps of the Gestapo."[71]

Offering an answer to their fears of such unjust treatment, von Galen moved on: "Justice is the only solid foundation of the State." The right to live freely is necessary to maintain the moral order of society. "How many Germans are now languishing in police custody or in concentration camps?" Again ignoring how many Jews might be in those camps or cellars, von Galen used Bishop Johann Sproll and Martin Niemöller as examples of suffering innocence. Because he cited Niemöller, he was able to tell his audience that "I am not talking about a matter of purely Catholic concern but about a matter of Christian concern, indeed of general human and national concern."[72]

Perhaps a few people in that warm church that day extended von Galen's speech to include Jews, but most would feel more comfortable in a Christian state; and because their bishop carefully avoided drawing their attention to the suffering of the Jews, perhaps they could avoid it also. No voice of opposition had been raised in Münster to defend Jews, so one could posit that most individuals had not made the connection between murder of the mentally ill and illegal actions perpetrated against the Jews.[73]

Von Galen cited the position of his office as reason enough to "speak up for the moral order." He acknowledged that some people would call his criticisms dangerous to the home front. He said he knew that he risked being classified as an internal enemy, just as Catholics had been labeled under Bismarck. But he believed that if he remained silent, the character of the national community would be weakened. To von Galen, the Gestapo actions were making men cowardly and apprehensive, full of distrust toward other Germans: "And therefore I raise my voice in the name of the upright German people, in the name of the majesty of

Justice, in the interests of peace and solidarity of the homefront; there-fore as a German, an honorable citizen, a representative of the Christian religion, a Catholic Bishop, I exclaim: 'We demand Justice!'"[74]

Von Galen used his position to warn the Nazi state that if it did not exercise authority properly, Germany would suffer rot and decay inter-nally. It is interesting that he emphasized his Germanness first and his Christianity second when voicing his demands. He was also quick to apply the language of "internal enemies," not to Catholics, but to the Gestapo.

Although this speech does carry a strong denunciation of some of the immoral practices of the state, it did not attack Hitler or the nation specifically. Instead it focused on the actions of the Gestapo and other related offices, and it called on all Christian Germans to worry about the state of affairs within their nation. By using the example of Niemöller, von Galen had carefully categorized Catholics with Protestants, reliev-ing Catholics of the fears of once again being relegated to outsider status with the Jews.

That same night, July 13, a terrible thunderstorm passed through Münster. In the driving rain, thunder, and lightning, priests from the Überwasser Church began arriving at the palace, begging for copies of the sermon. Portmann gave the "Gestapo" copy to one priest. Three hours later it was returned. Others began to copy and circulate the ser-mon. By Monday evening, copies had been sent to almost all West-phalian towns, leading clergy of Germany, and Field Marshal Hans Günther von Kluge. On that same Monday, von Galen sent letters of protest to Göring; Lammers; the ministers of the interior, of church af-fairs, and of justice; and the supreme commander of the armed forces. Only Lammers replied, and he only promised to forward von Galen's complaint to the Ministry of the Interior. Von Galen angrily replied to Lammers, asking him to tell Hitler that he was no god and that in the midst of war the Gestapo was destroying the inner front.[75]

Despite von Galen's first sermon and the shock waves it created, the confiscation of religious property continued. Missionary sisters were ex-pelled from their home following von Galen's first sermon. Hearing of the expulsion, von Galen went to the convent and tried to intervene. His cousin, Countess Helene von Galen, who was a sister there, had been arrested and jailed in a cellar of the convent. She later escaped through a window.[76] Von Galen's head must have been spinning by this time as he rushed from convents to seminaries only to find more expulsions and confiscations. He sent many of those who had been expelled to live in his ancestral home, Castle Dinklage.[77]

As the seizures continued, another Sunday approached. On July 20, 1941, von Galen again rose to the pulpit, this time at the Liebfrauen-kirche. He opened this second sermon by giving thanks that the city had not recently suffered "any new enemy attacks from without."[78] Then, in contrast, he immediately criticized the enemies within Germany who continued to attack monasteries, convents, missions, and all of their inhabitants. He listed all of the authorities he had contacted to protest these actions and argued that such actions resulted in the destruction of a sense of community. Although von Galen again strongly denounced Gestapo actions, the rest of his sermon urged, at most, passive resistance.

Encouraging Catholics to continue to obey the laws and do their duty, von Galen praised them for continuing the fight against the external enemy: "We Christians, of course, are not aiming at revolution. We shall continue loyally to do our duty in obedience to God and in love of our people and fatherland. Our soldiers will fight and die for Germany, but not for those men who by their cruel actions against our religious . . . wound our hearts and shame the German name before God and men."[79]

In reference to the enemy within, von Galen recommended that Catholics fight back not with arms but with endurance. Using the metaphor of hammer and anvil, he told his audience that the inner enemies were like the hammer, striking hard but eventually broken by the steadfast strength of the anvil. "The anvil . . . need not strike back. . . . The anvil . . . lasts longer than the hammer."[80] This would be in keeping with the goal of the Catholic Church. States could come and go but the church would be eternal.

The bishop did offer Catholics a mode of behavior that would ensure that the Nazis would be broken eventually. He gave the biblical instruction that they should "obey God more than men." This was not something novel for the Christian community of Westphalia: Pastor Martin Niemöller, a one-time resident of Münster, had given a similar sermon in the summer of 1937 and had subsequently been arrested for it. Von Galen, in his sermon, warned his listeners that one's conscience, formed by faith, must be obeyed even if it meant death, for it would be "better to die than to sin!"[81] Because this sermon echoed a theme emphasized by Protestant pastors, one could argue that von Galen was again seeking to place Catholics on an equal footing with Protestants, tightening the connection between two Christian confessions at the expense of other minorities. Reinforcing Catholic patriotism, the service ended with the customary prayer for Fatherland and Führer.

Hitler ordered the confiscations of religious houses in Münster stopped on July 30, 1941. But soon von Galen was going to have more to discuss in his sermons than Gestapo seizures of monasteries. In the final days of July, Father Heinrich Lackmann, chaplain at the asylum at Marienthal, made a secret trip to see von Galen. Father Lackmann explained that mentally ill patients were going to be removed from his institution at intervals, destined for euthanasia. He also mentioned that similar plans were in progress for inmates at Warstein in Sauerland. Although von Galen had known of the euthanasia of invalids since July 25, 1940, he had been advised by Cardinal Bertram to remain silent in order to avoid further troubles with the government.[82] Aware that the criminal code contained Article 139, the duty to expose an impending crime, von Galen approached the pulpit of St. Lambert's on Sunday, August 3, 1941. This sermon turned out to be the most important and the most outspoken one delivered by a member of the Catholic hierarchy during the Nazi era.

Opening with the information that the Gestapo's campaign against religious members of the community was continuing, he urged all listeners to file formal complaints with the authorities whenever they encountered slander. The parishioners heard the Gospel reading, Luke 19: 41–47, which includes this passage: "As he drew near and came in sight of the city he shed tears over it and said, 'Yes, a time is coming when your enemies will raise fortifications all around you, when they will encircle you and hem you in on every side; they will dash you and your children inside your walls to the ground . . . and all because you did not recognize your opportunity when God offered it!'"[83] Von Galen then related the words of Scripture to the events occurring in Münster in 1941.

Using the theme of Jesus weeping over others' missed opportunities, von Galen described the Fulda letter of June 26, 1941. This letter clearly stated that it was wrong for a Catholic to kill an innocent person under any circumstances except in war or in self-defense. Then he described, in specific detail, the killing of the mentally ill on the basis that they were "worthless life." Citing both Article 211 and Article 139 of the Penal Code, he used the sermon as a means of formally reporting the removal of patients from the Marienthal institution. Again wishing to impress on his audience their own vulnerability, von Galen pointed out that anyone could become unproductive at some time; no one's life would be safe in a society that viewed killing "unproductives" as justifiable. Using a very concrete example of a fifty-five-year-old institutionalized farmer recently euthanized while his son was fighting in the war, von Galen explained how the morale of soldiers would be deeply affected by these policies.[84] He then enumerated the Ten Commandments, stopping to evaluate how each commandment was being violated in Münster. He began the list with the Fifth Commandment, "Thou shalt not kill."

With each evaluation, the bishop painted a dismal picture of moral decay in German society: Sabbath broken, false witness given, property stolen, adultery committed, euthanasia practiced, and so forth. When he arrived at "Thou shalt have no other gods before me," von Galen made a link with his first sermon. He claimed that the Nazi state had set up false idols—the state, the race, their bellies—and that Catholics could not be expected to be loyal and obedient unless the state was exercising God's authority and justice. When describing violations of "Thou shalt not kill," von Galen reminded the people that they did not need a penal code to know that killing is always wrong and that the practice of euthanasia violated God's law.[85]

This sermon was a direct attack on certain policies of the Nazi state and as such has been cited since August 1941 as proof of resistance on the part of the German Catholic hierarchy. It was an outspoken denunciation of illegal seizures of monasteries and convents. It was a forthright accusation against the state for practicing euthanasia illegally. However, it was never a plea for protection of innocent Jews suffering and dying in ghettos or at the hands of the Einsatzgruppen, nor was it a call for insurrection against the Nazi state. (The Einsatzgruppen functioned as mobile killing units to destroy Jewish men, women, and children in Eastern Europe.)

Some listeners might have taken the message "Thou shalt not kill" one step further than the euthanasia of invalids to the murdering of Jews, but von Galen's sermon does not seem to suggest that parishioners should fight to protect another minority in the Reich. In fact, most published versions of von Galen's third sermon do not include its conclusion. Toward the end of the concluding remarks, he refers to his starting point: did Jesus weep only for Israel? This is the bishop's conclusion: "Is the people of Israel the only people whom God has encompassed and protected with a father's care and a mother's love, has drawn to Himself? Is it the only people that would not? The only one that rejected God's truth, that threw off God's law and *so condemned itself to ruin?*"[86]

Open, ideological hatred of Jews did not need to be explicitly expressed in a sermon by a member of the Catholic clergy. Jews could be comfortably portrayed as those who have been superseded by Christians, through Jewish rejection of Jesus as the Messiah. In keeping with traditional Catholic teaching, von Galen could blame the Jews for their own misfortunes because they had failed to recognize the "true Messiah." As Saint Augustine had written centuries earlier, Jews could be mistreated in order to be reminded of their "crime"; they did not need to be loved.[87] Following this line of reasoning, turning a blind eye to the misfortunes of the Jews would not necessarily make one an indecent person.

It might be suggested that von Galen could only rely on the support of his parishioners if he did not challenge their opinions too greatly and that that is why he did not attempt to connect the larger, humane question of euthanasia to the "racial" question. "The parish priest could generally count on the popular support of his flock in response to Nazi interference in local Church affairs as well as on full support from his superiors. In the Jewish Question, however, the clergy encountered primarily indifference or at the most abstract and latent anti-Semitism."[88]

Von Galen's three sermons were quickly reprinted and circulated widely among the German population. His words also reached an international audience, thanks in part to the efforts of the RAF, specifically the Political Warfare Executive Office (PWE), which was responsible for psychological warfare and propaganda. R. L. Sedgwick, a member of the PWE, stated that the PWE officers were "thrilled" with von Galen's sermons. They sent excerpts of the sermons through several BBC transmissions as well as leafleting them all over Germany. Directing the excerpts at German Catholics, Sedgwick explained why certain portions of each sermon were picked: "German Catholics had always disliked the Prussian hegemony in Germany. Memories of 1866 . . . and of the *Kulturkampf* were still alive, and were fostered by our propaganda."[89] The PWE chose to highlight those sections that stressed God-given natural rights, "since most were against democracy," and those portions that emphasized the need for Protestants and Catholics to work together to build a Christian community.[90]

The PWE was very successful in reaching the 30 million Catholics living in Germany in 1941. They were also able to reach an even wider audience by translating the sermons into English, Spanish, French, Czech, Polish, and Dutch. As the word spread, other bishops echoed von

Galen's words. On August 13, 1941, Anton Hilfrich, bishop of Limburg, condemned the killings going on at Hadamar. Albert Stohr, bishop of Mainz, preached against the taking of life. Because of others following von Galen's preaching, von Galen's three sermons did make it possible to mobilize an already existing public opinion. The protest not only resulted in an upsurge of publicity, but it also gave the Catholic Church a degree of credibility with opponents of Nazism. Unfortunately, von Galen and most other high-ranking clergymen chose to be silent once the killing machinery on German soil seemed to have stopped.[91] Von Galen's seeming success with the anti-euthanasia message should have encouraged him to preach further resistance to immoral policies. It does not seem to have had such an effect.

The Aftermath

Even though von Galen and the others did not openly challenge the Nazis on the Jewish Question, Nazi Party officials were incensed over von Galen's public denunciations. The question dominating their correspondence in the summer of 1941 was what to do with such a prominent figure. Several Nazi officials exchanged opinions on this dilemma. Even before the third sermon had been delivered, Gauleiter Meyer wrote to Lammers seeking to justify the Gestapo seizures of Jesuit property. Meyer argued in the letter that the Jesuits had been engaged in work against the state. As proof of this activity, he listed men such as Father Friedrich Muckermann (1883–1946), who had fled to Holland in 1933 and continued to agitate against the Nazis from exile, and Father Albert Maring, who had been arrested because of writings against the Reich. Meyer labeled both men, in traditional Kulturkampf language, *Staatsfeindlicher* (subversives). He also threw in that the nuns expelled from the cloister had insulted Alfred Rosenberg and were pacifists.[92]

He continued his defense by referring to von Galen numerous times as an enemy of the state who was inciting the population to act against the state police. Meyer asserted that the bishop did not have a clear understanding of the need for shelters and that he did realize that he should refrain from making references to "fanatics" such as Niemöller. In the end, Meyer asked the critical question of Lammers: how long can an enemy of the state be allowed to be seen and heard?[93]

Gauleiter Meyer became even busier at letter-writing once von Galen delivered his euthanasia sermon on August 3, 1941. Meyer sent Bormann a lengthy letter, selecting sections of von Galen's sermon and responding to them with counteraccusations. Because Bormann was the person who originally suggested that Gauleiters begin state action against Catholic property, the bulk of the letter sought to justify the seizures of religious houses.[94]

To Meyer, the problems with von Galen were his name-calling (referring to Gestapo agents as "inner enemies") and his plea to individual conscience, "Obey God more than men!" Meyer believed that the bishop was agitating against the Gestapo, the Führer, and the Volk. The highest crime, however, was not the call to conscience; the highest crime, as Meyer saw it, was von Galen's connecting the euthanasia of the mentally ill with the euthanasia of wounded soldiers at the front. At that point in the letter, Meyer referred to von Galen as *"Landsverrat"* (guilty of high treason) and recommended that he be hanged. Bormann agreed with his recommendation.[95]

In yet another letter to Bormann, Meyer raised the question of how long the bishop would continue to discuss the topic of euthanasia. His sermon had been read aloud in all of Münster's churches on August 10, 11, and 12. Meyer consoled Bormann with his belief that the population would soon forget about confiscation of cloisters and seminaries as long as their counterpropaganda could convince the people of the need for other uses of that property. However, he continued, "What will not keep the peace is the question of euthanasia."[96]

To Meyer's mind, nothing good could come of a public discussion of euthanasia, particularly because von Galen had so clearly linked it to the killing of wounded soldiers. Soldiers at the front were receiving copies of von Galen's sermon and asking their officers about its truthfulness. A police report from Münster attached a letter that the police had received from a Captain Fleiter. Fleiter was asking for a legal clarification of the question of euthanasia because his soldiers were reading von Galen's sermon and were becoming uneasy. Fleiter called von Galen "quarrelsome" and begged for guidance because "I already have enough to deal with my soldiers."[97]

Meyer was worried that von Galen might not be speaking as an individual priest but as the representative of a new vanguard of Catholic action. He asserted, "We know what von Galen is saying is nonsense and lies but we must be ready to answer—why can the Bishop get away with such lies?" "I believe that the arrest or expulsion of the Bishop must be enforced. In the final analysis, History has shown that states must lead the way in action against refractory bishops." He slyly suggested that an "action" against von Galen should come at a time when war reports would overshadow his "removal."[98]

Walter Tiessler, in the Ministry of Propaganda, also wrote his opinion to Bormann. Tiessler recommended that von Galen be hanged. He asserted that von Galen's comments only upset German mothers and wives about sons fighting in the field. In his official response, Bormann explained to Tiessler that he had informed Hitler of von Galen's speeches. In a private letter to Tiessler, Bormann agreed with Tiessler's suggestion about hanging the annoying bishop. He told Tiessler that when he made a similar recommendation to Goebbels, Goebbels had replied, "During the war the state would not move against the Church." The minister of propaganda realized that the good will of the Church was needed during the war but that after the war Hitler intended to take great measures against the church.[99]

What Bormann reported privately to Tiessler is confirmed both by a letter Goebbels had written and by a comment made publicly by Hitler. On August 12, 1941, Goebbels wrote a note stating that the arrest of von Galen would only make him a martyr, which might result in further unrest on the part of priests. Hitler told some intimates that "Bishop von Galen had irritated him . . . [and] assured his entourage that he would 'take care of him' at the end of the war, and in the settlement not a thing would be forgotten."[100]

In October 1944 Himmler also confirmed Bormann's assertions that no action could be taken against the bishop while the war continued. But those who associated with von Galen could be targeted without restraint. For example, in a letter to Lieutenant General Faeckenstedt, commander of the General Staff, Military District 4 in Münster, Himmler dismissed the lieutenant general owing to political untrustworthiness. Himmler wrote, "You cannot cultivate relations with a traitor to his country like Bishop von Galen . . . [who] has a way of thinking hostile to the State. . . . The Führer has met with nothing but opposition. . . . The whole set are enemies of the State." He continued, "We couldn't settle accounts with the traitor Galen for reasons of foreign policy. We shall catch up with him later on, and the whole Church with him." Comparing von Galen's actions with those of Stauffenberg, Himmler wrote, "There will be a thorough liquidation in that quarter. . . . Stauffenberg even wore a gold cross on a chain round his neck."[101]

Martyrs

Stauffenberg gave his life for his conscience. Von Galen appeared to be ready to become a martyr too, but only for what he deemed a Catholic cause. The Nazi government, because of its perceptions of what von Galen meant to the people of Westphalia, did not fulfill von Galen's desire for martyrdom. However, other, far less prominent people bore the cross of martyrdom because of von Galen and his three sermons. Some were arrested and interrogated; others were imprisoned and then released. Still others were killed. Examining Gestapo reports out of Münster, it is clear that "those priests or ordinary people who disseminated or discussed his sermon lost their jobs, were sent to concentration camps, or were executed."[102]

A young woman, Paula S., noticed transports of patients to a nearby asylum. She also noticed the smoke from the asylum's chimneys and made the connection. When some colleagues at work theorized about the sudden death of a patient, she confirmed the rumors of killing. She "mentioned that she had a copy of Galen's sermon. She was denounced and arrested. The copy of the sermon was discovered in a search of her home." Paula S. was not tried. She was imprisoned in Frankfurt for several weeks and then was transferred to Ravensbrück. She was kept in the concentration camp for six months. After her release she no longer had her job, and townspeople carefully avoided her. To this day, "she cannot describe what she experienced."[103]

A Mr. Thomassen in Leipzig reproduced von Galen's sermons by the thousand. For distributing them, several people in Leipzig met their deaths in concentration camps. Closer to home, Father Hermann Krahe of Münster was arrested by the Gestapo for distributing the bishop's "slanderous sermons" to soldiers at the front. For duplicating and spreading the sermons, Father Johannes Hogrebe was taken into custody, interrogated, and warned. Sister Anna Kellner was arrested for disseminating von Galen's sermons, and nurse Maria Lentze was taken into custody after she was caught distributing them. Because so many people were being punished, sometimes for simply having a copy of the sermons, the bishop's closest brother, Count Franz von Galen, filled with anxiety, asked his brother, "What are we to do if you are locked up?" "Nothing at all," was the response from the bishop.[104]

According to a report from the inspector of the Security Police, the commotion over von Galen's sermons was not showing signs of abatement. Nor did rumors cease to circulate that the bishop must be telling the truth. Using an example of a woman who would not leave the side of her elderly mother for fear that the police would come at any moment to take her away to be murdered, the report stressed that "in state-affirming circles, no one can understand why action has not been taken against the Bishop for all of his treasonous speeches." The Gestapo reports also emphasized that the sermons were affecting more than just Catholics: "Now not only Catholics but Protestants have it and are making remarks about it."[105] In yet another report sent to Goebbels, the writer worried that von Galen's remarks would find resonance among Protestants who had someone at the front. At the same time, the minister of propaganda recognized that prosecuting von Galen might lead to martyrdom for him and increased resistance on the part of other bishops.[106]

The belief that arrest or imprisonment of the bishop would trigger more open rebellion figures repeatedly in the reports of the Security Police and the Gestapo in Münster. "It is through von Galen's daily speech that he will be arrested, in order to play the role of a martyr and with the hope that the Catholic population will be seduced into open resistance against measures of the Regime."[107]

The problem with interpreting what von Galen wanted Catholics to do with the information he provided them is further complicated by the fact that the bishop brought lawsuits and filed police reports against individuals who smeared his reputation or who claimed to speak in his name. Von Galen filed numerous protests against local Nazi officials who had publicly insulted him. He also received warnings from other German nobles that the enemy was using the sermons to incite the German population against the state. In one such letter, Count Günther Oscar Bernhard von Stosch told von Galen that he was in danger of being a traitor because of this.[108] In each of these cases, von Galen cited Article 5 of the Concordat as his protection against slander.

Perhaps more interesting is a letter that appeared in Münster with no return address:

> My beloved Catholics! German men and women! My July sermons in St. Lambert's in Münster have caused a sensation in all of Germany. Not only Catholics but all freedom-loving Germans have seen the system of injustice. . . . My warning to the Gestapo appears to have been without success. Innocent men and women are still being taken by the Gestapo. The ill are still being killed by the hundreds. Because the Gestapo wants to fight against all upstanding and honest Germans,

we pick up the gauntlet. As your bishop—I say to you—abuse authority, struggle against godless systems, protect the world from godlessness. Thou shalt not kill! Christians! Germans! Practice passive resistance! Sabotage measures of the so-called movement! Fight to give the German nation peace, justice, and freedom![109]

Strong, direct words—but not the words of von Galen. Von Galen pressed charges against the anonymous sender of the letter.[110] Although the writer's call to passive resistance overlaps somewhat with von Galen's message, the bishop disassociated himself from his own message by threatening a lawsuit. The Office of the Vicar General sent a copy of the forged letter to all parishes in the diocese with an attached note explaining that von Galen could not possibly be the letter's author.[111] What did von Galen expect would happen after he made his famous sermons? What did he think the Catholic population would do?

The Gestapo was well aware of what others in Münster might be inspired to do with or without the bishop's approval. In August 1941 the police president of Münster received an anonymous letter warning him that as long as nuns and priests were called spies and traitors, Germany would be punished by God, and God would never allow the Germans to win the war. The author of this letter warned, "A country without belief and a soldier without belief are lost."[112]

Most of the reports from Münster's police force continually maintained that people who supported the party were at a loss as to why "a man who destroys the inner front in times of war is left untouched." Many asked why the bishop, "if he is a traitor is not imprisoned?" Constantly complaining that von Galen's sermons were the basis for further slander against the state and the party, the reports revealed that "Catholics see in Clemens August a stark and energetic man before whom National Socialism has stopped. . . . In Holland, a bishop who read von Galen's sermon in Dutch has been arrested. Clemens August attacks the State brutally during the war and the State remains silent."[113]

Recognizing the need to respond to the now very public knowledge of the euthanasia project, the Nazis produced a film, *I Accuse!* Based on the novel by Helmut Unger, the film tells the story of a beautiful young woman, Hanna, who has been stricken with multiple sclerosis. Her husband, Professor Heyt, and an ex-boyfriend, Dr. Lang, help her commit suicide. A courtroom drama unfolds, the pros and cons of euthanasia are debated, and the husband is acquitted. The film was released in August 1941 and was seen by approximately 18 million people.[114] The broad masses of people tended to react favorably to the glamorized version of "mercy killing," but in lengthy Security Police reports it was frequently noted that the starting point for discussion of the movie was von Galen's third sermon. Most people, the reports concluded, saw the film as the government's answer to von Galen's sermon.

The Halting of the Euthanasia Program

Lammers took note of all the Security Police reports on *I Accuse!* as well as the reports on disturbances among the population. He reported to Hitler that there was a growing distrust among the people. The euthanasia program, as applied to adults, was officially suspended, not stopped, by Hitler on August 24, 1941. The "mercy" deaths of incurably ill children continued, however, until 1945.[115]

Did the euthanasia project come to a halt because of von Galen's sermons of 1941? More than likely not, although von Galen's troublesome presence and endless lawsuits did have a powerful effect. Protestant leaders such as Braune, Bodelschwingh, and Wurm had been registering complaints a long time before the Catholic hierarchy got involved. In addition, recent research suggests that the project was in the process of being phased out in Germany by August 1941 anyway.[116] "The euthanasia program was not halted because of some local difficulties with a handful of bishops, but because its teams of practiced murderers were needed to carry out the infinitely vaster enormity in the East." Technicians, nurses, and doctors who had participated in the T-4 program were transferred to the East to assist in the death camps equipped with gas. Adding weight to this argument, Burleigh and Wipperman in *The Racial State* emphasize that by August 1941 the projected target of "disinfected" people had been reached. In all, by September 1, 1941, 70,273 people had been killed under the T-4 project and 93,251 beds "released."[117]

Nathan Stoltzfus, examining the possibilities of dissent in Nazi Germany, rejects Burleigh and Wipperman's argument by emphasizing that von Galen's sermons represented the public will. Once the regime noted that the public was openly discussing the question of euthanasia, it ended it. Stoltzfus asserted that "the euthanasia by gassing was stopped as a direct consequence of the force of popular opinion." Michael Phayer argued that Catholic women involved in charity work did more to stymie the T-4 project than public protests did. When state personnel came to take away patients from Catholic-run institutions for euthanasia, local women volunteers found themselves attempting to protect their wards. As the "murder box" pulled up in front of the facility, these women either falsified patient information or physically hid the intended victims.[118] These women were on the front lines of opposing the goals of the Nazi regime.

Von Galen's personal safety was ensured by the force of popular opinion. Hitler and other Nazi functionaries had already decided that they could not move against the bishop without risking loss of support from the entire Westphalian population. His troublesome presence continued to be irksome to the Nazis, but his one sermon, powerful as it was, was not enough to cause the ending of the euthanasia campaign. The euthanasia campaign was halted because of a combination of factors, one of which was the public discussion that von Galen's sermons helped to crystallize, along with the achievement of the targeted objectives of Aktion T-4 and the perceived need to move T-4 personnel to the East. Just as the Nazi leadership had realized that with the appropriate propaganda they could convince or at least confuse Germans over the question of sterilization, they now walked away from the T-4 project, filled with expertise and the assurance that as long as they used euphemisms, the public would not investigate and would accept them.[119] In this way, the euthanasia project functioned as a prelude to the "Final Solution" in the East.

The Fight Continues

Von Galen continued to register formal complaints after the August 3, 1941, sermon. In another strongly worded sermon on September 14, 1941, he pointed to the errors of Communism. Offering thanks to God for the brave Germans fighting the plague of Communism, he quoted from Hitler's speech of June 22, 1941, which justified the invasion by claiming that a "Judeo-Bolshevik conspiracy was attempting to start fires all over Europe." The bishop elaborated at great length on the rights violated by Communism, including the right to life and the murder of "unproductive men . . . invalids, and wounded." It did not take a great deal of perspicacity to understand that von Galen was drawing a parallel between Communism and National Socialism. The Security Police reports coming out of Münster quickly took note of the inference, as did Gauleiter Meyer in his correspondence with both Bormann and Goebbels.[120] What von Galen did not know when he gave the speech was that the Nazis had already met and issued a new directive: stop all measures "which might adversely affect the feeling of unity among the populace."[121]

This would lend credence to the argument that open protests against certain governmental policies, even under the Nazi government, could produce results. Yet von Galen did not pursue further resistance, even though he had not been prosecuted. The idea that open protests and notoriety could alter a dangerous situation could have been drawn from an anonymous letter that was delivered to von Galen in September 1941. The letter began by praising him for his courageous sermons and saying how rare it was to find a man willing to stand up for justice. The writer then brought up a matter that von Galen was unwilling to deal with: "The nation has stood by as public crimes have begun against the Jews." Eager to establish his own credentials as a "true" German, the person asserted that German blood ran through his father's veins as well as his own, and he justified his service to the nation by claiming to have fought bravely in World War I. The letter, written on the same day that legislation was decreed requiring Jews to wear the Star of David on their clothing, emphasized that no one was coming to the assistance of the Jews, not the nation or the army. He asked if von Galen was aware that Jews in conquered Poland were dying of hunger in ghettos and that the fate of thousands of other Jews remained uncertain. Then he asked the pivotal question, "Will you stand up and be our helper?" The author closed with an assurance that the bishop did not know him and that he had written to von Galen solely because of his hope that one day a defender would emerge to protect Jews.[122]

Von Galen was not that defender. He did not stand up and seek to help Jews specifically. He did not protest deportations of Jews even though he knew what it meant. In fact, quite tellingly, local Nazi leaders never even considered that von Galen might issue a protest once the deportation of Münster's Jews had begun. By December 1941, when deportations were in effect, the majority of Münster's Jews were being sent to Riga and Minsk. "Von Galen issued no word of protest."[123] Apparently the local Nazi officials knew von Galen well enough not to fear his interference in this matter.

As the Nazi government began to ease up on the church, the church responded by not creating situations that might cause problems for the state.[124] Attempts were made to decrease points of possible conflict between church and state. On September 22–23, 1941, Hitler ordered the Security Police to hold a meeting with church specialists to work to bring about a détente. Sweeping actions against the church were to be avoided, and actions against religious homes were to be suspended. At this meeting it was decided that the church would not be allowed to regain any lost ground but that further actions taken against the church would be limited from now on.[125] The church had won the new Kulturkampf, if winning was defined by successfully protecting the ecclesiastical institutions of the church on German soil. By choosing to avoid open confrontation against the state on the issue of the Jewish Question, the church had avoided being recategorized as a second-class minority within the nation.

The bishops did issue official statements at the end of 1941 and 1943 in which they noted again the continuing murder of the mentally ill and the Nazi campaign to sway the German conscience to approval of euthanasia. In 1941 they wrote, "We German Bishops shall not cease to protest against the killing of innocent persons. Nobody's life is safe unless the commandment "Thou shalt not kill" is observed." In September 1943 the German bishops issued their last joint pastoral during Hitler's regime, entitled, "The Ten Commandments as Laws of Life for Nations." When the Fifth Commandment appeared, it was not worded openly enough or directly enough to call attention to the systematic murder of Jews. Vaguely connecting euthanasia to mass murder, they offered this belated and weak insight: "Killing is wrong in itself."[126]

Offering such a meager defense for the plight of the Jews did not succeed in mobilizing Catholic support as had the strongly worded and forthright denunciations against euthanasia. Von Galen's sermons might have inspired some rare individuals to refuse to acquiesce and blindly follow the Nazi state, but it would be incorrect to credit von Galen's one euthanasia sermon with bringing about the end of the Nazi murder of innocents.

CHAPTER FIVE

Von Galen and the Jews

This is my commandment: Love one another as I have loved you. A man can have no greater love than to lay down his life for his friends.

—JOHN 15:12–13

"The manner in which these wretched folk are forced to abandon their homes and all their possessions—often with less than an hour's notice—makes one shudder. They are forced to make a written declaration to the effect that they are leaving voluntarily. Old and sick are taken to mass camps, relatives are put to forced labor, hundreds suffer rape, violence and robbery while crossing the border." At first reading, this might appear to describe a deportation of Germany's Jewish inhabitants during the war. However, these words, spoken by Bishop von Galen, were not about the fate of German Jewry. These were comments made in January 1946 at a postwar meeting of Catholic bishops and archbishops, called by the British zonal commander, General Gerard Walter Robert Templer. The comments had to do with postwar expulsions of ethnic Germans who had once been living in Eastern territories such as Pomerania, Breslau, and Upper Silesia.[1] The bishop never offered such words of public protest when Germany's Jewish citizens were being deported and killed.

Numerous explanations can be given for the silence on the part of the majority of the Catholic Church leadership regarding the Jewish Question. One factor was the repressive atmosphere of the Nazi state with its tactics of intimidation and terror. Another was the precarious position priests found themselves in, between public defamation in the scandalous morality and currency-exchange trials and private harassment with numerous banishments and arrests for transgression of Nazi laws. Add to this mixture the fact that the church had lost most of its traditional vehicles for protest: no Catholic unions, papers, organizations, or charities were allowed to continue under the Nazi government. For many German Catholics, the fear of a renewed Kulturkampf and its reclassification of Catholics as Reichsfeinde led them to conform to many government policies. Still others adhered to the traditions of religious anti-Semitism, limiting their defense to converted Jews. Too many had already compromised their principles on issues such as forced sterilization and euthanasia and were unwilling to question the anti-Semitic policies that the government had in place. They found the Catholic leadership speaking in cautious generalities, often overlaid with such patriotic sentiment that their words could not mobilize the general Catholic population to react to mistreatment of Jews. From the pope to the bishops, a policy emerged regarding the Jewish Question: Jews were "not immediately related to Church interests."[2] Silence followed.

Von Galen, winner of international acclaim for his very public denunciations of euthanasia and Nazi neopaganism, like so many of his colleagues, maintained his silence concerning the fate of the Jews, even when he had verifiable proof that deportation meant death. Even before the deportations began, von Galen did not protest the April 1933 boycotts, the September 1935 Nuremberg Laws, the pogrom of 1938, or the countless other discriminations and acts of violence perpetrated against men and women who had lived in his diocese for years.

He too had his reasons for silence. He had been a victim of Nazi terror when the Bishop's Palace was repeatedly vandalized. He had been pilloried in various Nazi publications and parodied in derogatory songs. He worried constantly about the fate of "his" priests in places such as Dachau or Sachsenhausen. He found it hard to believe stories of mass murder in the East; euthanasia in Germany could be seen and proved. As a representative of the church, he believed he was obliged to support church policies, including the decision to leave the Jews to their own fate. He was an ardent conservative and an ultranationalist, seeking constantly to prove that Catholics were truly Germans who could be just as loyal and obedient to the state as Protestants were. He was also vehemently anti-Bolshevik. His seething hatred of left-wing radicalism was going to make von Galen indirectly useful to the Nazis.

Many historians, when writing on von Galen, cite his attacks on Nazi racism as proof that the bishop could not have been anti-Semitic. Some, such as Heinz Mussinghoff, argue that von Galen's attacks on Nazi racism immunized Catholics against the anti-Semitism of the regime. Yet Mussinghoff cannot explain why Münster's Catholics refused to intervene on behalf of Jews from their own town or why, by 1934, visitors entering Münster were greeted by a sign, "Jews are Germany's misfortune. Trespassing of this community by Jews is unwanted."[3] Von Galen did not need to be openly anti-Semitic living in Nazi Germany. He was a rabid protester of Bolshevism, and that, in many people's minds, was Jewish.

Bolshevism, Communism, Marxism, atheism, and liberalism were lumped together and all seen by many as Jewish ideologies. To von Galen, these harmful and disruptive systems were destroying German culture and society in general. In a draft of a petition to Hitler, von Galen agreed with what Hitler had written in *Mein Kampf:* "International Communism is the greatest enemy of the people." Quoting extensively from *Mein Kampf,* von Galen wrote that Hitler's pronouncements on Ultramontanism only allowed men like Alfred Rosenberg to gain in importance. His letter claimed that the German bishops would continue to fight old and new opponents, and he listed some of them—rationalists, liberals, freethinkers, Marxists, Freemasons, and men like Rosenberg. The terms *rationalists, liberals, freethinkers,* and *Marxists* could all be used as ciphers for the Jews. The bishop ended his petition with an appeal to Hitler: continue the fight against the "terrible enemy" (Communism) of the beloved Fatherland, but also fight against the other enemies of Catholicism.[4] By emphasizing the shared enemy Communism, von Galen hoped to solidify Catholicism's place in the state. He, like Hitler, saw a link between Communism and Jewishness.

In a letter to Alfred Meyer, Gauleiter of Münster, von Galen, again revealing his mastery of *Mein Kampf,* quoted Hitler concerning the threat of international Communism. However, he went one step further in his letter to the Gauleiter, stating that, according to Hitler, an individual who helped create religious strife, as the Communists did, was "whether knowingly or unknowingly . . . a fighter for Jewish interests." The bishop reprimanded Meyer, advising him to stop distributing material that offended "Christian-thinking National Socialists."[5]

Until his death in 1946, the bishop refused to recognize that referring to Jews as "degenerate," "rejected," and "lost," combined with an ardent opposition to "Jewish" anarchy and liberalism, only aided the Nazi regime. Agreeing with the state that the true enemy was a "Judeo-Bolshevik conspiracy" and attempting to rally Catholics to the regime's fight against that enemy did not work to mobilize the Catholic population to defend a persecuted minority. The imagery of the Jews employed by von Galen in his sermons leaves one with the feeling that the Jews were responsible for their own damnation. His continuing fear of "godless Communism," the subtle suggestion that Jews were behind the forces of Communism, and his ultranationalism "made him and the whole German episcopacy useful in propping up the Third Reich."[6] They were unable to see that nationalistic values, combined with "normal" anti-Semitism, only contributed to the strength of the Nazis; as a result they sacrificed the very basis of their Christian faith, "Love one another as I have loved you."

A Climate of Opinion

By 1934 Neville Laski, working on behalf of the Board of Deputies of British Jews and the American Joint Distribution Committee, was able to relate the following story, revealing the crippling discrimination faced by almost all Jews in Europe. "Dr. Schramm, the State Commissioner, visited a school and asked a boy, 'Why do we shun the Jews?'" The reply, taught to pupils enrolled in the German-controlled Danzig school, was, "Because the Jews are destructive and communist."[7]

For many German Catholics, the idea that Jews represented a threatening, demoralizing influence on the nation was nothing new. Because of their experiences during the Kulturkampf, they saw their successful acceptance into German culture as dependent upon the exclusion of yet another minority. As they struggled for integration into the Second Reich, they denounced liberalism as a Jewish political ideology. The Catholic Center Party, founded on the heels of German unification, used anti-Semitic rhetoric quite frequently to denounce liberals and social democrats. Men such as Adolf Stoecker, inspired by noted professor Heinrich Treitschke, could write a petition asking that "Jewish influence" be banned from the new German nation.[8]

In Münster, following unification, the Jewish Question was also being discussed, particularly in pamphlets and newspapers. Professor August Rohling, a Catholic priest who lived in Münster for some time, was responsible for many anti-Semitic pamphlets published in the region. His most famous work, *Talmud-Jew*, appeared in 1871 and eventually landed him a position at the University of Prague. His writings portrayed Jews as masters of finance, captains of industry, organizers of terrorist groups, and members of another race.[9]

One of the men who encouraged Rohling to write his brochures was the chief editor of the *Westfälischen Merkur,* Christoph Cremer. Cremer was a member of the Catholic Center Party, and in 1880 he joined Stoecker's movement in Berlin. When Stoecker declared that a great chasm stood between Germans and Jews, Cremer quoted Stoecker in the *Merkur.* All three men, Cremer, Stoecker, and Rohling, believed that the worst thing for Christian salvation in Germany had been the emancipation of the Jews.[10]

One of the few "Aryans-only" organizations in Münster at this time was the German Reform Union, which lasted only from 1887 until 1900 and was both anti-Semitic and anti-Catholic. Its anti-Semitic rhetoric was guided primarily by religious and economic principles. Its anti-Catholicism included parodies of Catholic politicians and priests using slogans such as "The Jews are our Brothers" and "Germany Protect Poland and Jews." Although the German Reform Union elected to portray the Catholic Center Party as friendly to the Jews, in reality the Center Party did not work to assimilate Jews into German society.[11]

At about the same time that the German Reform Union was propounding religious and economic anti-Semitism, a more militant type of rhetoric entered the discourse. This aggressive, modern anti-Semitism was imbued with the racial, pseudoscientific teaching that biology had made it impossible for Jews ever to be fully assimilated into the German race. Many politicians adopted the language of anti-Semitism when trying to explain why people felt that their lives were out of control.

Hans-Joachim Bieber, writing on pre-1914 Germany, argues that politicians who were associated with antidemocratic, anti-urban, antimodern ideals most frequently adopted the rhetoric of anti-Semitism. According to Bieber's work, militaristic tendencies, community ideology, and cultural pessimism were also characteristics of the "syndrome which the strata of German society who were disquieted and irritated by the process of modernization developed as an anti-modern ideology of defense."[12]

Modernity, liberalism, and democracy were ideas that had been denounced by the pope in the 1864 encyclical *Syllabus of Errors.* These ideologies, along with "Jewish influence," were fought by many German Catholics. The Jesuit priest Gustav Gundlach originally believed it was permissible to combat "harmful" Jewish influences if the fight was for moral reasons. The vicar general of Mainz, after reading *Mein Kampf,* extolled Hitler's ability to reveal unwanted Jewish influence in literature and the press. Others, such as Father Wilhelm Senn, believed that the

Nazi movement was radical but that it seemed to represent Germany's last hope to end the "tyranny" of the Jews.[13]

Throughout the Weimar years, the leadership of the church spoke out against the Nazi Party's glorification of blood and race, yet it refrained from commenting specifically on the anti-Semitic propaganda that seemed to be flourishing in Weimar's unstable environment. One Catholic organization, the Katholikenbund, encouraged its members to fight against Marxists, Jews, and freemasons because all of them were thought to be enemies of the church and the German nation.[14]

To combat the radicalization of anti-Semitism, Cardinal Faulhaber declared in 1923 that every human life was precious—including that of a Jew. Such a backhanded defense as this alerted some Jews to the growing dangers around them. According to a report written by the Central Association of German Citizens of Jewish Faith (C.V.), that organization found itself fighting against alienation, rejection, and growing hostility to German Jews. The report noted that as the economy worsened, competition with Jewish firms increased, anti-Jewish thoughts grew, and many Jews found themselves defending their German identity.[15] To the C.V., anti-Semitism in Germany revealed the anxieties and resentments of those individuals aspiring to middle-class status.

Very few Catholic leaders recognized the danger of political anti-Semitism, although extraordinary individuals such as Father Bernhard Lichtenberg argued that the physical destruction of Jews would follow from the political rhetoric. Most Catholic leaders, by 1933, were stressing cooperation and moderation with the Nazi Party. Many priests, like Bishop Wienken and even Father Friedrich Muckermann, thought that the church and the state should support each other. Friedrich's brother, Hermann, also a Jesuit, went further. He became the leader of the Department of Eugenics at the Kaiser-Wilhelm Gesellschaft in Berlin and wrote articles that emphasized the danger of "foreign races" to the German nation.[16]

Many church leaders, in an effort to bolster their patriotic credentials, believed—partly out of religious anti-Semitism but also partly because they thought that the state's enemies had to be the church's enemies—that Jews should be denounced. In many warnings, Catholics were told that Jews were connected to any "ism" that threatened society. Archbishop Gröber wrote in a handbook, "Bolshevism is Asiatic state-despotism, practiced in connection with a Jewish group of terrorists." His definition of Bolshevism was not much different from Nazi Party

member Ferdinand von Lüninck's. Lüninck spoke at von Galen's en-
thronement as bishop of Münster in October 1933. In his comments, the
Nazi aristocrat told the assembled guests that Hitler would save all of
German Christian culture from the Asiatic pest. Praising the swastika
as a German symbol of victory, he declared a coming conflict between
Christianity and Asiatic Mongols.[17]

Perhaps Lüninck omitted a reference to the "Jewish group of terrorists" from his remarks because anti-Semitism played a rather small role
in Münster's local chapter of the Nazi Party (NSDAP). In 1929 a scandal
had occurred in Münster's Dresdner Bank, and the local Nazis had made
use of it by denouncing "Jewish capitalism" and by posting "No Jews
Allowed" placards at their meetings. In the wake of the bank debacle,
they also brought in a speaker whose theme was "Jewish Race—Your
Hour Has Come." However, by 1932 the NSDAP in Münster knew that
the anti-Semitic slogans were not an effective way to win over Catholic
voters.[18]

Anti-Semitic slogans may not have swayed the Catholic population
of Münster, but if those Catholics looked in 1933 to their new bishop for
leadership and guidance, they encountered an ardent opponent of Bolshevism, a fervent believer in the stab-in-the-back legend, an antidemo-
crat, antiliberal, antimodern man who believed that Catholics needed
to be obedient to God-given earthly authority. He did not endorse the
racial thinking of the Nazis, but he and other Catholics of Münster did
have at least a vague acceptance of the legitimacy of the Jewish Question.
Even upper-class resisters to Hitler "acknowledged the existence of an
alleged 'Jewish Problem' that required a more or less exclusionary and
prejudicial solution in a post-Nazi German state."[19]

Anti-Semitism was pervasive in all levels of Münster's society, and
whether it played a large role or a small role in Münster's branch of the
NSDAP, no voice of opposition was raised publicly when the government-sponsored discriminations, persecutions, and deportations began
—even though a Jewish community had existed sporadically in Münster
since the twelfth century.[20]

A Brief History

The oldest original document of the history of the Jews in all of Westphalia is a 1324 gravestone of a Jewish woman. That fragment is located

in Münster. The first recorded instance of a Jew living in Münster dates back to 1127–1128, when a man from Cologne, Juda ben David Halewi, came to the town. He later changed his name to Hermann Mönch and converted to Christianity. From that time forward, other Jews wandered in and out of Münster and its outlying regions, but by 1290–1300 enough of a settled community was present that a synagogue could be constructed.[21]

After the plague in 1350, Jews left the region to escape persecution, but those who remained continued to be involved with finance and currency exchange. The next major milestone to truly affect the Jews of this region occurred when Knight-Bishop Franz von Waldeck, a Catholic, destroyed the Anabaptists of Münster in 1536 and granted ten Jews the right of safe passage to live and work in the town. Waldeck did this primarily because he needed the financial support of the Jews after his expenditures in defeating the Anabaptist heretics. The Jewish community grew under Waldeck's guarantees of protection, and by 1550 approximately fifty to seventy Jews lived in the town. All this changed, however, when Waldeck died in 1553. The town fathers expelled the Jews by 1554 and passed a law decreeing that Jews no longer had the right to live in Münster.[22] By 1560 Jews were ordered out of the bishopric.

Despite the gravity of these laws and expulsions, numerous exemptions were granted. Many Jews were able to stay in town for months at a time, particularly if they were doctors. For nearly a century, Jews of Münster's regions were subjected to the whims of the city leaders. This changed somewhat in 1650, when Knight-Bishop Christoph Bernhard von Galen once again began the fight to "cleanse" the city of Anabaptists. Von Galen, before defeating the "heretics," consolidated the various Jewish organizations into one large group. He then split the Jewish community living in Münster by granting some Jews special status as "Court Jews" (a condition that lasted until 1803). Despite the cleavages produced, von Galen tended to be regarded as another protector, comparable to Franz von Waldeck. By 1661 the bishop had defeated the Anabaptists in the community, solidifying his hold on Münster until his death in 1678.[23]

The Jewish community continued to grow in Münster's surrounding regions, increasing from 75 families in 1720 to 203 in 1795. Jews were still banned from living in the town proper, owing to the 1554 statute. In 1810, however, the mayor officially granted Nathan Elias Metz the right to live in Münster. In two short years, 21 Jewish families had moved into the city. The general condition of Jews seemed to be improving over the course of the nineteenth century. For Münster's Jews progress meant the founding of a school specifically for Jews, the Marks-Haindorf Stiftung, and the naming of the first Jewish man as professor of medicine at Münster's university.[24]

Jewish emancipation in Prussian territory was included in the short-lived Liberal Revolution of 1848. By this time Jews were debating about orthodoxy or reform, separatism or assimilation. By law Jews did not become full members of Prussian society until 1869. Many went on to fight for German unification in the Franco-Prussian War of 1870-1871. Although many Jews believed that fighting as patriots would only improve Jewish life, the economic depression that hit Europe shortly after Germany's unification led to an increase in attacks against "Jewish capitalism."

Münster's Jews faced men such as August Rohling and his disreputable but highly popular anti-Semitic writings. Despite Rohling's attacks, the synagogue in Münster was consecrated in 1880. The Jewish community continued to grow, and with the outbreak of World War I, many enlisted, just as other patriotic Germans did. Fifteen Jewish men in Münster died fighting for Germany in World War I.[25]

Between World War I and 1933, the Jews of Münster became involved in all types of occupations. They were, for example, painters, bakers, horse dealers, engineers, postal workers, professors, dentists, doctors, and hairdressers. On the eve of the Nazi seizure of power, 697 Jews were living in Münster. Almost all of them were hurt by the Nazi-sponsored boycott in April 1933: 264 emigrated, 170 of them because of the events of Kristallnacht; 84 died of natural causes between 1933 and 1941; 4 survived by living illegally in Münster; 74 had an unknown fate; and 271 were deported beginning in 1941 to ghettos and concentration camps in Riga, Minsk, and Theresienstadt. Of those 271 deportees, 24 survived their ordeals. Only a few returned to resettle in Münster. Two of those who did return, Siegfried Goldenberg and Hugo Spiegel, established the Jewish Cultural Center in Münster in September 1945.[26]

Good Catholics, Good Nationalists

In April 1933 Hitler gave a speech addressing the Jewish Question. He vowed that he was doing the "work of the Lord" and performing a favor for Christianity by dealing with the Jewish presence in German life. In this speech, as in others, Hitler connected the Jews to Marxism, invoking the party platform that vowed to struggle against the "Jewish-materialistic spirit." Hitler's speech was not exceptionally new; the Jewish Question had been debated years before he had become chancellor. Even during the Weimar Republic, the right-wing extremists in the Parliament had raised the question whether the "Jewish race" belonged to Germany or whether it should be placed under foreign laws.[27] Hitler's regime moved quickly to address the Jewish presence in German life.

Beginning on March 5, 1933, Jews living in Berlin experienced the first terror action of the SA, aimed primarily at Jewish professionals. In the following days, such actions were perpetrated against Jews in other professions: doctors, lawyers, judges, and businessmen. On April 1 a national boycott against "international Jewry" was enacted. A handful of days later, a law was passed that resulted in the firing of Jewish civil servants. A few days after that came a law that attempted to define who was fully Aryan and who was not. The Catholic Church remained silent concerning the boycott. It did, however, refuse to hand over church record books that would have provided Nazis with information as to who should be considered fully Aryan.[28] Throughout 1933 there was a host of legislation designed to hurt Jews economically and to slowly take away rights that they had gained through the emancipation of 1871. The church did not offer to protest this legislation.

Von Galen did protest the racism of the Nazis at this time. In various sermons he warned Catholics to remain steadfast in their beliefs and not to fall prey to the exaltation of blood over common morality. In one sermon he claimed that he could not remain silent when false teachings were present. Explaining that neopaganism resulted from freethinkers and atheistic Bolsheviks, von Galen argued that the new Germany must be founded on principles of Christianity. One Nazi supporter, Carl Röver, charged von Galen with attempting to destroy the "will of the Movement" by linking the roots of Nazism to atheistic Bolshevism in his sermon.[29] No action was taken against the bishop.

Perhaps one reason why no proceedings were initiated against the bishop for his sermon was that he never challenged Hitler directly. In these and other similar sermons, he chose to attack Alfred Rosenberg, author of *The Myth of the 20th Century*. Rosenberg's writings were never officially incorporated into the Nazi Party platform; therefore attacks against his writings were technically not attacks against the Nazi state.

In October 1934 von Galen agreed to write the introduction to Professor Wilhelm Neuss's rebuttal to Rosenberg's publication. Originally Cardinal Schulte of Cologne had been slated to write the introduction, but at the last minute he declined to do so.[30] In selecting his opponents, the bishop carefully avoided the risk of a direct attack on the government; he sent the message to Catholics that they could support certain aspects of the Nazi state while not wholeheartedly endorsing the regime.

A good example of this mixed message occurred in January 1935 when the people living in the Saarland were getting ready to vote. They could, according to the Treaty of Versailles, return to Germany or be incorporated into France. Von Galen, in several strong statements, told the Saar's voters that Germany's peacefulness was dependent upon German Catholics' voting to return to Germany. Six bishops of the province of Cologne used von Galen's statements to influence Saar voters. The bishops' words were such a powerful endorsement of the German nation that the voting commission board registered a complaint about the use of undue influence at the polls.[31] Von Galen truly occupied an ambivalent position. He was an ardent supporter of German aggrandizement and revision of the Treaty of Versailles, yet he chose to protest certain government policies selectively. His careful selection of areas to be challenged was generally so overlaid with patriotic sentiment that the message of the challenge was dissipated.

Some of the ambiguity of von Galen's mixed message toward the Nazis was evident in 1937, when General Erich Ludendorff died. Von Galen recommended that church bells should chime and that the church should be decorated with flags to honor the dead. Many church members thought von Galen's actions were scandalous, considering that Ludendorff had fought against the Catholic Church, the papacy, and the Jesuits. Publicly, von Galen wanted the dead general honored. Privately, he sent a letter to all clergy stating that Ludendorff's service to Germany in the war should be respected but that they should also keep in mind that he held many misguided opinions of Christianity.[32] The letter of explanation was not to be read before Catholic parishioners.

Picking and choosing what to endorse and what to oppose was getting more and more complicated under the Nazi government. Praising a war veteran while ignoring his persecution of Catholics sent a very complicated message to Catholic parishioners. Bishop Preysing in Berlin, looking at von Galen's recommendations on memorializing General Ludendorff, began to believe that the bishop of Münster "sympathized with the National Socialist system until the final end."[33] The confusion only worsened as the years progressed.

The Image of the Jew

Some historians, such as Heinz Mussinghoff, argue that by criticizing Rosenberg's racism, von Galen had effectively immunized the Catholics of Münster against the infection of anti-Semitism. However, when one analyzes how the bishop portrayed Jews in his sermons and letters, a picture emerges that reveals the Jews to be a condemned people, superseded by Christianity and left to their own devices. In this respect von Galen is quite typical of the Catholic Church hierarchy. From the time of Thomas Aquinas on, it was popularly accepted by many Christians that Jews did not need to be loved. One could therefore remain unmoved by the plight of the Jews and still have a clear Christian conscience. As the teachings went, Jews had failed to accept Jesus as the Son of God, and by that they had damned themselves. Only those Jews who had "seen the light" and had converted were worth working to protect.

Jews had also historically been portrayed as a force of disorder and upheaval. Depictions of Jews over the span of centuries built on images of anarchy, terror, and radicalism. According to the forged "Protocols of the Elders of Zion," Jews were sowers of chaos, greedy for world domination. With the advent of the Enlightenment and the French Revolution, many conservatives thought that liberalism was a Jewish ideology because Jews, they thought, benefited the most from concepts of equality and emancipation. All of these images coalesced to construct the stereotype that all Jews everywhere represented a threat to order, hierarchy, and stability. Their questioning of God-granted earthly authority seemed to threaten the very foundations of Christianized Western Europe. By the time of the Russian Revolution, Jews were associated not only with the liberalism of the nineteenth century but also with Communism and Bolshevism in its Russian revolutionary incarnation.[34]

On September 14, 1941, von Galen delivered a sermon in which he directly quoted Hitler's words about the need to fight the "Judeo-Bolshevik conspiracy." Drawing on a speech Hitler had given in the Reich Chancellery on June 22, 1941 (the day the Nazis invaded the Soviet Union), von Galen used Hitler's words, "For two decades the Judeo-Bolshevik rulers in Moscow have taken great pains to start fires not only in Germany but in all of Europe." Revealing the dangerous threat that all of Europe was now facing, von Galen relied on Hitler's own descriptions and tropes to prove his point.[35] He could use words such as *Communism, Marxism,* and *Bolshevism* interchangeably, and many people would immediately understand that these words were ciphers for the Jews. The bishop, by clearly linking Jews with Bolshevik radicalism, did not need to openly attack the Jews. He certainly did nothing to improve their situation when he referred to Jews in his sermons in language reminiscent of traditional religious anti-Semitism. Here, Hitler's messianic narrative of redemption overlapped with von Galen's Christian one.

In a sermon delivered in June 1935, the bishop explained a four-hundred-year-old tradition in Münster. In 1535, when Franz von Waldeck defeated the Anabaptists in town, the conquering bishop dedicated the city to the Sacred Heart of Jesus. Von Galen connected the heresy of the Anabaptists to the "sins" of the Jews. Telling the audience that "whoever does not listen to the Church is a heathen and officially is a sinner" would naturally mean that Jews were sinners.[36] He continued by describing how the "Israelites debased the Savior" and how anyone who resisted Jesus as the Christ appeared on the "side of the blinded Jews" who had called out on Good Friday, "We don't want you [Jesus] to rule over us!" In this sermon von Galen equated the rejection of Christianity with rejection of worldly authority, leading to anarchy, disorder, and chaos. Anabaptists, Jews, atheists—anyone who did not accept Jesus' message—promoted a questioning of authority, to the bishop's mind. In particular, von Galen pointed to modern-day Russians as people who were suffering because they had not respected God-given authority and were therefore deprived of their natural freedoms.[37] Calling the Russians an "unfortunate people," he emphasized that worldly authority was sanctioned by God and should not be challenged. In a single sermon von Galen had successfully combined the imagery of disorder, Russian "terror," heresy, and Jewishness. He was not immunizing Catholics against Nazi racism; he was immunizing them against feeling the need to intervene on behalf of their suffering neighbors.

In another sermon, in 1940, the bishop was concerned that Catholic parents might need to give religious instruction to their children in their own homes because of state cutbacks in the school system. He emphasized that in an "enemy-filled world," the Holy Spirit was needed to guide and to protect innocent children from harm. Who might bring these children harm? Specifically, von Galen referred to the "degenerate Jews" as one possible threat. The bishop explained how the "rejected Jews" had denied Jesus as the Savior, and he quoted from John 3:19, "On these grounds is sentence pronounced: that though the light has come into the world, men have shown they prefer darkness to the light because their deeds were evil."[38] Although von Galen did not read the preceding verse, many listeners in church could be presumed to be familiar with it: John 3:18, "No one who believes in him will be condemned; but whoever refuses to believe is condemned already, because he has refused to believe in the name of God's only Son." *Condemned, rejected, degenerate, harmful.* All of these words carry a powerful message. Jews were responsible for their own damnation. Although not necessarily preaching overt racial hatred, von Galen was not working to improve the image of the Jew in German society. All of this language contributed to the image of the "sinful Jews," creators of their own problems and destroyers of Christian-based culture.

By offering sermons such as these, the bishop showed Catholics that there was a way to exist somewhat comfortably under the Nazi government. They should be loyal, obedient Germans, who accepted the legitimacy of their rulers. They might object to specific laws, but overall they could support the values of Volk and Vaterland. In a series of seemingly minor moral compromises, many Catholics had decided that "the 'Jewish Question' was basically a matter of indifference."[39] The Nazis did not need active hatred of the Jews. They only needed apathy to succeed. After all, Jews had stood condemned as "official" sinners in all of Christian Europe long before the advent of Hitler's new, false messianism.

Münster's Local Population

In 1933 the German Catholic bishops issued a statement after the signing of the Concordat. They declared "their unwavering support of the important national values of ethnicity and culture and limited dissent to an insistence that this goal would not be achieved by resorting to immoral means."[40] The issue of limited dissent came to the fore in 1935 when the church began complaining about a law affecting the sacrament of marriage.

The proposed Nuremberg Law stated that racially mixed marriages were not permitted. The church responded by claiming that a priest would be obligated to marry two baptized people despite their racially mixed stock.[41] This conflict further intensified once the September 1935 Nuremberg Laws were passed, prohibiting mixed marriages. Although there were individual priests who circumvented the law by using a clause in the Concordat that referred to "great moral emergency," the church as an institution obeyed the 1935 legislation. In an article in the *Klerusblatt*, the new anti-Jewish decrees were lauded as necessary "'safeguards' for the general character of the German people."[42]

Articles pertaining to the Nuremberg racial laws began appearing in a Nazi-controlled paper, *Der Stürmer*. In the Münster edition of the paper, lists of Aryan women who had been impregnated by their Jewish husbands were printed alongside denunciations of the yet-to-be born "Bastards."[43] Other citizens found their names listed in the paper because they had been spotted shopping in Jewish-owned stores. Issues of *Der Stürmer* appeared in destroyed shop windows beside placards that generally read, "A . . . Jew lives in this store." In a postwar interview, one citizen of Münster recalled that the local Nazis took photographs of people shopping and then published their pictures with captions such as "This woman buys from a Jew."[44] All of these were strategies designed to intimidate the local citizenry. Unfortunately for the local Nazis, these methods were not deemed very successful.

Many of Münster's local police and NSDAP reports include bitter complaints that the population seemed to be completely ignorant of the Jewish Problem. The reports reveal an intense drive on the part of the Nazis to override what they believed to be the influence of the church over this question. *Der Stürmer* sought to equate Catholicism with Judaism and Communism by publishing articles that suggested a link between the international "isms." They included songs that called for the removal of the influence of the Jews and the pope from German soil. Again, despite *Der Stürmer*'s efforts to make the link believable, they reported, "*Der Stürmer*'s attempts to win over the population . . . [are] proceeding with considerable difficulty. Many still drivel about 'decent Jews' from whom they continue to buy despite all the propaganda of the movement. In this respect the influence of the Church appears to be predominating."[45]

The reports reveal party members' preoccupation with settling the Jewish Question while simultaneously teaching the local population how to properly treat the Jews. Numerous reports lamented that the average citizen was still dealing with Jews.[46] Perhaps an even larger problem faced by the local Nazis was convincing their own party members as well as uniformed soldiers to stop frequenting Jewish-owned businesses.[47] For party members, Aryans who failed to comprehend the seriousness of the Jewish Question were "worse than the Jews themselves."[48]

To enlighten Münster's population, various party members made suggestions such as increasing public humiliation through more lists in *Der Stürmer*. Others called for stricter action against party members and their wives who were still buying from Jews. One report from Christmas 1936 expressed shock and dismay that at such a time of year, Christians were still purchasing from Jews. This report recommended pillorying these people for educational purposes. As for dealing with the uniformed soldiers, the party suggested that a list be prepared for the men so that they would know which businesses were run by Jews. The list would be accompanied by instructions that would explain why they should no longer shop there. In another case, party members appealed to the Ministry of War asking for a statement on what it meant to see German soldiers buying in Jewish stores.[49]

Resolving that the Jewish Problem was "a burning issue of general interest," the local Nazis decided that they should work to increase propaganda aimed at Jewish business owners, put identification marks on the windows of Jewish shops, and set an example for the other citizens by personally not purchasing products from Jews. They believed this was necessary because "the Catholic population has little understanding . . . that the time has come to solve the 'Jewish Question.'"[50]

Despite party members' determination to resolve the Jewish Problem, a January 1936 account disappointedly related, "This month's report for this region does not have many offenses against Jews. Merely unknown culprits turning over a row of gravestones in the Jewish cemetery in Münster."[51]

1936: The "Real" Enemy Exposed

Two major events dominated von Galen's world in 1936: the remilitarization of the Rhineland and the outbreak of civil war in Spain. On March 7, 1936, German troops marched into what had been the demilitarized zone of the Rhineland. Von Galen quickly sent a telegraph to Werner von Fritsch, supreme army commander, welcoming him to the region "in the name of true German Catholics" and telling the leader that German soldiers on the Rhine were symbols of renewed German honor.[52]

In the case of the Rhineland occupation, von Galen reassured German Catholics that they wanted to walk in step with all "true German citizens." He also reminded them that "a large part of National Socialism should be welcomed, especially the anti-Communism and the national-aggressive foreign policy." Seeking to prove that Catholics had much in common with the Nazi state, von Galen pointed out the common enemy, Communism, and stated, "For thousands of years Germany has been Christian . . . we were true Germans then and now."[53]

Reiterating that the new German state must be a Christian one, von Galen gave a sermon beginning with Mark 16:16: "He who believes and is baptized will be saved, he who does not believe will be condemned." Jews, neopagans, and atheists who were not baptized would not be saved. Catholics, however, "who did their duty and remained true in time of class struggle and revolution, who gave their lives for their country,"[54] had already proved that "We German Catholics stand unshakably true to our *Volk* and *Vaterland.*" Believing that Germany was in the midst of a religious crisis, the bishop urged Catholics to keep Hindenburg's admonishment alive: "Let Jesus be preached in Germany!"[55] He told Catholics that he understood that their loyalty to the state was often questioned when attempts were made to link Catholics with Communism: "I know how deeply this hurts you, helplessly suffering in the attempts to classify you as 'enemies of the people,' although you helped resist the Red Flag and . . . proved your loyalty to the German nation." Praying for an end to the religious crisis, von Galen ended the sermon by clearly stating that it was possible to do one's duty to God and still love and serve the German nation.[56]

Von Galen believed that the real threat to Germany's future, if not all of Europe's, was atheistic Communism and socialism. Once civil war broke out in Spain in 1936, his sermons were dominated by concerns for Christianity menaced by the spread of Marxism. The only way he could see of combating the spread of radicalism was to maintain the practice of Christianity, for "atheism and Bolshevism go hand in hand."[57] In this respect, von Galen wholeheartedly endorsed the Nazi portrayal of the events in Spain. Hitler had told the German people that defeat of Franco's forces would mean the victory of Bolshevism over all of Europe. As the Nazis exploited the civil war to gain support for their struggles against Bolshevism, von Galen also encouraged Catholics to fight against the dangers posed by such a godless system.

Quoting 1 Corinthians 12:27, "Now you together are Christ's body, but each of you is a different part of it," von Galen preached that Spain's fate was linked to all of Christian Europe's. Only through prayer and watchfulness could the "pestilent Communistic infection"[58] be overcome. Telling his parishioners that Communism produced estrangement from the teachings of Christianity, hatred of God, and self-destruction, he prayed that the "infection" would not spread to his beloved Germany.[59]

At the Fulda Conference of bishops in August 1936, the discussion of the Spanish civil war dominated the meetings. All of those present offered to share in the fight against the spread of Bolshevism. By the fall of 1936, Hitler had invited Cardinal Faulhaber to his Berghof residence. Reportedly, the two men spoke of the Spanish civil war for three hours. Hitler's aim was to convince the cardinal that church-state cooperation was vital in this dangerous struggle. Approximately one month after Faulhaber's visit, the Fulda Conference produced a letter that criticized National Socialist oppression of the church's institutions but gave unconditional support to Hitler in his battle against Bolshevism.[60]

The civil war in Spain gave von Galen an opportunity to remind listeners that Communism stood in direct opposition to Catholicism, despite what Nazi propaganda was telling them. In one sermon von Galen listed various articles that had appeared in Nazi publications such as *Das Schwarze Korps* where suggestions were made that the German bishops and the pope were somehow in league with Communist forces. Von Galen emphasized how many times the pope had denounced Communism as a threat to Christian culture and to the peace of the world in general. He told the audience that he had been in Rome in 1936 and had heard the pope himself speak for almost an hour on the dangers posed by Bolshevism. In defense of the German bishops, von Galen noted that they had raised their voices in protest of socialism and Communism even when Germany had been ruled by those same groups. Years later, after Pius XI had died, von Galen could still be found defending the deceased pope's warnings against Communism and Bolshevism. Although von Galen rejected the claims made by Nazi publications, he ended the sermon with prayers for the Führer and for Christians suffering in Spain.[61] The fear of being classified as an enemy of the state once again seems to have resulted in displays of loyalty taken to absurd lengths.

At other times he complained that the Gestapo were closing down Catholic organizations because the organizations were supposedly in league with the Communists. He would then point out that Catholics and Hitler had similar goals: Hitler wanted to destroy Communists, and the pope wanted to convert them. Von Galen believed that ultimately, both leaders had the same goal: the complete eradication of Communism from European soil.[62]

When the Spanish civil war ended in 1939, von Galen joyfully exclaimed that the outcome had proved God's power over atheistic Communism. Noting again how the church had fought Communism for decades, von Galen warned Catholics that godless Communism was still a threat, because of Moscow and its desire to defeat Christian states.[63]

1938: "No One Helped Us"

"*Kristallnacht* [November 9–10, 1938], appeared to us to be the highpoint of Nazi barbarism, cruelty and misfortune that could befall us. It was, however, only a first beacon, a link in the chain of cruelty, a beginning of inhumanity, whose object was . . . murdering all Jews." These words were written by Rabbi Fritz L. Steinthal, born in Berlin in 1889. He became a rabbi in 1911 and a few years later served in World War I and earned the Iron Cross. He became chief rabbi in Münster, serving in that capacity from 1919 to 1938.[64]

In Dr. Steinthal's letter, written from Argentina in 1966, he related his memories of the events of Kristallnacht. He described the terror that he and his wife, Gertrude, experienced as they hid in the attic while downstairs their home was being ransacked by SA members. Later they were found in the attic and brought downstairs at gunpoint to be interrogated. The SA men took Dr. Steinthal and drove all over Münster that night looking for more Jews to harass and arrest. The rabbi noted that these were not Münster's SA men. The local members of the SA had been sent to another town. Theoretically it would be easier for SA men to terrorize strangers.[65]

After driving around all night, the SA men dropped the rabbi off at the local jail. He remained there until he could secure emigration papers for Argentina. Dr. Steinthal and his wife left Münster forever on December 9, 1938. His successor in Münster, Rabbi Julius Voos, his wife Stephanie, and their infant son, Daniel, all perished in a concentration camp.[66]

How did the pogrom detailed by Rabbi Steinthal's letter begin in

Münster? The night before, November 8, 1938, one of Münster's papers, *Der Münsterische Anzeiger*, ran commentary on Herschel Grynszpan's attempt to assassinate Ernst vom Rath, concluding: "This bloody deed . . . of the criminal gang of international Jewry, Free Masonry and Bolshevism . . . provokes chaos[;] because of this bloody deed in Paris, the Jews of Germany must suffer the consequences."[67]

Following the news of the death of vom Rath on the night of November 9, 1938, orders were given to SA men to destroy Jewish businesses, synagogues, and homes. In Münster, the SA arrested at least fifty Jews in one night. They mistreated and harassed countless others, including the elderly and infirm. Rabbi Steinthal tried to find comfort while imprisoned by holding onto the belief that the bishop cared about his welfare. This belief allowed him to focus his energy on working to save other Jews from arrest or deportation.[68]

Rabbi Steinthal's undying belief in von Galen's support remains a point of controversy. Although the rabbi was convinced that the bishop had sent a messenger on November 10 to see what had happened to him, the man who actually went to see the rabbi's wife, Dr. Hans Kluge, denied that the bishop had sent him.[69]

According to Kluge, on Thursday morning he went with two other students, Adolf Lillich and Albert Maring, through the streets of Münster, surveying the damages. Lillich and Maring knew that the bishop had called from Münsterland to Ignatius House, where they lived with the other Jesuits in town. Von Galen had been out of town on November 9, performing confirmations, when he heard about the violent attack. The Jesuits' home was very close to the synagogue as well as to the Jewish school, the Marks-Haindorf Stiftung. Mussinghoff has interpreted von Galen's call to the Jesuits as an expression of concern for the Jews in Münster.[70] More cynically, one could interpret the call as indicating concern that the Jesuits' close proximity to both the synagogue and the Marks-Haindorf Stiftung might have resulted in damage to Ignatius House.

Whatever the motivation for the phone call, Kluge reported that he heard the Jesuit brothers discussing the night's events and asked permission to go see Steinthal's Catholic maid. Kluge went to Steinthal's residence, spoke to the maid and to Mrs. Steinthal, and returned to the Jesuits with the information he had gathered.[71] Kluge had no contact either in person or via telephone with the bishop. Von Galen did not directly send Kluge to inquire after Dr. Steinthal's welfare. What his intentions were regarding the phone call to the Jesuit brothers remains unclear.

Rabbi Steinthal's 1966 letter also mentioned, as further proof of von Galen's concern for the Jews, that the bishop had ordered prayers to be said for Jews in all of the bishopric's churches. This is simply unfounded. No instructions were given by von Galen, ever, for prayers to be offered for Jews. This does not mean that there were no prayers given. Prelate Joseph Leufkens offered prayers for Jews in the Servatii-Kirche, next door to the burned-out synagogue. Father Joseph Reukes and Vicar Johannes Klumpe were both arrested in 1941 for praying openly for the Jews. Both were eventually sent to Dachau.[72]

Lower-level clergymen spoke out, even if minimally; but why did von Galen choose to remain silent after such blatant criminal activity had taken place? The immediate answer given by Mussinghoff has to do with a delegation of Jewish citizens and their meeting with the Catholic Caritas director, Theodore Holling. Mussinghoff claims that von Galen wanted to help the Jews and that this meeting proved it. In this meeting the Jews asked Holling to act as the intermediary with von Galen, who at no time had personal contact with any member of the Jewish delegation. The delegates told Holling that they would like the bishop to publicly protest the events of November 9–10. Von Galen responded, through Holling, that he would need the Jews to write down their side of the story, because he could not believe that all the guilt belonged to them in this case. His response also came with a warning that his public condemnation of the violence might lead to more severe reprisals against the Jewish community. Not surprisingly, the Jewish delegation then told Holling very politely that the bishop should refrain from protesting on their behalf. They made no further attempts to enlist the bishop's support for their plight.

Although it is hard to imagine that von Galen actually believed that the Jews had had some hand in the destruction of their own homes, businesses, and places of worship, he asked them to explain their side of the story. This seems to suggest that von Galen had bought into some of the Nazi myth that Jews were an international force out to destroy all Germans everywhere. Even though those particular Jewish delegates left the impression that von Galen should remain silent regarding the events of November 9–10, that incident alone does not fully exonerate von Galen for his continuing disregard of the constant violations perpetrated against Jewish citizens. Simply stating that von Galen honored the Jewish delegations' wishes and said nothing is not a sufficient explanation for his silence.

Joachim Kuropka claims that von Galen's silence had to do with the fact that he was not in town to witness the violence for himself, that he had missed seeing schoolteachers lead their classes to view the burning synagogue, singing hate-filled songs; or hearing some in Münster's crowds call out for death to all Jews in exchange for a murdered diplomat in Paris. Being out of town, he had missed the November 10th edition of the local paper, which portrayed the violence and destruction as "the answer of the National Socialist population" to the murder of vom Rath.[73] Somehow not being present at the time is used as a valid reason to ignore what had happened.

Kuropka also argues that the bishop might have been intimidated because he was aware that Cardinal Faulhaber's palace had been invaded on November 11, 1938, with the explanation that Jews, "Blacks and Reds" were all in league together.[74] Both Bishop Johann Sproll and Cardinal Theodor Innitzer in Vienna were terrorized during Kristallnacht as well. Perhaps von Galen feared that a similar event would happen at his palace if he spoke out.

Another of Kuropka's explanations is that von Galen worried that Nazi retaliations would be in the offing if he condemned their misdeeds. The examples most frequently cited in connection with von Galen's silence are the arrest of Münster's priests following the bishop's three famous sermons of 1941 and the reprisals carried out against the archbishop of Utrecht, Kardinal Johannes de Jong.[75] De Jong, in Holland, publicly protested the deportation of Jews in July 1942. Several days later, the Nazis responded by deporting Catholic "non-Aryans," including Edith Stein, a Jewish convert who had once studied in Münster. All of these were real, vivid incidents of Nazi terror tactics. However, one obviously cannot use these subsequent events to explain the bishop's silence in 1938.

It would be appropriate to point out the terror faced by the Catholic Church in 1938: the morality trials, the money trials, the closing down of Catholic local papers, the coordination of the Catholic Press, the elimination of Catholic religion teachers, and the banning of Catholic youth groups. Von Galen's sermons reveal his worries about the loss of these

Catholic institutions; he was convinced that the church was indeed battling to keep Catholic influence a presence in German daily life. He also would have recognized the popularity of Hitler's regime in 1938. The annexation of Austria and of the Sudetenland had occurred before Kristallnacht. For a German nationalist such as von Galen, the incorporation of these territories was something to be welcomed and supported by Catholics. Taking a public position on the Jewish Question might detract from Germany's successes and might endanger the Catholic Church's inclusion in the celebration of the new Germany.

Von Galen's abandonment of the Jews after the events of Kristallnacht shows him to be more in step with the church's official 1933 policy than has generally been portrayed. The Jewish Question was not an immediate concern of the church, nor was it an immediate concern of von Galen.[76]

When the church leaders met at Fulda in 1938 for their annual conference, they had to choose between two drafts of a joint pastoral for publication. One draft condemned the racism of the Nazis, and the other focused on the church struggle. They decided to adopt the draft dealing with the church's battle rather than circulate a condemnation of racism practiced in the Nazi state. In the document chosen for a wide audience, the bishops did refer to racism, stating, "In the church there are no differences between Volk and race. . . . All men in this way are God's children, without difference in rights and rank[.] As members of the Church, we are called together to be comrades."[77]

"Members of the Church" automatically excludes Jews from this statement. From the papacy down, most Catholic leaders only took an interest in Jewish policies when converted Jews began to be classified as full Jews. After Kristallnacht, the German Catholic Church did increase aid to Catholic Jews who were seeking to emigrate to Palestine. Organizations such as St. Raphael's Union were accused of aiding only Catholic Jews in their emigration to Palestine, "so that the whole land would not be lost to the Jews."[78] Unconverted Jews were left to solve their own emigration problems.

A few days after Kristallnacht, Hermann Göring held a conference on the Jewish Question. He maintained the same view that many top Nazis held; if war ever broke out, Jews would "face a major reckoning." Once the war did begin, further radical solutions to the Jewish Question appeared to be more feasible.[79]

War

In the opening weeks of the war, many local mayors enacted further discriminatory measures against German Jews. These measures ranged from curfews to banishment from restricted areas. As the war continued, additional decrees were passed, designed not only to discriminate against the Jews but also to humiliate them personally. A labor court in Cologne decided that Jews were not entitled to any vacation time, adding that "employers . . . have no particular duty to care for Jews."[80]

Despite the complications of war, many German authorities continued to push emigration as a possible solution of the Jewish Question. With the defeat of France in June 1940, some government officials turned their focus to the Madagascar Plan, until the Vichy government complained that it already had too many Jews in its region. In the early fall of 1940, Baldur von Schirach, then Gauleiter of Vienna, asked Hitler to send Viennese Jews to the General Government region of Poland. Hitler agreed to Schirach's request.[81]

Hitler later told two Gauleiters that "in ten years time there was only one report he would want to have from the Gauleiters, namely that their areas were German and by that he meant completely German. He would not ask questions about the methods they had used . . . and could not care less if sometime in the future it was established that the methods used to gain territories had been unpleasant or not absolutely legal."[82]

Jews were being sent eastward in the effort to make occupied lands "German." At the same time, the Reich Security Main Office continued to press for emigration. However, with the June 1941 invasion of the Soviet Union, an entirely new situation emerged. With every kilometer the German Army conquered, more Jews were added to Reich territory. It was becoming obvious that emigration of all Jews from conquered lands would not be feasible. The war against "Judeo-Bolshevism" triggered "the most extreme solution of the 'Jewish Question.' With the actions of the SS *Einsatzgruppen* the persecution of the Jews was transformed into systematic extermination."[83] For Jews living in Germany, the invasion of the Soviet Union meant a further radicalization of Nazi policies. For Münster's Jews, already forced to live in special housing since an April 1939 decree, the invasion brought the threat of deportation. To von Galen, the war in the East represented the ultimate battle for Christianity's cause. Concerning the war against the Soviet Union, he remarked, "If I were able, I would go fight against Bolshevism."[84]

On the eve of the invasion of the Soviet Union, it was clear to many German generals that this war was going to be unlike any other. It was an ideological war to be waged against "Judeo-Bolshevism." General Franz von Halder, commander of the army general staff, noted in his diary after a meeting with Hitler, "It is a war of extermination. . . . We are not fighting a war in order to conserve the enemy." The campaign itself was guided by "ruthless and energetic action against Bolshevik agitators, guerillas, saboteurs, and Jews and the total elimination of all active or passive resistance."[85]

Hitler claimed that war against the Soviet Union was necessary in order to protect all of Christian Europe from atheistic Bolshevism. Many of the German Army leaders believed that the center of "Judeo-Bolshevism" was indeed Moscow. "The association of the Jews with Bolshevism had become widely current among the European upper and middle classes after the Bolshevik Revolution. The fear that . . . Jews were prominently represented among the leading Bolsheviks appeared to confirm traditional anti-Semitic beliefs about the subversive nature of the Jews." When many people in Germany imagined the Soviet Union, they envisioned a "country in which hordes of culturally if not racially inferior Slavs and 'Asiatics' were led by a group of Jewish Bolsheviks bent on subverting the holiest values of Western Civilization."[86]

A police report explained just how the German population was struggling to put together a picture of the enemy. Previous propaganda, said the report, had described the Soviet Union as a gray, terrible place for a German man to be, a place filled with oppression and poverty brought on by a Bolshevik system run by Jews. The report noted, however, that despite the earlier propaganda's attempts to depict all Soviets as beasts and subhumans, German soldiers who had encountered Soviet POWs were contradicting Nazi propaganda. The German soldiers wrote letters home telling their families how the "beasts" were actually intelligent, quick to learn new skills, clean, hard-working, and, in some cases, blond and blue-eyed. To counter these assessments, the report suggested a concentrated effort to reveal more racist images, including pictures of the "animal-like" character of Mongolian and Turkic soldiers fighting in the Red Army. In addition to stressing racial differences between Germans and Soviets, the report urged Nazi Party members to remind Germans of the need for Lebensraum in the East.[87] Clearly, the Nazis recognized that the population still might have ambivalent feelings regarding the Soviets. They also recognized the need to place greater influence on differences between the two peoples in order to sway public opinion. In this respect they had some help from the German Catholic Church.

The Church and the Invasion

How did the Catholic Church respond to the invasion of the Soviet Union in the summer of 1941? The bishops of western Germany met at Fulda for their annual conference only a few days after the invasion had begun. Without directly mentioning the new campaign in the East, they urged Catholics to fulfill their patriotic responsibilities. Some bishops, however, broke the uneasy silence, offering their own personal opinions about the new campaign.

The bishop of Paderborn rejoiced that the battle had begun "for the protection of Christianity in our Fatherland, for the rescue of the Church from the threat of anti-Christian Bolshevism." The bishop of Eichstaett regarded the campaign "as a crusade, a holy war for homeland and people, for faith and church, for Christ and His most holy cross."[88]

The bishop of Münster delivered his three famous sermons in July and August 1941, censuring the Nazi practices and policies against the church and the mentally ill, but then he wrote a pastoral letter praising Hitler for finally breaking the terrible Nazi-Soviet Nonaggression Pact with Stalin. The bishop prayed for God's intervention to protect German troops fighting against the errors and heresies of Bolshevism.[89]

It would appear from von Galen's sermons that he had at least a vague suspicion that there was a "Judeo-Bolshevik conspiracy." Hitler had continually told the German people that such a conspiracy existed and that he was a crusading prophet, come to free Europe from the hands of Jews and Bolsheviks: "Today I will once more be a prophet: if the international Jewish financiers in and outside Europe should succeed in plunging the nations once more into a world war, then the result will not be the Bolshevizing of the earth, and thus the victory of Jewry, but the annihilation of the Jewish race in Europe."[90]

Once the invasion of the Soviet Union had begun, Hitler wanted to make clear what his intentions were in the battle of ideologies: "We are clear about the fact that the war can only end either in the extermination of the Aryan nations or in the disappearance of Jewry from Europe.

... This would not end as the Jews imagined, namely with the extermination of the Euro-Aryan nations, but rather ... the war will result in the destruction of Jewry. This time, for the first time, the old and typical Jewish law will be applied, 'An eye for an eye, a tooth for a tooth.'"[91]

A police report after Hitler's speech indicated that the general population reacted most favorably to those parts of the Führer's address that touched on the struggle against Bolshevism and the renewed denunciations of Jewry. The report claimed that the revival of Old Testament proverbs such as "An eye for an eye" revealed the Führer's renewed attacks on Jewry and predicted that such sayings would result in "the expulsion of the last Jew from European soil soon enough."[92]

Although the general report alleged that the population at large reacted favorably to denunciations of Jews and Bolshevism and seemed to have accepted the idea that a conspiracy of the two groups existed, one man who had murdered Jews and Bolsheviks from 1941 to 1945 testified to the contrary. His testimony, however, came much too late to alter the millions of murders based on a false belief. That man was Erich von dem Bach, antipartisan chief and higher SS police leader, Russian Center. At the end of the war, he concluded, "Contrary to the opinion of the National Socialists that the Jews were a highly organized group, the appalling fact was that they had no organization whatsoever. . . . Never before has a people gone as unsuspecting to its disaster. Nothing was prepared. . . . It was not so, as the anti-Semites say, that they were friendly to the Soviets. That is the most appalling misconception of all. The Jews in the Old Poland, who were never communistic in their sympathies were . . . more afraid of Bolshevism than of the Nazis."[93]

Bach's conclusions that no Judeo-Bolshevik conspiracy had ever existed came much too late to help the Jews. By September 1, 1941, Heydrich issued the directive that Jews were to wear the Star of David on their clothing.[94] Once Jews were visibly marked, it would be easier to isolate, control, and, ultimately, murder them. The Catholic Church did not protest the new decree. It did disagree, however, with the Gestapo's orders that baptized Jews were to wear the star as well. Bishops Wilhelm Berning and Wienken wrote to the Gestapo and asked that baptized Jews be exempted from wearing the star while they were attending Mass. The Gestapo refused the request.

Von Galen said nothing publicly about the decree, delivering a sermon only a few weeks later in which he focused on the dangers of a "Judeo-Bolshevik conspiracy." He began the sermon with "Communism is terrible to its innermost core and seeks to destroy Christian culture" and proceeded to speak of the pestilence of Bolshevism and what its goal was: to bring death to German culture and death to Christianity. Before all, with God as his witness, he stated, "I wish success in the struggle against atheistic communism."[95] What he could not believe was the Nazi effort to imply that Catholics were in collusion with the Jews and the Bolsheviks.

Reichsfeinde: The Church under Attack

Von Galen wholeheartedly endorsed the fight against godless Bolshevism. He was baffled, however, when the Nazis attempted to portray "the Blacks," or clericals, to be in league with the "Reds and Golds" (Bolsheviks and Jews). Particularly when he was addressing Catholic unions or Catholic workers' associations, he argued that it was still possible in Nazi Germany for a Catholic worker "to be true to the church and simultaneously be true to Germany."[96] He often reminded his listeners that class struggle had been condemned in numerous papal encyclicals. Von Galen believed that the class struggle was against the natural social order, and he called on Catholics to fight against the "pestilence" of Communism. He suggested that by supporting God, church, and Fatherland, Catholics could defeat atheism and Bolshevism.[97] He also acknowledged the dangerous situation the church now found itself in, recognizing that Catholics were oftentimes categorized as "enemies of the State," even after so many Catholics had given their lives fighting against the forces of radicalism in Germany.[98] Being classified as an enemy of the state only reinforced his belief that now more than ever Catholics needed their unions and associations in order to protect themselves.

Von Galen did not confine his expression of fears to his parishioners and other clergymen. He drafted a letter to Hitler asking him why the chancellor had endorsed the Concordat in one breath and had denounced Ultramontanism in another. Quoting again from *Mein Kampf,* the bishop sought to prove to Hitler that Catholics were good and true Germans, unlike the enemy Bolsheviks. In a personal letter to the Führer, he informed Hitler that the Gestapo had closed down several Catholic organizations based on the February 1933 anti-Communist law. He explained that Catholicism and Communism were in opposition to each other. He admonished Hitler to use the power God had given him judiciously, encouraging him to stop the attacks on Catholics that only resulted in the destruction of a sense of community.[99]

Despite von Galen's letters and sermons combating the classification of Catholics as enemies of the state, charges of Communist sympathy continued. The Union of Catholic Women and Mothers and the Marion Young Ladies Congregation in Münster were closed down, charged with violating the February 1933 law. Cloistered nuns in Münster were labeled *Volksfeinde* and were expelled from their convent by the Gestapo. When news of this event reached the bishop, he said that the blood rushed to his head and his heart began to beat faster and he found himself pacing in his room for ten minutes before he could calm himself down. Von Galen rallied and responded to the action by arguing that labeling cloistered nuns as enemies implied that all German Catholics were the state's enemies. He then listed all of the Catholic places currently under siege by the Gestapo, defending their honor. In particular, he focused on Jesuit priests who were off fighting in combat for Germany, the numbers killed and wounded, and those who had received the Iron Cross. He pointed out the injustice that while these men were fighting and dying for Germany, their workplaces and homes were being taken from them. He reminded the audience that he had encouraged Christian soldiers to fight against the spread of Bolshevism, but he believed that these soldiers' rights were being violated. The bishop stated that it was his understanding that German Catholics were just as entitled to German justice as any other citizen of Germany would be.[100] He seemed to be able to ignore the fact that German Jews were consistently being deprived of their rights, along with so many other minorities under the Nazi state.

Von Galen picked up the theme of justice again in 1942 when he drafted a letter for the German bishops. In the draft von Galen said that Catholics were doing their patriotic duty by serving in the war; but, he noted, "German Catholics are not given the same rights as the rest of the population." Again, unwilling or unable to see that there had been a general, steady decrease in citizens' rights under the Nazis, von Galen blindly continued his argument, stating that there seemed to be an attempt to rid Germany of its Catholic heritage. He enumerated ways in which he believed Catholicism was being denied equal treatment and concluded that fighting against the Catholic Church while its members were fighting against Bolshevism in Russia was "terrible."[101] Both of these letters ended with a call to Catholics to remain true and loyal to

Germany as well as to their faith and with prayers for Hitler and the Fatherland.

These writings reveal von Galen's fear that once again Catholics were being relegated to second-class status in Germany, that they were not considered to be truly German, and, perhaps worst of all, that they were being placed into the same category as the "real" enemies of Germany, the Jews and the Bolsheviks. He believed that Hitler was missing the point that the Catholic Church and the state could align themselves in the battle against their common enemy—Judeo-Bolshevism.

The Common Enemy: Church and State United

Von Galen believed that Germany was the last bulwark against the spread of godless Bolshevism. Hitler noted that and remarked, "I can speak of peace and still have my war." And Hitler was correct in that his battle against Bolshevism found general approval in Vatican circles. Ambassador Diego von Bergen at the Vatican said, "Hitler's appeal to God, his assurances that the government would take Christianity as the basis ... of the nation ... and his declaration that he would combat Bolshevism had all made a good impression." Cardinal Faulhaber, in Rome in 1933, met with Pope Pius XI. Publicly, the pope praised Hitler because he was the first leader to "raise his voice against Bolshevism."[102] Privately, the pope instructed Faulhaber to seek accommodation with the new Germany.[103] The church was going to work with the Nazis in the battle against the common enemy, atheistic Communism.

When von Galen thought about the war in the West, he thought about attaining a just peace. When thinking about the war in the East, however, von Galen remained steadfastly convinced that the war was justified. In a sermon in 1943 in Telgte, the bishop exclaimed, "The war is true and just." He made German soldiers into martyrs fighting to save all of Europe from ruthless Bolshevism. His address was so moving and so passionate that the Nazis used excerpts of the sermon to enlist Dutch men to voluntarily join the SS.[104]

In a March 1942 letter, von Galen stated that nothing terrible could come of a war against Communism. He said that any German soldier who gave his life fighting for the state had become a victim for all Germans. He claimed that God wanted the Germans to overpower Bolshevism, not just because God was pro-German, but also because God

wanted to keep all of Europe safe from the loss of Christianity and protected from the satanic philosophical system. Sounding more and more
like those who once preached plenary indulgences for the First Crusade,
von Galen claimed that Christian soldiers who had given their lives out
of duty to God and country had earned eternal rewards. When the news
reached the bishop that the Soviet offensive, begun in December 1943,
was victorious in February 1944, he reminded those present that all of
us are mortal and then said prayers for Germany's soldiers, asking God
to protect them from the power of Bolshevism.[105]

Von Galen's fears of Bolshevism did not stop at the end of the war.
Even in defeat he worked to prevent the spread of Communism and attempted to mold postwar Germany into a Christian state. To the end he
was unable to recognize that his anti-Bolshevik opinions and his extreme
nationalism might have aided the Nazis in their crimes against individuals he had once known personally.

Deportations and Death

On September 18, 1941, Heinrich Himmler wrote a letter in which he
described Hitler's desire to "clear" the Reich of Jews. The Nazi machinery worked quickly, and by October 10 Heydrich held a meeting where
he mentioned the idea of deporting 50,000 Jews to Riga and Minsk. He
even considered shipping Jews to concentration camps originally set up
to hold Communist POWs. One day after Heydrich's meeting, the commander of Einsatzgruppe A, Franz Stahlecker, told the commissioner in
Latvia, Dr. Otto Drechsler, that because the Führer wished it, "a 'big
concentration camp' was to be established near Riga for Jews from Germany and the Protectorate."[106]

Ten days later, Drechsler received an order to construct a camp for
25,000 Jews, twenty-two and a half kilometers from Riga. By October 24
the chief of the Order Police, Kurt Daluege, had signed deportation
orders for Riga and Minsk. This followed the October 23 decree forbid-
ding emigration of Jews from Germany and German-controlled areas.[107]

In the initial roundup procedures, various Jewish communities were
required to submit lists of Jews; the Gestapo then made the selection.
There were so many possible victims and so few transports at this time
that in the beginning a Jewish Community Office could request an exemption or a deferment for specific individuals. Occasionally the Ge-

stapo would grant the request. In the initial phases, the victims on the deportation lists were informed where they were going. The victims often received instructions about what items they should bring with them on the transport. Throughout November and December 1941, approximately 25,000 Jews from Germany and Austria selected from those first deportation lists arrived in Riga and some 7,000 in Minsk.[108]

All of these upper-level bureaucratic decisions concerning deportation and transport hit the Jewish community in Münster in full force in December 1941. On December 13, 135 Jews of Münster were deported to Riga. The list included the names of four- and nine-year-old children. The Gestapo and the SS in charge decided to try to keep the transport a secret, arranging for the deportation train to leave Münster at eleven in the evening.[109] Their report claimed that the evacuation of the Jews was designed to avoid any "unwelcome occurrences." There were no unwelcome occurrences when the train arrived, maybe because, as the report noted, Aryan citizens were allowed to "make a dash at property and apartments" belonging to the departing Jews.[110]

Other deportation transports from Münster followed. For example, 11 Jews were sent to Riga in January 1942, and 11 more were sent to the Warthegau in March 1942; 50 old and ill Jews were removed from their "special" home in the Marks-Haindorf Stiftung and deported to Theresienstadt in July 1942. The last to go in 1944 were "mixed blood marriage partners and mischlinge." These individuals were sent to work in Gestapo prisons. Of the 271 Jews deported from Münster, only 24 survived.[111]

One of the men to be deported from Münster was twenty-two-year-old Siegfried Weinberg. He survived transports and camps and came to testify before a U.N. commission at the end of the war. Weinberg and his younger sister Ruth were put on a deportation list, but their parents and their oldest sister, Hedwig, were not. Siegfried Weinberg, an automotive and electrical mechanic, was arrested on December 11, 1941, by the Gestapo. They placed him under watch in a restaurant in town. While he was detained there, most of his possessions packed for the transport were taken from him. At eleven o'clock on a rainy December night, he and thirty-five to forty other people from the Münster region were loaded onto a train, which departed December 13. It did not arrive at its destination until December 16, 1941. Those who were not already dead from the arrest and the three-day journey were forced to march five kilometers to a ghetto near Riga.[112]

Weinberg's letter, offered as his testimony, gives the vivid details of *Appelle* (prison roll calls), indiscriminate murders by ghetto police, starvation, disease. He was marched to the worst prison in Riga, called Salaspils, where he lived in unimaginable and inhumane circumstances. Eventually he worked with some Jews from Latvia, and they all escaped on July 13, 1944. They met up with and joined the Red Army. His letter ends with his gratitude to the United Nations but also with "Long live the Red Army and their great Marshall Stalin!"[113] In case Weinberg wondered what the Christian population of Münster thought about his and other Jews' disappearance from town, rumors circulated by mid-1942 that they were being murdered. Church leaders were informed by SS officer Kurt Gerstein that Jews were being murdered systematically. Closer to home, one woman, who had been a playmate to a Jewish girl, blandly noted, "I only know that we noticed one day that the E.s were no longer there."[114]

The early deportations of Jews to Riga, unknown to Mr. Weinberg, usually resulted in mass killings as the trains were unloaded. Just a week before Weinberg's transport, 13,000 Jews were slaughtered immediately upon their arrival in Riga. Those sent to Minsk from Germany and Austria were originally housed in what was left of a former ghetto. At the end of the war, there were 9 survivors. Of the old and sick of Münster who were sent to Theresienstadt, many died in the abysmal conditions of the camp; others were "liquidated" in Auschwitz.[115]

Knowledge

Did the Bishop of Münster, a man in a position of power, know about the deportations of Jews from his diocese, and did he know what deportation meant? Following the invasion of the Soviet Union, rumors spread about the fate of German Jews in the mysterious East. "By the end of 1941, the fate of German Jews deported to Riga and Minsk was known." In 1942 the student group the White Rose published a detailed letter about the murder of 300,000 Jews in Poland. Von Galen refused to believe the unconfirmed reports of mass murder.[116]

In early 1942 Margarete Sommer, a leader of Berlin's Aid Society, sent Bishop Preysing a report documenting the deportations and deaths of Catholic Jews. She had received much of her information from Nazi leader Hans Globke, who spent his days writing anti-Semitic legisla-

tion and his nights channeling details of the murders of Jews to Sommer. Sommer's report was circulated, and on February 5, 1942, Bishop
Berning referred to it in church. Cardinal Bertram received and read the
report on February 14. At the bishops' conference held February 22–
24, 1942, a discussion about the fate of evacuated non-Aryans appeared
on the agenda. Von Galen attended this conference. He remained silent.
Cardinal Bertram, the leader of the Fulda Bishops' Conference, cut off
contact with Sommer to avoid being labeled a traitor. This effectively
interfered with the transmission of her information to the clergymen.[117]

In September 1944 von Galen received a letter from theology professor Wilhelm Neuss. Von Galen had known Neuss since 1934, when
he wrote the introduction to Neuss's rebuttal of Rosenberg's work. In
the letter of 1944, Neuss gave specific information about the conditions
he had personally observed at Müngersdorfer Prison and the deportations of Catholic non-Aryans. Stating that the deportations had become
a "burning question for the Church," he provided von Galen with concrete evidence of the terrible things happening at the prison as well as the
conditions of the transports themselves. He even mentioned that he had
tried to get Bishop Wienken to stop the transports, adding that Wienken
feared that a "sharp demeanor" might lead to an increase in the suffering. The professor believed that immediate action was urgently needed
in the matter. He wrote to von Galen hoping that he would have "a better
command of the situation than I do."[118]

Von Galen took the information Neuss had given him and prepared
a letter to priests in his diocese. The October 1944 letter asked clergymen
to report on the fate of deported non-Aryan Catholics only. The results
of his inquiry are not known.[119] One might question why von Galen refrained from using the German legal system as he had in the battle over
euthanasia. In that case he had argued that according to German law,
he would be guilty of committing a crime if he had information about
murders and remained silent. He used this argument to justify his August 3, 1941, denunciation of euthanasia; yet he did not do this in the
case of Catholic non-Aryans being shipped off, nor did he do this for
unconverted Jews.

Perhaps one of the more convincing explanations for von Galen's
silence, besides intimidation, is the gradual easing of antichurch policies as the course of the war turned against Germany. After the defeat
at Stalingrad and in North Africa and the fall of Mussolini and Italy's
surrender, there was an attempted decrease in internal tensions. Hitler,

recognizing the need to stop antagonizing his base of support, exempted priests and nuns from national defense work in 1943. Bormann issued a directive to Nazi leaders about lessening confessional tensions in order to calm the population. By May 1943 Bormann had decreed that all agitation against the churches should be stopped. Heydrich, relentlessly anti-Catholic, had earlier written a request for the end of state support to seminaries. His report, considered posthumously in 1943, was ignored. The minister of education also asked citizens to continue confessional instruction despite the constant aerial bombardments.[120]

Once it was clear that Germany's very existence was at stake, the church sought accommodation and cooperation with the state rather than to attempt resistance. The bishops still occasionally offered minor protests on specific issues, but nothing was directly aimed at the mass murder of Jews. "Unlike the mentally retarded and handicapped, [the Jews] found no champion of the likes of Bishop von Galen to attempt to stop their murder through a calculated appeal to the public." Instead, Cardinal Bertram focused his complaints on the compulsory divorce decree for those in mixed marriages. He was quick to point out, however, that the protest was not out of a "lack of love for the German nationality, lack of feeling of national dignity, and also not to [sic] underestimation of the harmful Jewish influences upon German culture and national interests."[121]

Von Galen protested against the German Press and its call for revenge in the face of aerial bombardments. He told Germans that as Christians they were superior to the "old Jewish law, 'An eye for an eye, a tooth for a tooth.'" He was part of a bishops' joint protest in September 1943, in which they weakly noted that "killing is bad in itself."[122] Apparently the word *Jew* would not cross the bishop's lips when defending Christian Germany.

By 1941–1942 the German Catholic hierarchy, including von Galen, knew what deportation meant. Yet they did not speak out, as the French, Belgian, and Dutch bishops did. Statistically, the German Catholic bishops had a potential base of support within the killing machinery itself. As of December 31, 1938, 22.7 percent of the SS were registered as Catholics. Yet only a minor number of Jews were saved by German clergy. Given the combination of a lack of forceful leadership from Rome, the terror practices of the Nazis, and the subtle hint that Jews were forces of disorder out to destroy Christian culture, Donald J. Dietrich claims, "It is not surprising that the bishops did not assume a leadership role."[123] It is, however, a highly disturbing moral legacy.

Those who argue that the church maintained a position of silence in order to avoid even worse things should consider that the church apparently did not have the same fears when it spoke out about the disappearance of Catholic unions, workers' associations, and other organizations.[124] Nor were its representatives afraid to speak out when the Catholic presses and newspapers were censured. They were not silent when cloisters, seminaries, and convents were confiscated or when crucifixes were taken down from classroom walls. They were not silent on the issue of divorce or euthanasia. They were silent on the most vicious and deadly issue of Jewish persecution. They had fought to protect Catholic institutions, and in a sense, as the war turned against Germany, they won the second Kulturkampf that had been waged against them. Their institutions were safe. Germany would be a Christian state.

1945–1946

At the end of the war, von Galen continued to be an outspoken critic of Bolshevism, still holding onto his belief that the greatest danger Europe had ever faced was this "godless" movement. His fears of anarchy, lawlessness, and a general overturning of society's hierarchy predominated during the last year of his life. He also steadfastly refused to admit to German guilt concerning the unimaginable atrocities that had been committed against innocent civilians. Instead, he chose to equate crimes committed by recently freed Russian POWs and liberated foreign workers with those committed by Germans in concentration camps.

A month before his death, von Galen drafted a joint statement for the bishops of western Germany. It began, "Religion alone is the fundamental basis for community life." This draft shows that von Galen had not learned very much from postwar revelations. He called on the true believers to recognize God's authority over all other types of leadership. He openly condemned both socialism and Communism and said nothing to condemn National Socialism.[125] To the end, he remained nationalistic, a fact that was doubtlessly quite irksome to the new zonal commanders.

As the British and American troops were rolling into Münster, von Galen openly exclaimed in an interview that no matter what occurred, "I am and remain German." He made it desperately clear to the occupying forces that not only would he remain true to the Fatherland but that he also regarded the Allied Powers as the enemy. This attitude earned von Galen a sharp reproach from the exiled Thomas Mann. Mann wrote an open letter to the German nation, urging its people to recognize that their freedom would only come from the Allies. The exiled writer advised the German people not to model themselves on Bishop von Galen when he referred to the liberators as enemies.[126] Von Galen was probably never aware that when the Supreme Headquarters Allied Expeditionary Forces prepared a white list of who they might approach in postwar Germany, they described the bishop as "anti-Nazi but not necessarily pro-Allied."[127]

Although the bishop refused to think of the Allied Powers as liberators, he was quick to assure them that they had conquered a Christian land, where hierarchy, authority, and order were obeyed. He despised the postwar chaos and refused to understand why recently freed foreign workers might seek revenge on the German citizens who had held them captive. He constantly wrote to and had meetings with British zonal commanders to register his complaints regarding the fight against hunger, crime, and possible Communist agitation. His correspondence reveals his lingering racism regarding Slavic people and American blacks; he formally requested that blacks not be permitted out at night, believing that they were raping women and stealing.[128]

General Dwight Eisenhower had ordered Allied commanders to maintain discipline among the recently freed prisoners as well as the Allied Troops, but the bishop charged that all of these forces were running wild and committing crimes, while hunger spread. He feared that under such conditions of anarchy and suffering, the German population might be more open to Communist agitation. Repeatedly appealing to various British authorities for aid, the bishop often listed specific crimes committed against his own family and the family properties.[129] To von Galen these were the indications that Germany and ultimately all of Europe were in danger.

In most cases the British authorities replied graciously, thanking the bishop for the information and gently reminding him that under the circumstances they could only do so much. In only a few instances did the British try to impress on von Galen the severity of Germany's crimes. Military Commander J. Spottiswoode, who served in that capacity from April 1945 to July 1946, once responded to von Galen's pleas for restoration of order and repression of Communist activity by apologizing for the upsurge in crime but also reminding von Galen that the men he was accusing of criminal activity had been brought into Germany against their will for forced labor. He then put pressure on the bishop to reveal names of prominent and ardent Nazis, because, he said, "we have as yet no instance . . . of any Nazi being reported to us by the Church."[130]

Spottiswoode requested a meeting with the bishop after several newspapers printed a discussion notice placed by von Galen. Some of the topics for discussion included "Pastors in Danger! What does England want—only negatives? Anti-fascist, anti-militaristic . . . Positives? Democracy . . . Democracy brought us Misfortune before 1933. Democracy brought Hitler to power, now Democracy brings Communism. . . . Put forward Positive Christian Doctrines."[131] According to eyewitnesses, the meeting became very heated and lasted two and a half hours.

Three main topics were addressed during the meeting: the question of guilt, the problem of starvation, and the increase in crime. The bishop remained adamant that the entire German nation could not be condemned, because most people recognized that "active or public resistance ended in death or internment in a concentration camp." He continued, asserting that he himself had been spared these possibilities only because the general population would not have stood for a Nazi attack against him. One could question at this point why, if von Galen believed himself to be so protected, he did not go further in his criticisms of Nazi policies. Spottiswoode himself tried to enlighten the stubborn bishop by pointing out that the extreme actions of the Nazis would never have been possible if there had been extensive, active resistance. Both men refused to alter their opinions. They did agree, however, that the problems of hunger and crime were being actively addressed by the Allied Powers.[132]

The day after their encounter, Spottiswoode wrote a private letter to Bishop von Galen. In the final analysis, Spottiswoode claimed, they both wanted the same thing: permanent peace. Their major point of difference was the position of the foreign workers. The British commander asked von Galen to try to see from the newly freed men's perspective. They had been taken against their will, abused, and forced to work for Germany's cause. Spottiswoode asked, "Is it surprising that they have lost any Christian ideas and civilized inhibitions which they may have previously possessed?" He then attempted to further drive home the reality of Germany's crimes: "I admired still more the restraint of our interpreter, Lt. Klink, who had himself, as a captured Polish officer suffered far more in the last years in physical and mental torture than any unfortunate German in the recent affairs of which we are speaking. I myself took him out of Belsen. . . . He can be well understood to feel all Germans guilty of the failure to control the leaders who acted in such an inhumane way in their name."[133]

Spottiswoode did not convince the bishop. Upon receiving the commander's letter, von Galen offered to print a clarification for the newspapers. In the notice he stated nothing about war guilt and only succinctly conveyed the fact that the British military authorities were working to alleviate hunger and crime.[134]

Von Galen continued to fight against the idea of German guilt despite what he knew about the crimes committed. He denounced the International Military Tribunal at Nuremberg as "show trials" aimed at defaming the German people.[135] He equated postwar sufferings of Germans with the horrors experienced by inmates in concentration camps. Writing to the pope in August 1946, von Galen suggested the need for a conference that could discuss treatment of German POWs, crimes committed by foreign workers in Germany (notably those committed by Russians and Poles), and the expulsion of ethnic Germans from "acquired" territory in Poland and Czechoslovakia. Describing the loss of life in Münster and the destruction of the town, he warned the pope that "there is a growing danger of proletarianization. . . . Apostles of godless Communism are agitating in the industrial section. . . . We fear that the victory of Bolshevik ideas will spread from the Russian zone."[136] He also threw in the evaluation that the English and the Americans "either do not see the danger or do not have the courage to see."[137]

The overriding fear of Communism and the unconfirmed suspicion that all Jews were Communists had helped to blind von Galen to the persecution of innocent people during the war. His concerns that postwar Germany remain Christianized were further intensified by letters he received from German POWs. Many of the letters emphasized that there was a growing radicalism among the devastated Germans. One anonymous letter, received by von Galen on September 23, 1945, came from a Catholic officer who claimed to have never been a member of the NSDAP, the SS or the SA. The officer said he had been imprisoned since May 1945. He wrote to von Galen because he believed that the Catholic Church was the only institution that had not forgotten the imprisoned. Perhaps he remembered the bishop's passionate prayers for German soldiers. He complained that Germans were suffering, that many POWs were dying from exposure, typhus, overcrowding, malnutrition, and a lack of medical treatment. After describing these conditions, the man rhetorically asked, "And all the Christian Democracies are crying out about our Concentration Camp-Prisons?" The officer did generously note that the English guards at the camp were "correct and not hateful"; but, he countered, he had heard of other places where "uniformed Jews—German-speaking Jews—took out their Old Testament hatred on us."[138] Adding that his imprisonment represented the "saddest chapter" in history, he fed von Galen's fears further still by claiming that the POW camps were becoming breeding grounds for Bolshevism.[139]

The POW's final words can be related to von Galen's postwar bewilderment at the thought that Germany as a nation should be held accountable for Nazi crimes against humanity. The officer bitterly wrote, "I cannot believe that I must now make amends for National Socialism." The fear of Bolshevism, "normal" anti-Semitism, and nationalism all contributed to the power of the Nazis. Von Galen's commitment to dualism, that is, "good Catholics" versus "bad Communists"—possibly "bad Jewish Communists"—led him to betray his earlier commitment to the very foundations of Christian principles.[140] He continued this betrayal by refusing to acknowledge the severity of Nazi crimes in the postwar world.

CHAPTER SIX

The Construction of an Image:
Von Galen in Retrospect

I was born for this, I came into the world for this: to bear witness to the truth; and all who are on the side of truth listen to my voice.

—JOHN 18:37

In order to fully evaluate von Galen's place in the history of resistance to National Socialism, it is necessary to examine how he came to be portrayed as a famous and staunch anti-Nazi resister. One of the reasons he appeared so prominently in the postwar resistance literature was that the majority of historians interpreted his nomination to the position of cardinal as a reward for his resistance to National Socialism. Therefore one must consider the role that the supreme pontiff played in influencing von Galen's decisions as well as how the pope's nomination came about.

The presentation of von Galen as churchman-resister was augmented by apocryphal stories and legends that surrounded his name and contributed to the process of turning him into a mythical figure. The postwar attempt to begin the canonization process of Münster's "Lion" also fed into and perpetuated the idealized portrait of von Galen that had come to predominate assessments of his behavior during the twelve years of Hitler's reign.

Some historians of the 1980s and 1990s, such as Joachim Kuropka, have argued that von Galen found resonance with Münster's population because he showed his followers what could be achieved within a totalitarian state. Others, such as Heinz Mussinghoff, argue that von Galen's anti-Nazi struggles worked to immunize Münster's population against the racism and anti-Semitism of Hitler's regime. I would argue that von

Galen might have indeed resonated with Münster's population, but perhaps his words found a receptive audience because he was not truly challenging his listeners to put their faith to the ultimate moral test; that is, he was not urging them to embrace people who had been labeled by government authorities as outcasts.[1] The persecution of the Jews provided Catholics with a unique opportunity to turn the preaching of the Gospel into action. But for von Galen and the majority of the church leadership, that opportunity was lost.

Nec Laudibus, Nec Timore

In October 1933 von Galen became the first Catholic bishop to be appointed under the terms of the Concordat.[2] Unlike the Seventh Day Adventists or the Jehovah's Witnesses of Münster, von Galen took the oath of loyalty required by the Nazi state. The enthronement ceremony took place on October 28, 1933. His sermon provided the new bishop with an opportunity to let the members of his diocese know what he would do for them as their leader. A close look at this sermon will help us evaluate him as a guardian of the moral order and assess his place in the pantheon of resisters.

Following the opening formalities, von Galen told his audience that he would take on the burden of being their bishop because God had called him to serve as a priest. He then gave some personal information as a way of introducing himself to those not already familiar with his history, "I know you and you know me. I don't know all of you individually, but I know in general the loyal Catholic people that I shall lead." He promised them that he would struggle daily to be a better person with the aim of becoming a "light of the world."[3]

He continued to define what he believed a bishop should be, setting an incredibly high standard. Some of the characteristics von Galen believed that a bishop should embody were the ability to suffer in silence, the love of speaking the truth regardless of the consequences, and the steadfastness of belief expressed in his motto, "Neither men's praise, nor fear of men, shall move us."[4] Referring to himself as a "high priest," the new bishop believed that he was required to watch over the "Holy Temple of the Lord." Then he reiterated what Pope Pius XI had listed as the duties of a bishop: to confirm, to baptize, to ordain priests, to consecrate holy places, to bring people to Christ, and to lead the diocese in sacrifice. Most importantly, however, the bishop was "obligated to pronounce the truth and to watch over the purity of teaching and beliefs. He also had the duty to give an opinion on the difference between justice and injustice, over good and bad actions . . . to bring about good and to prevent evil."[5] The bishop, by this definition, was to function as a living witness to the message of the Gospel.

Von Galen explained that his heaviest responsibility would be to act as the guardian of Christian morality. Taking the responsibility for each member's soul seriously, he warned that he would provide admonishments and teachings as often as required so that no soul would be in jeopardy. He would work with parents to ensure that children were receiving proper moral instruction. He hoped to continue his work with charitable organizations, so that he could be a true example of Jesus' teaching, "Whatsoever you do for the least of my brothers, that you do unto me." He saw himself as the upholder and enforcer of canon law. And he reminded his congregation of their duty to obey him, using the analogy that as the pope is to the entire church, so the bishop is to his entire diocese.[6]

The new bishop said he wanted his life to be an example,[7] and he set inordinately high goals and copious duties for himself. What is most intriguing on his list of duties is the responsibility to testify to the truth, reveal evil and immorality, and function as a local "mini-Pope" in his diocese. By his own words, von Galen set himself up as the supreme moral arbiter of Münster. He promised to act as the pope, guarding canon law, protecting the church's institutions, and saving Catholics from committing sin. What he could not foresee in October 1933 was the dilemma he was going to face in attempting to fulfill his long list of responsibilities. Under National Socialism he was forced to confront the question of what the role of the church should be: should he focus his energy on safeguarding the church's institutions, or should he speak out forcefully, unambiguously, regarding all questions of morality and ethical behavior?

Von Galen did attack Rosenberg's neopaganism and Bolshevism's atheism, yet he never protested the immoral actions perpetrated against the Jews, the Russian POWs in Münster, or the other persecuted minorities. Instead, he chose to fight to keep the church's institutions functioning on German soil. Using Pope Pius XII as his role model, von Galen followed the example and dictates of the supreme pontiff. The bishop had told his audience that obeying the pope was equivalent to the commandment "honor thy father,"[8] and if the pope did not take an openly defiant stand on the overarching issue of morality and ethical behavior, clearly condemning Nazi aggression and brutality, then von Galen would not allow himself to do so either. In his choice of what to oppose and what to obey, von Galen was heavily influenced by the example set by Pius XII. What choices did Pius XII make, and how did those decisions affect von Galen and the rest of the church hierarchy?

Illuminate the Conscience

The Roman Catholic Church is based on a hierarchical, authoritarian principle of order. Von Galen, as bishop of Münster, was part of that hierarchy and was the pope's representative in his diocese. He functioned as the enforcer of the pope's will. If the Holy Father was willing to go only so far in his public pronouncements regarding Nazi atrocities, could von Galen have reasonably been expected to go further? Given von Galen's devotion to the pope, his respect for hierarchy and order, his endorsement of Nazi expansionist aims, and his own German nationalism, it would have taken an extraordinary willingness to question all that von Galen held dear in order to openly condemn Nazi barbarism. Von Galen did not prove to be that willing. Yet why did the pope, who was not German and who was not living directly under the National Socialist government, choose to remain silent over the discrimination, persecution, and annihilation of European Jews? Why did he remain silent on the question of German aggression? Why did he counsel members of the hierarchy to do as he did, in effect leading them in many respects to collaborate with an immoral government?

The silence of Pope Pius XII has been heavily debated, particularly since the publication of Rolf Hochhuth's *Der Stellvertreter* (The deputy) in 1963. Hochhuth charged that the pope had stood by silently while Jews were sent to their deaths, with the implication that the entire church had also watched in silence. Hochhuth's play presented Pius XII as a cold, remote individual and seemed to imply that the church had more influence in the modern world than Pius had originally believed. It also revealed Pius's exaggerated belief in the power of his own diplomatic adroitness. Despite the play's weak historical accuracy, it succeeded in raising the awareness of larger issues, such as the relationship between Christianity and Judaism and the place of the church in the twentieth century.[9] Upon his election to the office of supreme pontiff, Pius XII faced a dilemma that ended up affecting all members of the Catholic Church.

On March 2, 1939, with war looming on Europe's horizon, Cardinal Eugenio Pacelli was elected supreme pontiff. The Sacred College of Cardinals had decided that Pius XI's successor needed to have superior diplomatic skills in order to steer the Catholic Church through the increasingly menacing international scene. In choosing Pacelli, fluent in seven different languages, they hoped he would bring all of his accumulated diplomatic experience to the table to work to prevent strife and resolve conflicts peacefully. Their interests coincided with the new pope's, for Pacelli expressed the wish to be remembered as the "Pope of Peace."

Pope Pius XII stood in sharp contrast to the machismo of Benito Mussolini and tended to be compared to the British prime minister, Neville Chamberlain. Both Pius and Chamberlain were firmly convinced that maintaining peace superseded all other concerns. Both men also held rather inflated beliefs about their own power and diplomatic abilities. The main difference between the pope and Chamberlain seems to have been that by March 1939 even Chamberlain was beginning to recognize that peace was not one of Hitler's aims. The pope, however, continued to work for peace despite his ambivalent attitude toward the "revolutionary upstart" leading Germany.[10]

Despite the new pope's personal feelings about Hitler, Pius XII had a special fondness for Germany and thought he could play a historical role in bringing to an end the new Kulturkampf being waged in Nazi Germany against Catholics. Comparing his position to that of pope Leo XIII, the pope decided to send Hitler a letter similar to the one received by Emperor Wilhelm I in February 1870. Leo's letter of reconciliation was believed to have begun the gradual winding down of the Kulturkampf and had led to an increase in respect for Vatican diplomacy. Pius's letter to Hitler, which announced his appointment as the new pope, was written in German rather than the customary Latin. It emphasized the need for church and state to work together. Behind the scenes, the pope ordered the Vatican press to stop attacking the government in Germany.[11]

Although the pope had made an amazingly conciliatory gesture, Hitler did not relax the persecution of the church in Germany, nor did he alter his plans for European expansion. A few days after receiving the pope's letter, Hitler seized the rump state of Czechoslovakia. The pope not only dismissed the illegal seizure but also met with an audience of

German pilgrims that very day, joining them in singing German songs. At that moment, the pope declared the takeover of Czechoslovakia to be one of those "historic processes, in which, from the political point of view, the Church is not interested."[12]

Whether the pope was unable to admit that his diplomatic efforts were failing or whether, more cynically, he was responding to the knowledge that there were more Catholics in Germany than in Czechoslovakia, he did realize that the Catholic stronghold of Eastern Europe, Poland, might be the next target of the Führer. He moved quickly and proposed that a five-power conference be held in May 1939. On the preliminary discussion schedule were possible causes for war, including boundary disputes between Poland and Germany and problems between France and Italy. Hitler rejected this idea, claiming that no disputes existed between Germany and Poland.

With the invasion of Poland in September 1939, the pope was again presented with the question of how to work for peace and still safeguard the interests of Germany's Catholic population. He was also compelled to think about what the church actually is and what it should aspire to be. In searching for his answer, Pius echoed his predecessor's beliefs, summarized in the 1922 encyclical *Ubi arcano Dei,* which defined the church's role as teacher and peacemaker: "as teacher and head of all other societies . . . to perfect them as grace perfects nature." In Pius XII's own encyclical *Summi Pontificatus,* issued in 1939, he addressed similar themes but tended to imitate Leo XIII in his discussion of the interaction between church and state authority. He defined the pope as Vicar of Christ, as the teacher, guardian, and interpreter of dogmatic and moral truths. He reminded Catholics that the pope was infallible and, as supreme leader of the Catholic community, was owed complete obedience.[13]

The pope, like von Galen, encouraged testifying to the truth regardless of dangers or difficulties. On two separate occasions, he spoke about delivering the truth and doing one's duty despite reservations and fears: "This duty necessarily entails the exposition and confutation of errors and human faults; for these must be made known before it is possible to tend and to heal them."[14]

By Pius's own definition, it was the papal mission to reveal errors in morals and dogma and to guide the consciences of the faithful about oppression and illegality. Pius XII also expected that local bishops in Germany would work to safeguard the institutions of Catholicism. The dominant advice given to the bishops throughout the course of the war was to remain loyal to the Concordat and to protest violations of that legal document whenever they occurred. The fight in Nazi Germany was narrowed to terms set down by the treaty, and the pope came to view any overt threat of political resistance on the part of an individual bishop as contrary to the desired behavior.[15] His decision had a profound impact on the priorities of the Catholic Church. Under Pius XII, Catholic leaders were expected to place their greatest emphasis on maintaining Catholic institutions. They had been instructed to criticize moral outrages only insofar as they collided with what had been defined as church interests.

War

Once the war had broken out, the pope did not apply the "just-war" theory of Aquinas to the situation. Instead, he focused on Benedict XV, the pope who had served during the First World War and who had established the papal prerogative of remaining neutral juridically in such a conflict. This did not mean that Benedict XV remained spiritually neutral. His position was ratified in the Lateran Treaty of 1929 under Pius XI. This document provided the papal office with the right to "bring its moral and spiritual pressure to bear in all circumstances in conjunction with its desire for peace."[16] Despite having a legal document that would have given Pius the leeway to denounce Nazi crimes against humanity while simultaneously allowing him to remain "neutral," the legalistic pope never utilized the Lateran Treaty to directly condemn the war of aggression; nor did he issue a statement about Germany's responsibility for war crimes.

Public silence does not mean that Pius was not privately questioning his choices. He was constantly praying, fasting, and performing other acts of penance, searching for guidance. His emaciated appearance revealed an inner struggle, but in the end he succumbed to his most natural inclination—diplomatic reserve. At one point, during the Phony War (winter 1939–1940), he was willing to meet with German resistance members, represented by Dr. Joseph Müller. Müller had traveled to Rome to seek the Vatican's help in contacting both the British and the French governments to see if they would be willing to open negotiations with a non-Nazi German leadership. For a brief moment, the pope was willing to consider supporting an illegal revolutionary activity with the hope that the outcome would be peace.[17] However, the negotiations came to nothing when he refused to be drawn too far into the conspiracy. Even privately, the pope was unwilling to let down his guard of neutral reserve with respect to Germany.

In the pontiff's Christmas Eve radio broadcast of December 1939, he violated his own self-imposed standards of strict neutrality. It was not that he condemned the Nazi war of aggression; instead he denounced the Soviets' taking of Finland and made clear that extended warfare would only create chaos. In the midst of chaos, he explained, Communists would rise up and attempt to destroy European civilization. Apparently, when it came to fighting and the Soviet Union, impartiality was not part of the pope's concern. Unlike the case with Nazi Germany, there was no discussion of remaining diplomatically neutral, and there was no desire to seek conciliation with Stalin. Pacelli's fears of Communist-induced anarchy and barbarism had been reinforced years earlier when a Communist revolutionary held a pistol to his head and threatened to kill him. Eyewitnesses reported that Pacelli, who was then a nuncio, remained eerily calm and was able to avoid any injury to himself or to the others present as he faced down the would-be shooter. He was, however, haunted by this 1919 incident for the rest of his life, still noting that he relived the incident in his dreams even into his eighties. This brief but powerful encounter with German Communists in Munich in 1919 had left an indelible mark on Pius XII.[18]

As the war dragged on, many people waited hopefully for a papal denunciation of German aggression. Norway and Denmark fell. Then Belgium, Luxembourg, and Holland were overrun. Latvia, Estonia, and Lithuania followed. The pope said nothing. He did send telegrams to the leaders of the Benelux nations following their invasion, but the messages were only inquiries after their welfare, not condemnations of Nazi military power. Once the Nazis invaded the Soviet Union, the pope found himself in a difficult position. He did not want to do anything that might aid the spread of atheistic Bolshevism, but he could not afford to alienate the Allied Powers either. As one American diplomat wrote, "The militant atheism of the former [Russia] is still regarded as more obnoxious than the modern paganism of the latter [Germany]."[19]

The Vatican unrealistically began to hope that the American and British forces would finally understand the terrible threat that Bolshevism represented to the world and would join Germany's efforts to defeat

Stalin. The pope at one point remarked in his frustration, "They [the Germans] are a great nation who, in their fight against Bolshevism, are bleeding not only for their friends but also for the sake of their present enemies." So great was the pope's conviction that Communism represented a much more fundamental danger to Christianity than National Socialism that the German ambassador at the Vatican, Ernst von Weizsäcker, could write to Berlin, "A diplomat who enjoys special connections with the Vatican assured me yesterday the Pope sternly condemns all plans aimed at weakening the Reich. . . . In the Pope's view a powerful German Reich is quite indispensable for the future of the Catholic Church."[20]

By the spring of 1943, the Allied Powers had already landed in North Africa and the German military had surrendered at Stalingrad. Russian victory appeared imminent. Although the pope had detailed knowledge of German atrocities committed in Eastern Europe, he continued to state that "the Bolshevik danger would henceforth override every other consideration and that, since Germany was the sole rampart against the specter of Bolshevism, nothing must be done to weaken the Reich."[21] The pope was so committed to the policy of defeating Communism that in October 1943, when the Nazis had occupied Italy and had begun to round up eight thousand Jews from Rome and upper Italy, Weizsäcker could comfortably report to Berlin, "By all accounts, the Pope . . . has not allowed himself to be stampeded into making any demonstrative pronouncement against the removal of the Jews from Rome." The report also went on to praise the pope's diplomacy, stating, "He has done everything he could . . . not to injure the relationship between the Vatican and the German Government." High praise from the Nazis seems damning in and of itself, but the German diplomat was also correct that the pope had not allowed himself to be swayed by appeals for a public statement regarding Nazi war atrocities, nor would he allow other representatives of the church to be so influenced.[22]

"Every Man Will Be Answerable to God for His Own Actions"

Despite the pope's insistence that the church hierarchy follow his example of neutral reserve, he received numerous and varied appeals that pressed him to lead Catholics in the matter of conscience. Perhaps the best-known appeal came from Cardinal Eugene Tisserant of France.

Tisserant wrote to Cardinal Cesare Orsenigo, warning him that the Italians and the Germans meant to destroy everyone. He also wrote, "Since the beginning of November, I have persistently requested the Holy See to issue an encyclical on the duty of the individual to obey the dictates of conscience because this is the vital point of Christianity. . . . I fear that history may have reason to reproach the Holy See with having pursued a policy of convenience to itself and very little else. This is sad in the extreme, particularly when one has lived under Pius XI."[23]

Not only defeated French priests were asking the pope to guide millions of Catholics in the matter of conscience. In 1941, following von Galen's boldly successful denunciation of euthanasia, approximately twenty German bishops signed a pastoral letter asking the decisive questions: "What is our duty in the present moment? What does conscience require? What does God, what do German believers expect of their bishops?" Cardinal Bertram, believing that he understood the pope's dictates, refused as the leader of the German Bishops' Conference to allow the pastoral letter to be published. He objected to the publication on the grounds that compromise and collaboration were the only ways of preserving the church's institutions.[24] Bertram was correct in his assessment of the pope's goals, but he had failed to ask whether the church would lose some of its moral authority in so choosing.

Waldemar Gurian, a German exile living in Switzerland, begged the German bishops and the pope to speak out in defense of moral principles. Fearing the destruction of all moral authority of the church in Germany, he wrote, "The Church is not an association which adapts itself to particular circumstances of power; it is the guardian and protector of the moral order. . . . The Church must speak out when worldly power endangers and breaks up this order."[25]

Other leaders echoed Gurian's call for a clear pronouncement. The president-in-exile of Poland, Wladislaw Raczkiewicz, wrote personally to Pius, not asking for diplomatic or material assistance but calling on the pope, in the name of all Poles, "that a voice be raised to show clearly and plainly where the evil lies and to condemn those in the service of evil." Raczkiewicz, like so many others, demanded that the pope show the world that "divine law knows no compromise." He remained steadfast in his opinion that if the pope denounced Nazi actions, the Poles would "find the strength to resist."[26]

Raczkiewicz wrote his appeal from London in January 1943. The timing is relevant because he had undoubtedly been disappointed by the pope's Christmas Eve message of 1942. Out of a twenty-six-page address, Pius had one small paragraph that he claimed was an appeal to Catholics to help the Jews. The text ran, "Humanity owes this vow to hundreds of thousands of people who, through no fault of their own and solely because of their nation or their race, have been condemned to death or progressive extinction." Lost in the twenty-six-page announcement, this was not recognized by most people as a forthright call to action. According to Saul Friedländer's research, the papal Christmas message was considered innocuous—so much so that no German documents even bothered with an analysis of the statement.[27] Reacting to the message, the American ambassador to the Vatican, Harold Tittman, met with the pope and tried to suggest that the Holy Father needed to be more severe in his condemnation of Germany. Pius responded succinctly. He believed he had spoken clearly enough. He refused to say more.[28]

Silence

Apologists for the pope often claimed that he had to remain silent on the issue of Jewish persecution because the information received by the Vatican could not be verified or was generally attributed to enemy propaganda. However, on June 2, 1945, Pius XII addressed the Sacred College of Cardinals. The war in Europe had ended only twenty days earlier, and no official information regarding the Nazi concentration camps had yet been released. Yet Pius was able to provide detailed information about Nazi death camps that, he said, "used scientific methods to torture and suppress people who were often innocent."[29] He did possess accurate information, and it was in his hands long before June 2, 1945.

Others argue that Pius refrained from speaking out because various victims of Nazi atrocities had asked him not to interfere: a papal denunciation might produce a worse situation. Some of these requests for silence came from groups of Jews, one came from Archbishop Adam Sapieha of Kraków, and there was also a letter from the 1943 German Bishops' Conference at Fulda. The pope's diplomatic training of weighing and reweighing all sides of the issue was revealed when he counseled reserve out of fear of reprisals in a letter to the bishop of Berlin; he claimed that "in spite of good reasons for Our open intervention, there are others equally good for avoiding greater evils by not interfering." In the summer of 1943, the pope addressed the College of Cardinals and stated that denunciations only endangered the intended victims of crime.³⁰ Certainly some of those requests for silence were valid, but one must consider the fact that the truly weakest and most powerless people being rounded up to be killed had no opportunity to counter the requests for papal noninterference. In addition, the requests for papal action far outnumbered the requests for continued silence. By counseling others to remain silent, the pope was essentially collaborating with the Nazis.

Another explanation for Pius's silence reasons that the pope had weighed the arguments for and against action and had decided that even if he issued a statement, it would be useless. Part of this argument hinges on the idea that throughout the course of the war, Pius had seen all of his diplomatic efforts fail and that he was conscious of the decline of the church's authority in the modern age. He had come to the point, so the argument goes, of believing that the only way to restore the Vatican's power was to maintain strict neutrality. He would not risk a public condemnation "of war-time activities which, even if morally justifiable, would be dangerously impolitic."³¹

A corollary to this explanation is that the pope had assessed the conditions inside Nazi Germany and had decided that a statement about atrocities would not move German Catholics to action. He examined von Galen's very public denunciation of euthanasia and wondered "whether a protest about other crimes, such as the much more secret atrocities against the Jews, would make the same appeal to legality, and receive sufficient response within Germany to make Hitler think again."³²

He considered the obstacles to getting this information out: no working church press in Germany, no open travel between Germany and Rome, only infrequent broadcasts of Vatican Radio in Germany. He realized that he would have to rely on verbal transmission of his information. In addition, the information would have to be worded strongly enough to somehow convince the German Catholic population that their consciences would be impaired if they did not oppose Nazi practices.³³ The pope did not believe that German Catholics, if faced with such a blatant choice, would choose their religion over their nation.

If the pope had forced the issue, challenging Catholics to side either with National Socialism or with Catholic morality, he feared that the church would lose its battle for their loyalty. Although this argument has its merits, it is interesting to note that the pope never even tried to prepare the German public for protests against its own national government. He did not circulate the few but courageous statements made by various bishops, and this allowed those individuals who lacked concern for the Jews to continue in their path of indifference. John S. Conway charitably argued that the pope did not wish to unburden his conscience, thereby laying "upon each individual member the guilt of association and weighing down the consciences of priest and people alike." But even Conway later asks "whether it was the Pope's responsibility to witness to the truth of the Gospel regardless of the consequences."[34]

Did not Pius himself define the church as teacher and supreme guardian of the moral realm? How much worse could a protest from the pope have made the situation for millions already imprisoned and destined for death? The church's self-defined task was to bear witness to the truth, to fight for justice, and to reveal evil wherever it was found, regardless of the circumstances or dangers in doing so. Carlo Falconi wrote, "The Church is not the International Red Cross. It is supposed to testify to the Gospel's message and bring the faithful to live in accord with that message; it is the guide of their consciences." Certainly a papal statement regarding the murders of Jews would not have halted the Holocaust, but "it would have constituted an . . . unmistakable appeal for compassion towards Jews everywhere. It would have provided moral guidance to the faithful."[35]

Because the pope had come to believe that Catholics in Germany were psychologically unready to hear a call to action, he embarked on a course to preserve the institutions of the church on German soil. The overriding motivation was not to mobilize political resistance but to maintain the status quo. Klaus Scholder, after examining the Vatican's policies, remarked, "There was no Catholic resistance in Germany, there were only Catholics who resisted."[36] There were men like Lichtenberg or Delp, but on the whole the German episcopacy, including von Galen, embraced the Vatican's policy.

Konrad Adenauer, in a postwar comment, addressed the question "What If?" What if the German bishops had sponsored a joint call to action? He responded, "I believe that if all the bishops had together made public statements from the pulpits on a particular day, they could have prevented a great deal. That did not happen and there is no excuse for it. It would have been no bad thing if the bishops had all been put in prison or in concentration camps as a result. Quite the contrary. But none of that happened and therefore it is best to keep quiet."[37] Neither

the pope nor the German bishops were going to wear crowns of martyrdom in the fight to save Jews from annihilation. They all lived to fight
for the church's institutional interests.

Von Galen and the Pope

Many of the notes exchanged between von Galen and Pius XII were
destroyed in fires following the heavy aerial bombardment of Münster.
When von Galen wrote to the pope about the devastation of Münster,
describing in great detail how the city lay in ruins, he noted sadly that the
most serious loss for him had been his collection of handwritten letters
from the Holy Father.[38] What letters did survive reveal von Galen's loyalty and respect for the pope as Christ's representative on earth, under-
scoring his belief that the supreme pontiff commanded absolute obedience, just as a biological father would expect from his son.

The remnants of their correspondence also reveal that they were fundamentally in agreement in philosophy and outlook on life. The pope,
like von Galen, was an aristocrat who valued stability in the social order.
Both men were opposed to liberalism, egalitarianism, and Communism.
Pacelli, who had been one of the major contributors to the 1917 monumental compilation and centralization of all church law in the *Codex
Juris Canonici,* shared von Galen's respect for the law. They also shared
a passionate conviction of the evilness of atheistic Communism.

The letters from the pope generally begin with a word of thanks to
the bishop for his letters and information on the state of affairs in Münster. These remarks are usually followed by a reassurance that the Holy
Father was still sympathetic to Germany. Each letter typically closed
with still further assurances that the pope loved all Catholics, without
respect to country, and would continue in his ceaseless efforts to bring
about peace.[39]

The body of each letter showed Pius's deep concern about the education of young people. He feared that German youths were not being
inculcated with proper religious values and that they were being exposed
to immoral, un-Christian beliefs. He also discussed the difficult position
the Catholic Church now found itself in in Austria, the Sudetenland,
and the Warthegau. More than likely he did not know that Himmler and
Heydrich had increasingly argued for suppression of all churches, classi-
fying them as ideological enemies of the state. He might have been aware

that it was Martin Bormann who had begun the systematic liquidation of churches by pushing a strict church-state law, privatizing churches and depriving them of all state privileges. He did recognize that in places such as Austria and the Warthegau, the state now controlled all of the churches' revenues and that state-sponsored donations were forbidden.[40] He definitely believed that the Catholic Church was embattled as never before in these regions.

In von Galen's side of the correspondence, he showed himself to be the loyal and obedient son of the church. His letters almost always expressed his thankfulness whenever the Holy Father wrote to him. He often mentioned the "fatherly love" of Pius and signed as the "son and servant" of the pope. He also wrote of his desire to come to Rome and kneel before the papal throne. Most of his letters provided the pope with detailed accounts of Münster's wartime situation, particularly the destruction caused by wartime aerial bombardments, as well as the postwar increase in crime and violence. He shared the pope's concerns about the morals of young people and worried incessantly over the fate of Christianity in Europe.[41]

In one surviving letter, von Galen lamented that he had not heard very much from the Vatican, stating that he could no longer receive copies of the Vatican newspaper, *L'Osservatore Romano,* and that it brought him pain to hear that the Holy City was surrounded by warfare. Von Galen felt isolated from Rome at the time, but what he did not know was that one diplomat and later resister, Ulrich von Hassell, felt the same isolation from Rome and wrote in his diary, "Why does Rome allow von Galen to fight all alone?"[42]

Neither the bishop nor the diplomat would have been immediately aware that Pius had written to his close friend Bishop Preysing about von Galen. This letter is far more revealing of how the pope regarded von Galen's outspokenness than anything exchanged between Münster and Rome. In the letter to Bishop Preysing, Pius honestly praised von Galen for his courage in denouncing euthanasia and other injustices suffered by Catholics in Germany. However, Pius assumed that Preysing had mailed copies of von Galen's three sermons of 1941 in an attempt to show the pope how resolute behavior had produced results and had not ended with von Galen's imprisonment. Pius noted in the letter that he believed Preysing did not want to miss an opportunity to encourage further acts of public defiance over other issues and injustices. Pius then wrote, "We emphasize that, because the Church in Germany is dependent upon your public behavior . . . in public declarations you are *duty bound to exercise restraint.*" He continued his admonishment by claiming that although bishops such as von Galen who championed the things of God and the Holy Church would always have his support, he nevertheless "require[d] you and your colleagues *not to protest.*"[43]

The pope, leader of an institution based on hierarchy, would not encourage individuals to behave like mavericks. If he could not unburden his conscience publicly, then they would also be expected to restrain themselves and operate within the limits of the church's authority. The pope's statements in this letter relate to the issue of von Galen's appointment as cardinal. In most studies, von Galen's nomination is portrayed as a reward for his public denunciations of National Socialism. I would suggest that although this may partly be the case, it is also plausible that von Galen was named a cardinal because Pius XII wanted to reward him for staying within the boundaries of the church hierarchy, for being a true and loyal son of the church. By adopting the pope's priorities and curbing his own behavior after the 1941 denunciations, von Galen had contributed to the prestige of papal authority in overriding individual "upstarts." He had agreed to preserve the image of a united Catholic Church hierarchy. In so doing, von Galen had also aided the Nazi regime.

Rome

On December 23, 1945, Vatican Radio and *L'Osservatore Romano* announced that thirty-two bishops from all over the world were to be raised to the College of Cardinals. That announcement was followed by Pius XII's Christmas Eve message, in which he emphasized the internationalism of the church and the need to build a lasting, universal peace. In that vein, he had chosen to nominate three Germans, so that their country would not experience the isolation it had felt at the end of World War I. He had selected Bishop Frings of Cologne, leader of one of the largest dioceses in Germany; Bishop Preysing of Berlin, a long-time friend; and Bishop von Galen of Münster, nicknamed by this time the Lion of Münster. In Rome, a German Jesuit, Ivo Zeiger, reported the reaction to the news: "It was clear that the naming of the Cardinals was like a bomb. In German Catholic circles, it was . . . thankful jubilation for Germany; especially the raising of Galen. . . . The jubiliation in Westphalia was the greatest."[44]

All three German bishops originally had their doubts about the veracity of the announcements. If the pope had truly decided on them, they believed he would be fighting against the majority of world opinion, but they reasoned that this might be a way for the pope to show there was a distinction between being German and being a National Socialist. The day after Christmas, as rumors were flying, von Galen wrote to his brother Augustinus, still uncertain about the reliability of the reports. "According to the 23rd reports on radio and in the paper, I shall be a Cardinal. I still have no official report. I still hope that it is not true. The thought is unsettling: I am unqualified and unfit, and not least of all, unworthy."[45]

Despite his personal humility, von Galen did eventually verify the reports. On January 6, 1946, wrote to Pius, letting the pope know that he had finally received the official news of the appointment. Von Galen interpreted the pope's decision as a reward for his diocese's behavior, that the majority of Münster's Catholics, himself included, had remained true to the Holy Church: "It is a solace to me if I may see in this nomination a recognition of the brave steadfastness shown by the majority of Catholics in my diocese of Münster, of their loyalty to Christ, his Holy Church, and to the Holy Father during years of persecution and their witness to the Rights of God and for the God-given rights of the human individual." A similar interpretation was offered by von Galen when he wrote to his sister-in-law Countess Paula von Galen. "It is also manifest that he wished to reward my brave diocese for making it possible for me, by their support, to speak the truth openly however unpleasant it may have been."[46]

Von Galen also believed that his nomination to the position of cardinal was a way for Pius XII to show the world that not all Germans were guilty of shameful behavior. The theme of receiving a fair judgment for Germany, of not subscribing to the notion of collective guilt, ran through almost all of von Galen's postwar sermons. Both von Galen and Preysing remained convinced that the Holy Father was working to restore German honor through their nominations.[47]

Actually receiving the cardinal's hat proved to be even more difficult than confirming the first announcements of the nominations. The first biographers of von Galen, Portmann and Bierbaum, both included copious information on the physical difficulties of getting to Rome for the ceremony. All three bishops had numerous troubles in leaving their respective occupation zones in order to arrive in Rome in time for the ceremony. Bishop Preysing had a relatively smoother time, because the French zonal commander gave him a special flight to Paris and then put him on a train for Rome. Bishops Frings and von Galen were to travel together. They encountered almost insurmountable obstacles, from canceled flights to broken-down cars.[48]

What these earlier biographers did not write about were the behind-the-scenes diplomatic difficulties that arose once the appointments had been announced. The diplomatic wranglings are worth examining, because they reveal what the British Foreign Office thought about the position von Galen had come to occupy in postwar Germany.

Initially the British Foreign Office was not certain that Münster belonged in the British occupation zone. This was an honest mistake; it had been American troops whom von Galen first saw enter Sendenhorst at 2 P.M. on March 31, 1945. According to witnesses, he turned very pale and went to the chapel to pray. The British reported that the Americans had "captured" the bishop, and so the confusion persisted for a few days. When Rome first inquired whether the bishop might be allowed to leave Germany, the Foreign Office decided to imitate the Americans with the vague response, "We are not officially sponsoring the application."[49]

Debates in the Foreign Office and the Intelligence Office fluctuated over the question of von Galen's visit. Some voiced the fear that because von Galen was so nationalistic, he represented a political threat in postwar Germany. Others admired von Galen for his frankness, even in defeat. One diplomat assessed von Galen as "the most outstanding personality among the clergy in the British zone. . . . Statuesque in appearance and uncompromising in discussion, this oak-bottomed old aristocrat, who acquired renown for his forthright denunciation of the Nazis, is by no means effusive of the Allies. He is a German nationalist . . . and sticks up for German rights against all comers. In a recent address he repudiated the accusation that the whole German people were responsible for Nazi cruelties and made the . . . point that Germans themselves were inmates of concentration camps."[50]

Other workers in the Foreign Office feared that if von Galen was allowed to go to Rome, he would reveal his bias against British zonal command. They resolved at that point to cancel von Galen's trip but to allow an American bishop the right to travel through Germany, because his account to Pius would be "less biased in Germany's favor than that of the Bishop of Münster."[51]

The matter was by no means solved. The debates continued, and other solutions were offered. One seasoned diplomat, G. W. Harrison, wanted to leave a loophole so that von Galen could go to Rome, reasoning that organized religion could be useful in reeducating Germany in the postwar world. Harrison's advice was ignored at first, and a telegram was drafted, primarily by John Munro Troutbeck, to the effect that the British would not sponsor the visit, because German nationals were not permitted to leave Germany unless there were exceptional circumstances.[52]

When news began to leak that the bishop's trip was going to be denied, the Vatican sent word that von Galen was held in high esteem, and a demonstration in support of von Galen's trip was held in London. Nevertheless, the Foreign Office wanted to adhere to the collective-guilt thesis and worried that von Galen would use the trip to change people's perceptions of Germany. Finally, Colonel R. L. Sedgwick wrote to the Foreign Office explaining that they would be missing an excellent opportunity to connect with the German people if they failed to give the bishop permission to travel. Sedgwick, who had been in the Political Warfare Division, also believed that the church was one of the few institutions left in Germany through which they could "make contact and find understanding, so far as regards internal order and political stability in Germany."[53]

Although von Galen was a thorn in the side of the occupying powers, permission was finally granted for him to go to Rome. The trip to the Holy City itself proved to be a series of minor disasters. Originally Frings and von Galen were to go to Frankfurt, then Vienna, and then Rome, but their flight did not work out. Eventually they boarded a train that took them to Paris and then on to Rome. The entire journey was physically exhausting and took nine days. Von Galen left Münster on February 8, 1946, and returned to Germany on March 7.

In Rome, the ceremonies for the thirty-two new cardinals extended over several days. Celebrating Mass in one church, von Galen thanked the pope for being fair to Germans at a time when the world "had declared the entire nation guilty. . . . He referred to the heroism of many Christians in Germany during that period of satanic tyranny."[54] The Italian population loved "the Giant" and began to pick up on the theme of the "other" Germany, just as the British Foreign Office had nervously anticipated.

Their worries must have increased astronomically when, during the part of the ceremony in which the pope places the cardinal's hat on each new member's head, Pius embraced von Galen and said, "God Bless You and God Bless Germany." There was a swell of applause that washed over the crowd like a tidal wave. Frings dryly remarked, "As I came, no one clapped. Germans were not there and the others knew nothing of me." It seemed that von Galen's trip was doing exactly what the proponents of collective guilt dreaded, rebuilding the image of the "uncoordinated" Germany. One senior diplomat, after witnessing the applause, noted, "When Bishop von Galen came down the steps of the Papal throne, it seemed to me that at that moment the German name, covered so long in shame and infamy, recovered something of its former luster in the person of this great bishop."[55]

Before completing his visit to Rome, von Galen made time to confirm a converted Jewish boy and then left for a tour of Tarent, Bari, and Foggia to visit interned German POWs. On March 7, 1946, all three cardinals reunited and flew to Paris. Frings and von Galen then boarded a train to Frankfurt. They took a car from there to Cologne and Münster, spending a night stuck in the mud during a driving rainstorm. The trip home had been fraught with delays and troubles that exacted a physical toll on von Galen.[56] Before proceeding to Münster, the tired Cardinal von Galen stayed with his brother Franz. He was sixty-eight years old and had only a few weeks left to live.

A Triumphant Return

Arriving back in Münster, von Galen found the city still in ruins but decorated to welcome him home. One eyewitness, a major in the U.S. Airborne Division, remarked that the inner city looked "like Pompeii." The cathedral, which had been completed in 1215 and "which had weathered the storms of war and siege for eight centuries," was in ruins. Von Galen stood amid those ruins on March 16, 1946, and addressed a crowd of approximately fifty thousand people.[57] This was his last mass.

Looking around him, the new cardinal spoke emotionally of the destruction. He spoke of the city in ruins, the homes turned to rubble, and the church destroyed. Yet, he claimed, there was optimism present in the crowd, optimism for the opportunity to rebuild God's house and to renew the spirit of Jesus. The Cardinal said it had been his duty to speak for Truth and Justice and that he had spoken in the name of all Catholics. Crediting them with protecting him, he said that he knew why the pope had called him to be a cardinal.[58]

Elaborating on earlier themes, von Galen told the anxious crowd that it was the loyalty of Münster's people, specifically their loyalty to Christ and to the church, that had brought him this honor. He continued his explanation by attempting to destroy the theory of collective guilt. Claiming that the pope was not like the rest of the world, he said Pius had "shown the entire world that he knows Germany better than those who judge us, condemn us, and want to damn us." Applause followed this. Comforting the crowds, von Galen assured them that the pope's choice proved that "despite the injustices and criminality of many Germans . . . a large portion of our nation did not subscribe to this destructive, pagan ideology." The applause grew still louder. In closing he thanked the citizens for making it possible for him to struggle for God during the dark times and said that the Holy Father had blessed all of Germany when he placed the red hat on his head.[59]

The crowd went wild with von Galen's stirring sermon. He had said what they all wanted to hear. If they had maintained Catholic values, in the sense of attending Mass or teaching their children Catholic beliefs, then they had "resisted" Nazism. They were heroes just like their famous cardinal. According to von Galen, they had all been part of a great fight for church interests, and despite the physical destruction of the cathedral, they had won. The pope had rewarded all of them for struggling to protect the Holy Church. No one at the ceremony asked where the Jewish citizens who had once lived in Münster were.

"Fearless Witness to Earthly and Spiritual Truth"

Most individuals who wrote congratulatory notes to von Galen following his nomination to the College of Cardinals did not refer to his anti-euthanasia sermon of 1941 specifically. Rather, they interpreted the cardinalship as von Galen's reward for serving the church in Germany. One British leader, Spottiswoode, picked up on the theme of fighting to save Christianity: "I see in this distinction a recognition of your courageous attitude in the defense of the Christian principles which had been jeopardized in Germany during the last years." The city Freemen of Sendenhorst praised von Galen in their note for his struggle to create the ideal church while still protecting the honor of the German name.[60] Representatives of the postwar Refugee Union thanked von Galen for being the first to "openly and fearlessly make remarks to the Allied Powers about the fate of millions expelled from their homes in the East" and for his admonishments to the victors of the war to practice Christlike charity and justice. None of them referred directly to the cardinal's famous 1941 fight but instead focused on his lifelong commitment to protecting Christianity in Germany.[61]

Because von Galen died so soon after receiving the red hat, the congratulatory notes were still arriving when condolence notices began to appear. The sympathy notes were strikingly similar to the notes of congratulation in their interpretation of why von Galen would be remembered as a resister.

Death

On March 23, 1946, the local papers ran von Galen's obituary, announcing that von Galen had died peacefully on the day before. In the notice, von Galen was called a "courageous protector of the Church and a champion of the Rights of Man." He was also praised for remaining loyal to the pope while still holding onto his "German-ness." The combination of loyalty to Catholicism and German nationalism was the way most individuals who sent notes summarized von Galen's career. One letter-writer, Karl Zuhorn, wrote to Franz von Galen describing the grief that the entire city was experiencing. He called von Galen a "true citizen" whose great energy in serving both the church and the Fatherland would be sorely missed. Spottiswoode, who had only recently sent his note of congratulations, echoed Zuhorn's sentiments of condolence, asserting that it would be a difficult task to find a suitable successor for von Galen. Praising von Galen for his courage and frankness, Spottiswoode said that Germany had lost a great man at a critical time, one who had "fought for Catholicism in Germany."[62]

Ernst W. Stählin, a leader in the Evangelical Lutheran Church, wrote that although he had never met von Galen personally, members of his church had told him stories of how von Galen had tried to bring Christians closer together. He believed that von Galen's passing represented a terrible loss for the Christian Churches in Germany. Despite the difference in their denominations, Stählin said he and his church members admired the deceased as a "fearless witness to earthly and spiritual truth."[63] Stählin was not the only non-Catholic German to praise von Galen for his convictions. The remnants of the Jewish communities of Cologne and the North Rhine Province also sent messages of sympathy.

Philipp Auerbach, leader of the North Rhine Province Jewish com-

munity, said his community shared in the loss of von Galen because they
believed him to have been "one of the few responsible men who had
led the fight against racial persecution in a difficult time." This theme
was reiterated by the Jewish community in Cologne, which chose to remember von Galen as a "courageous fighter for human rights." Rabbi
Steinthal, who had fled Münster following Kristallnacht, years later still
wrote letters about von Galen's deep devotion to God and his strong
love of justice. In one letter he testified that von Galen had wanted to
use his authority as bishop to practice justice and charity to his neighbors. It is particularly interesting to read the letters from Jews in light of
von Galen's complete silence regarding their persecution. Somehow, the
Jews of these communities managed to believe that von Galen had cared
about them and had tried to inspire others to feel the same way. It should
also be mentioned that Auerbach and Hubert Lewin were the only two
Jews who sent sympathy notes at the time of von Galen's death.[64]

Some individuals said that von Galen's words served as inspiration.
Author Ricarda Huch once wrote a note to the bishop thanking him for
speaking out against injustice and the violations of conscience. She had
protested against the National Socialist banning of Jews from the Prussian Academy of Arts. She claimed that she felt bound to the bishop because of his example. Rudolph Pechel, a member of the Kreisau Circle,
credited von Galen and Martin Niemöller with strengthening his resolve
to resist. Speaking of von Galen, Pechel noted, "Through his sermons
and pastoral letters which were secretly distributed from hand to hand
throughout the whole of Germany, he gave comfort and strength to millions of Germans. This brave and resolute man belonged to the entire
German people."[65] From these notices and letters, one can begin to see
how the image of von Galen as a tireless fighter for human rights came to
be constructed. Germans could take comfort in the fact that the bishop
had maintained his international Catholicism while keeping his credentials as a thoroughly German man. Others focused on his denunciations
of men like Rosenberg and concluded that his words transcended the
separation of denominations and had come to speak for all of mankind.
This was not entirely the view of the officials of the Catholic Church.

On March 28, 1946, Cardinal Frings delivered the sermon at von
Galen's burial mass. He began with John 6:63, "It is the spirit that gives
life, the flesh has nothing to offer." Describing von Galen's vitality and
popularity, Frings attempted throughout the service to teach those present that von Galen's spirit still remained and that they could keep it alive

by emulating his behavior. He praised von Galen for his manly courage, his fight for justice, and his childlike belief in God and the Holy Church. He said von Galen had presented them with the unforgettable picture of "a true German, unshrinking and with a deep spirit, a thoroughly Catholic bishop."[66]

Von Galen would probably have been pleased to be remembered in just such a way. He had once remarked to Friedrich Muckermann, "We von Galens are neither particularly clever nor good-looking, but Catholicism is in our bones."[67] Von Galen may not have been interested in being remembered as a resister, but rather as a defender of the interests of the church. Works that followed von Galen's death, however, began to claim that von Galen had played a significant role in a monumental battle to defeat all elements of National Socialism.

The Construction of a Legend

Long before the war ended and death overtook von Galen, the image of the bishop was building to almost mythic proportions—so much so that many people could not wait to meet the famed bishop in person. One British officer wrote after an encounter with von Galen, "Here visible in the flesh was the legendary being: the defier of Hitler and all his works . . . the Lion of Münster himself. . . . I could not remember ever having seen a more distinguished and Olympian figure."[68] The officer was not the only one to respond to the image of von Galen. Many Allied soldiers heard stories of the famous bishop and traveled to Münster's cathedral to see "where the 'giant Bishop' lived." One Belgian major remarked, "If there is one German to whom I would take off my hat, it's this Count von Galen."[69] How had von Galen's image become so inflated?

Contributing to the image of von Galen as churchman-resister were several newspaper articles that appeared during the war. In 1942 the *New York Times* ran a series entitled "Those Who Defy Hitler" and included references to the bishop as one who fought to protect Catholic institutions against Nazi paganism. The London *Times* also portrayed von Galen as a symbol of Catholic opposition to the National Socialist regime. The American army newspaper, *Stars and Stripes,* carried a story claiming that von Galen's commitment to Catholic values had so angered Himmler that he sent Gestapo agents to arrest the bishop. The story also asserted that von Galen had calmly asked the agents to give him a moment, changed into the full regalia of his bishop's office (including the miter), and then pronounced that he was ready to be arrested. According to the story, the Gestapo agents promptly left without the bishop.[70] Although the story is undoubtedly entertaining, no such incident ever occurred.

Other stories also circulated to reveal the moxie of the bishop. One story frequently appearing in the literature on the bishop asserted that once von Galen was sermonizing on the sanctity of marriage, and "a young Nazi thug, who was posted at the back of the nave, called out, 'You as a celibate have no right to talk about marriage and children!' Clemens August . . . brought his huge fist thumping down on the edge of the pulpit, and retorted, 'I will not tolerate in my cathedral any reflection upon the Führer!'"[71]

Another anecdote had von Galen at the midnight mass on Christmas Eve beginning his sermon this way: "Notices have appeared on the authority of the Gestapo that all persons of non-Aryan stock must leave the church before the sermon begins. If this be so, then we must expect to hear a Child's voice say from the crib, 'Come along, Mummy, we are not wanted here.'" Von Galen privately clarified to Colonel Sedgwick that he had never said this from the pulpit but had occasionally related it publicly.[72]

Von Galen was aware of the growing rumors surrounding his person, and to combat them he decided to give an interview to an American newspaperman, Hans Fleischer, on April 6, 1945. He wanted to make it clear in the interview that he was a German patriot and that he would not discuss political issues. Fleischer added, "The Bishop makes clear, although he and other Germans were anti-Nazis, they nevertheless remain true to the Fatherland and regard the Allied Forces as the enemy." Not being fully satisfied by Fleischer's article, and angered about the *Stars and Stripes* story of his alleged Gestapo encounter, von Galen decided to publish his own press statement. In the clarification notice, he said that as a German bishop he was suffering along with all other Germans, that he would refuse to comment on political issues for the duration of the war, and that he no longer wished to be named in the press or on the radio.[73]

Eventually, von Galen overcame his desire for anonymity and granted another interview, in October 1945 to Fritz R. Allemann of Switzerland. The interview appeared in a Zurich newspaper, *Die Tat,* and was reprinted in January 1946 in the *Glasgow Observer* under a new title.

In this interview, Allemann contributed to the image of churchman-resister by referring to von Galen as "the old resister of National Socialism"[74] and by comparing the bishop to Martin Niemöller.

Allemann allowed von Galen a free voice, and the bishop seized the opportunity to critique the British occupying forces, equating their leadership tactics with those of the Nazis. He castigated the British for arresting German men who had taken party membership or a Nazi title "in order to stave off something worse." Portraying an inaccurate picture of Nazi concentration camps, von Galen claimed that "even the National Socialists permitted inmates of camps to exchange letters twice a month with relatives and to receive food parcels." The bishop insensitively compared the suffering of postwar German wives and their children to that of inmates of Nazi concentration camps, because he had heard that many of these German women could not receive pensions and other funding owing to their husbands' temporary imprisonment in British camps.[75]

In the section of the article entitled "His Greatest Sorrow," von Galen did not chose to address war guilt or crimes against humanity, as might have been expected. Instead, he complained that the British were inadequately supplying the now destitute German people and expressed his fear that the lack of material goods would turn them to Bolshevism. He also criticized the expulsion of Germans from "newly-created" Polish territories. He concluded the interview claiming it was his duty to speak out against injustice: "I am not only a bishop, but also a German man, a Christian with sympathy for poor men." He said it was necessary "to raise his voice, knowing that before all else, it is my duty to see that men find their way back to the one true God, but that they must also have justice."[76] Allemann was too polite to force the bishop to address the issue of war crimes.

One might think that such a vigorous and outspoken comparison of the British with the Nazis would have lead to criticism of von Galen, yet the *British Zone Review* carried a flattering article just one month later, in November 1945, crediting von Galen with immunizing Münster's citizens against National Socialist ideology and claiming that Hitler called the town "Black Münster" because of the bishop's influence: "Although the city, like the rest of Germany, must be held guilty of at least passive acceptance of Hitlerism, its citizens contend, by reason of its religious and cultural traditions, it was somewhat unreceptive of Nazi doctrines. . . . Undoubtedly this was largely due to the influence of Graf Clement [sic] August von Galen . . . who on many occasions spoke from the pulpit in condemnation of the Nazi's doctrines . . . and the Bishop who enjoys much popularity among his flock continues to reign over his diocese."[77]

Apparently the British were willing to overlook the bishop's accusations that they were behaving as badly as the Nazis had. They continued to praise von Galen's wartime behavior. Perhaps they had realized what the shrewd diplomat G. W. Harrison had already concluded; that organized religion could be used by the British to reeducate the German population. Or perhaps they needed to foster the image of the "other" Germany as the Cold War began heating up. Von Galen had warned the British that there would soon come a time when they would need Germany as their ally in the fight against the danger of Bolshevism, stating in 1946, "I prophesy that before much time is out you will ask us to arm again, so that we may be a bulwark between you and Russia."[78] In any event, both British and American newspaper reports, interviews, and unconfirmed rumors contributed to the image of von Galen as churchman-resister. This image was further compounded in 1956.

Monuments

Ten years after von Galen's death, it was suggested that the late cardinal be considered for canonization. This suggestion sparked a debate about von Galen's place in the roll call of resistance fighters. Von Galen's associates and earliest biographers, Heinrich Portmann and Max Bierbaum, were the most prolific proponents for canonization, taking the position that von Galen had an inherent saintliness about him and had been part of a kind of grand resistance against the regime.[79] Their idealized portraits of the bishop had dominated the literature on Catholic resistance until 1956 and were representative of the more general studies of resistance that emerged in the immediate postwar era with their attempts to prove that collective guilt was unfair and that there had been Germans who refused to "coordinate" with Nazi ideology.

One of the first individuals to publicly challenge the stylized portrait of von Galen was a Catholic publicist, Johannes Fleischer. His little-known article, "The Myth of the Holy Resistance Fighter," leveled the charge that von Galen, along with all the other German bishops, had not performed the duties of their offices and had caused their Catholic followers to sin by endorsing both nationalism and militarism. Fleischer pointed out that so long as church leaders remained at peace with the regime, their followers would choose to do the same. In the end, he concluded, their silence had aided National Socialism.[80]

Another individual who began to voice some criticism of the bishop was Ernst-Wolfgang Böckenförde, who argued that the leadership of the Catholic Church, von Galen included, had worked to protect its own interests by ratifying the Concordat and had inadvertently contributed to the stabilization of the regime. He also accused von Galen and other Catholic leaders of abandoning persecuted minorities.[81] What made Böckenförde's article most intriguing was that it was published in 1961 in a Catholic magazine, *Hochland.*

This somewhat minor publication event was symptomatic of a larger change in the treatment of the theme of resistance in church historiography that began in the 1960s and 1970s. A much more critical interpretation of church leadership had begun to appear, and the focus had started to shift to individual Catholics who had behaved heroically rather than the actions or inaction of the institution.[82] Cracks were beginning to appear in the wall of "Grand Resistance" literature.

A few years later, Karl-Heinz Deschner published a sweeping work that argued that there had been no Catholic resistance to Nazism. He explained the lack of resistance quite simply: the pope and the German bishops had commanded obedience to earthly authority, and the majority of German Catholics followed their instruction. Deschner's study further indicted the church for its silence when he pointed out that even those bishops who, like von Galen, had denounced some government policies, had never been touched.[83] His implication was that they should and could have gone much further in denouncing fascism in general and National Socialism in particular.

Despite the works of individuals such as Fleischer and Deschner, the idealized portrait that earlier biographers such as Portmann and Bierbaum had fostered continued to predominate in the literature.[84] Their creation was challenged again in 1978 from an unexpected source, when the local papers carried reports that a monument to von Galen was going to be established at the cathedral square.

The majority of papers, drawing on the image in the studies by Portmann and Bierbaum, called von Galen a "fearless fighter for human rights and freedom of conscience against the totality of Nazi rule." One reported that von Galen had been a "fighter for human freedom and the rights of man." At that point a seventy-five-year-old Communist and freethinker, Reinhold Schmidt, entered the discussion. Schmidt, who had been arrested in 1935 for his anti-Nazi leanings, published sermons and speeches given by von Galen revealing that the "fearless fighter" had perhaps endorsed some of the aims of National Socialism.[85] His publications embarrassed the local papers, and once again the door seemed to be open for some new, more critical evaluations of von Galen to appear.

Although Schmidt had hoped to stop the ceremony of 1978, the church fathers of Münster went ahead and revealed the bronze bust of the cardinal. Some of Schmidt's followers appeared at the ceremony, handing out leaflets that attacked the Catholic Church and its involvement with the Nazi regime. After the ceremony there were some minor scuffles, but in the end von Galen had been officially memorialized by the church as a "symbol of Resistance for men of all beliefs."[86]

Since that time, others have investigated von Galen's opinions. Barbara Vennenbernd, examining resistance among workers in Münster, has pointed to von Galen's silence regarding the early establishment of concentration camps for Communists. Rahner's work has revealed the execution of Russian POWs in Münster's local prison and the bishop's silence. Forty years after Münster's liberation, on May 8, 1985, a bronze plate was added to a stone in the town, praising the individuals who had spoken out against militarism and fascism. By August 1985 the bronze plate had been broken and stolen from its memorial stone.[87]

The memorial to von Galen remained, but the canonization question was still unresolved. Pope John Paul II went to Münster in 1987. Eventually he announced that von Galen would not be canonized, but rather another one-time resident of Münster would be. He named Edith Stein, for her witness to the horror of Nazi brutality.

Conclusion

Happy are those who are persecuted in the cause of right: theirs is the kingdom of heaven.

—MATTHEW 5:10

Although the canonization process was officially closed in 1987, historians of the 1980s and 1990s have continued their search for a definition of resistance and how best to interpret von Galen's actions. Joachim Kuropka, Heinz Mussinghoff, Marie-Corentine Sandstede-Auzelle, and Stefan Rahner and his collaborators are some of the individuals who have most recently reexamined von Galen's role during the Nazi period.[1] Rahner's work tends to be the most critical depiction of von Galen, concluding that he was not a universal antifascist, as earlier depictions had sought to prove. He contends, nonetheless, that von Galen had a symbolic significance for many of Münster's citizens. Kuropka, Sandstede-Auzelle, and Mussinghoff, who are generally less critical than Rahner, focus on what Ian Kershaw has called "the art of the possible," claiming that von Galen achieved symbolic importance because he came to represent what could be achieved under a totalitarian system. Of the three, Kuropka is the most committed to keeping von Galen's name firmly ensconced in the annals of resistance, seeking to prove that the bishop did engage in political resistance with notable effects while simultaneously finding support from the nonelite segments of German society. All of these historians define von Galen's actions as resistance based on the categories created by the Bavaria Project.[2] Those scholars determined that symbolic acts of noncompliance could be termed resistance.

I disagree with these works and their definition of resistance. I do not dispute that von Galen, like various other individuals, functioned as a symbol of what was possible in terms of resistance under the Third

Reich. However, not all of his actions, symbolic or otherwise, can be defined as resistance. To say otherwise would detract from the memory of those individuals who risked their lives against great odds or who were actively persecuted in their efforts to stop the Nazi regime. It would be more useful to portray von Galen as a person who practiced selective opposition and who revealed the fluid nature of the boundaries between conflict and consensus in Nazi Germany. Above all, he missed bringing Catholicism's universal moral concerns to the aid of other beleaguered subjects of the regime.

In his essay on resistance, Michael Geyer discusses the Nazis' ability to use the language of collectivity to divide German society and exclude portions of it. Geyer argues that what resistance leaders should have been looking for were new ways to reconnect a torn society.[3] In my evaluation of von Galen, I searched for proof that he recognized the need to work for a new solidarity with those groups in German society that had been deemed radically "other." Von Galen could have benefited many, because of his office, by impressing upon his parishioners and anyone else who would hear him that the bonds of human solidarity should transcend the bonds of a religious affiliation. I do not find convincing evidence that von Galen recognized this need to seek bonds with those members of German society who had been labeled as "other," despite his keen awareness of the attempt to place Catholics in such a role (i.e., Nazi attempts to designate them as second-class citizens and ideological enemies of the Reich).

Finally, I conclude that von Galen's resistance is more like what Claudia Koonz has defined in her essay in *Resistance against the Third Reich, 1933–1990,* as "single-issue dissent" to specific Nazi policies.[4] As in many of the individual cases Koonz presents in her essay, von Galen did not set himself against Nazi policies in general, but he did vigorously oppose particular aspects of National Socialism. What seems to be most true in von Galen's case is that he objected whenever he perceived that the interests of the Catholic Church were under attack by the state authorities. His opposition, I argue, did not generally reach beyond those boundaries, despite his position and training to do otherwise.

As Koonz's "single-issue" individuals sometimes became more obedient and compliant to other Nazi policies, von Galen, too, sought to prove his obedience and loyalty to the state. His sermons were often so overlaid with patriotic sentiment that listeners would have had to strain to find challenges to Nazi authority. His nationalistic sermons failed to convey effectively the message that there was a difference between loyalty to the state and loyalty to the Nazi Party. His attempts to show such a difference were watered down every time he blessed the Führer at the end of his sermons or endorsed Nazi foreign policy. By taking such ambiguous positions, von Galen led many Catholics to believe that they could continue in their everyday lives, operating under the illusion that it was still possible to be loyal both to Catholicism and to the German state.

One reason for my conclusion that von Galen practiced at best selective opposition is that von Galen was not an ordinary citizen, unaccustomed to assuming a public leadership role in society; therefore, more could have been expected from him. He came from a socially and politically involved family, with both his father and one brother, Franz, serving in the Prussian parliament. He had witnessed a long family tradition of public service and assumed such a role from the moment he became a bishop. I do not believe it is unfair to judge him according to his self-imposed standards, which included his responsibility to guide the consciences of his followers in questions of morality and legality. He had many of the tools necessary to become an extraordinary leader; the majority of recent studies do not consider these facts, however, when they evaluate the bishop's position and possibilities under the Nazis.

Furthermore, these most recent studies do not examine the limitations that von Galen would have had to overcome if he had sought or given guidance regarding contemporary theological justifications for the idea of revolution. Nor do these studies make a connection between the lasting social memory of the Kulturkampf and its tremendous implications for von Galen's misunderstanding of his own position in the Third Reich. I argue that von Galen's memory of this past persecution on the part of the state and his desire to avoid such persecution again were major factors in limiting his dissent.

In addition, there is a great need to reexamine the grave misconceptions about von Galen stemming from his three famous sermons of 1941. Most studies do not make it clear that the first two sermons never addressed euthanasia; they leave the impression that all three were devoted to denouncing this Nazi project. They also de-emphasize von Galen's intention in disseminating the information regarding the killings. I argue that von Galen did not expect or desire individuals to take the information he had given them and use it as a reason to participate in active resistance. This would be supported by his metaphor of the hammer and the anvil, through which he advised his listeners that passive disobedience to specific Nazi laws was all he expected of them. He never endorsed active resistance against the regime. In addition, when addressing the issue of euthanasia, no researcher to my knowledge has integrated the role that Protestant individuals played in gathering the physical, verifiable proof of killings that von Galen demanded before he would issue a public statement. Without the help of Protestant pastors, von Galen might never have preached his sermon of August 1941. After he had successfully launched his public denunciation of specific Nazi immoral practices, why did he not go further in his criticisms of other illegal actions? The fact that he was never interrogated or arrested by state authorities after delivering the sermons suggests that he could have risked more if he had so desired.

Finally, most historians of von Galen have neglected to study the relationship between the bishop's ideas of Bolshevism and his portrayal of Judaism.[5] This is a highly significant link, for it allowed von Galen to find a redeeming feature in National Socialism. Good Catholics could support a government whose aim was to destroy a "Judeo-Bolshevik conspiracy." When von Galen promised that any German soldier who had given his life in the fight to save Christianity would find eternal reward in heaven, he made the struggle in the East the equivalent of a new, cleansing crusade. In his boundless encouragement of Nazi aggression in the East, von Galen led his followers to believe that they were performing a moral good by supporting the actions of their government. Thus von Galen allowed his Catholic listeners to believe in many of the regime's overarching goals while putting clearly illegal and immoral acts into categories of "mistakes" or "excesses."

Von Galen, and many of his scholar-interpreters, believed that he had cleverly escaped the Nazis, because he had been able to criticize aspects of the regime without punishment. Although these criticisms might have lessened his own feeling of being oppressed, he did not work to mobilize public opinion to alleviate oppression experienced by other minority groups in his society. He was limited in his opposition by what had been defined by Pius XII and the Concordat as "Church interests." He did not emerge as a person who challenged the ultimate basis of Nazi rule. As Susan Zuccotti wrote, "If intolerance and segregation are to be challenged and destroyed, someone must raise the initial questions. The economic, political, and social elites of a nation have a vested interest in the preservation of the status quo. Religious leaders suffer from the same constraints, but they, at least, might be expected to rise above them."[6]

Koonz, in an article titled "Ethical Dilemmas and Nazi Eugenics," states that hers is a cautionary tale "to those who conclude that every sign of dissent indicates resistance."[7] Von Galen's life under National Socialism was one of selective opposition, accommodation, and sometimes outright support. His life revealed the very fluid nature of these categories. There are many explanations for his selective opposition: his particular social construction of the world (shaped by his youth); his lack of theological tools that might have encouraged him to embrace a broad-based resistance; his belief that the Catholic Church was experiencing another Kulturkampf, which mainly threatened to exclude Catholics from the German nation-state; his support for Germany's cause against the spread of Bolshevism; his loyalty to Pius XII; and his respect for church hierarchy and the conservatism for which it stood. All of these factors worked against von Galen in that they held him back from becoming one of those extraordinary individuals who were willing to risk everything to rescue victims outside their social kin or to help end the Nazi regime.

To those who might think my assessment of von Galen is too harsh, I would respond that I believe von Galen should be held to a higher standard of accountability because of the office he held and the beliefs he affirmed. If church leaders will not publicly witness to the truth, to act as guides for their followers' consciences, then whom should we expect to fulfill this task? Asking these questions of von Galen is not imposing late-twentieth-century values and expectations on an earlier time: one can find contemporaries of von Galen pleading with the church representatives to lead them in a larger spiritual and moral mission against Nazism as a whole. Pope John Paul II, speaking of the tragedy of the Holocaust and the duty to remember, said that the church should recall "all those times in history when they departed from the spirit of Christ and his Gospel and, instead of offering to the world the witness of a life inspired by the values of faith, indulged in ways of thinking and acting which were truly forms of counter-witness and scandal."[8]

I would not go so far as to say that von Galen was scandalous in his behavior, but I do believe that he lost sight of the larger, more humane questions involved in the brutality of the Nazi regime. He failed to build solidarity with other persecuted segments of society and thereby left a questionable moral legacy for Catholics struggling to live up to the universalizing, moral elements of their faith. At some point von Galen might have meditated on Luke 10:25–28: "There was a lawyer who, to disconcert him, stood up and said to him [Jesus], 'Master, what must I do to inherit eternal life?' He said to him, 'What is written in the Law? What do you read there?' He replied, 'You must love the Lord your God with all your heart, with all your soul, with all your strength, and with all your mind, and *your neighbor as yourself.*' 'You have answered right,' said Jesus, 'do this and life is yours.'"

"Neighbor" was not defined as Catholic or Jew. It meant *human being.* As a bishop, von Galen should have offered living testimony to the truth of that statement.

Appendix: Three Sermons in Dark Times

Sermon by the Bishop of Münster, Clemens August Count von Galen, on Sunday, July 13, 1941, in St. Lambert's Church, Münster

My dear Catholics of St Lambert's:

I have longed to read personally from the pulpit of this church today my pastoral letter on the events of the past week and in particular to express to you, my former parishioners, my deep-felt sympathy. In some parts of the parish of St Lambert and also in other parts of the city, the devastation and loss have been particularly great. I hope that by the action of the municipal and government authorities responsible, and above all by your brotherly love and the collections taken today for the work of the Caritas Union and the Parish Caritas, some of the hardship and suffering will be relieved. I had in mind also, however, to add a brief word on the meaning of the divine visitation: how God thus seeks us in order to lead us home to Him. God wants to lead Münster home to Him. How much at home were our forefathers with God and in God's Holy Church! How thoroughly were their lives—their public life, their family life, and even their commercial life—supported by faith in God, directed by the holy fear of God and by the love of God! Has it always been like that in our own day? God wants to lead Münster home to Him!

Concerning this I had meant to put some further reflections before you. But this I cannot do today, for I find myself compelled to openly and in public speak of something else—a shattering event which came upon us yesterday, at the end of this week of calamity.

The whole of Münster is still suffering from the shock of the horrible devastation inflicted on us by the enemy from without during the past week. Then yesterday, at the end of this week—yesterday, the 12th July—the State Secret Police (i.e., Gestapo) confiscated the two residences of the Society of Jesus in our city, Haus Sentmaring in the Weseler Strasse and the Ignatius-Haus in Königstrasse, expelled the occupants from their property and forced the fathers and lay brothers to depart without delay on that very day, not merely from their residences, not merely from the city of Münster but from the provinces of Westphalia and the Rhineland. Yesterday, too, the same cruel fate was inflicted on the missionary sisters of the Immaculate Conception in Steinfurter Strasse, Wilkinghege. Even their convent was seized and the nuns are being expelled from Westphalia: they have to leave Münster by 6 o'clock this evening. The premises and possessions of these religious orders are confiscated and assigned to the authorities of the Gau (i.e., administrative district) of Northern Westphalia.

Thus the attack on the religious orders which has long been raging in Austria, South Germany and the newly acquired territories of the Warthegau, Luxembourg, Lorraine and other parts of the Reich, has now stricken Westphalia. We must be prepared that in the near future such terrifying news will accumulate—that even here one religious house after another will be confiscated by the Gestapo and that its occupants, our brothers and sisters, children of our families, loyal German citizens, will be thrown on to the street like outlawed helots and hunted out of the country, like vermin.

And this is happening at a time when we are trembling from fear of further nightly air-raids which may kill us all or make us homeless refugees! Even at such a time innocent and deserving men and women, who are greatly esteemed by countless people, are expelled from their humble possessions; at such a time fellow Germans, fellow-citizens of Münster, are made homeless refugees.

Why? They tell me, "for reasons of state policy." No other reasons have been given. No occupant of these religious houses has been accused of any offence or crime; not one has been brought before a court, still less found guilty. If any one of them were guilty, let him be brought to justice; but is one permitted also to punish the innocent?

I ask you, under whose eyes the Jesuit fathers and the sisters of the Immaculate Conception for many years have been leading their quiet lives dedicated solely to the glory of God and the salvation of their fellow-men—I ask you: who holds these men and women to be guilty of an offence meriting punishment? Who dares to level any charge against them? If any dare, let him prove his assertion! Not even the Gestapo has made any such charge, let alone a court or the public prosecutor.

Here I testify publicly as the bishop who is responsible for the supervision of the religious orders that I have the greatest respect for the quiet, humble missionary sisters of Wilkinghege Bahlmann, mainly for missionary service in Brazil. There he worked himself, and his untiring and fruitful activities—not least in the name of German culture and civilization—lasted until his death three years ago.

I testify as a German and a bishop that I have the greatest respect and reverence for the Jesuit order, which I have known from the closest observation since my early youth, for the last fifty years, that I remain bound in love and gratitude until my last breath to the Society of Jesus, my teachers, tutors and friends, and that today I have all the greater reverence for them, at a moment when Christ's prophecy to his disciples is once again fulfilled: "If they have persecuted me, they will also persecute you. If ye were of the world, the world would love his own: but because ye are not of the world, but I have chosen you out of the world, therefore the world hateth you."

And so from this place, speaking also in the name of the true Catholics of the city and diocese of Münster, I greet with profound love those who have been chosen by Christ and are hated by the world as they go into unmerited banishment. May God reward them for all the good they have done for us! May God not punish us and our city for the unjust treatment and banishment which here has been meted out to His faithful disciples. May God's omnipotence soon return to us these our beloved banished brothers and sisters!

My dear diocesans! Because of the heavy visitation brought on us by enemy air-raids I originally resolved to keep silent in public about certain recent acts of the Gestapo which simply called for some public protest on my part. But when the Gestapo pay no heed to the events which have made hundreds of our fellow-citizens homeless, when they at this very moment continue to throw innocent fellow-citizens on to the street and to expel them from the country, then I must no longer hesitate to give public expression to my justified protest and my solemn warning.

Many times, and again quite recently, we have seen the Gestapo arresting blameless and highly respected German men and women without the judgment of any court or any opportunity for defence, depriving

them of their freedom, taking them away from their homes and intern-
ing them somewhere. In recent weeks even two members of my closest
council, the chapter of our Cathedral, have been suddenly seized from
their homes by the Gestapo, removed from Münster and banished to
distant places. Since then I have received no reply whatever to the protests which I addressed to the Minister for Ecclesiastical Affairs. But it
has at any rate been established by telephone enquiries to the Gestapo
that neither of the canons has been accused, or is suspected, of any punishable offence. Without any guilt on their part, they have incurred the
penalty of banishment, without any charge against them and without
any opportunity to defend themselves!

My Christians, hear what I say! It has been officially confirmed that
Canons Vorwerk and Echelmeyer are accused of no crime. They have
done nothing meriting punishment. And yet they have been punished
with banishment.

And why? Because I did something that did not please the government. Of the four appointments of canons made in the past two years
the government informed me that they objected to three. Since the Prussian Concordat of 1929 expressly excludes any right of objection by the
government, I confirmed the appointment in two of the cases. In doing
so I committed no wrong, but merely exercised my established right, as
I can prove at any time. Let them bring me to court if they think that I
have acted contrary to law. I am sure that no independent German court
could condemn me for my actions in the appointment of these canons.

Was it because of this that the matter was handled not by a court but
by the Gestapo, whose actions in the German Reich are unfortunately
not subject to any judicial review? Against the superior physical power
of the Gestapo every German citizen is entirely without protection or
defence. Entirely without protection or defence!

In recent years many Germans have experienced this in their own
person, like our beloved teacher of religion Friedrichs, who is held pris-
oner without any legal process or sentence, like the two canons who are
now living in banishment; and again it is experienced by those religious
orders who yesterday and today have been suddenly expelled from their
property, their city and their province.

None of us is safe—and may he know that he is the most loyal and
conscientious of citizens and may he be conscious of his complete innocence—he cannot be sure that he will not some day be deported from
his home, deprived of his freedom and locked up in the cellars and concentration camps of the Gestapo.

I am aware of the fact: This can happen also to me, today or some other day. And because then I shall not be able to speak in public any longer, I will speak publicly today, publicly I will warn against the continuance in a course which I am firmly convinced will bring down God's judgment on men and must lead to disaster and ruin for our people and our country.

When I protest against these actions and these punishments by the Gestapo, when I call publicly for an end to this state of affairs and for the judicial review or reversal of all actions by the Gestapo, I do no more than Governor-General and Reichsminister Dr Hans Frank has done, writing in January of this year in the Journal of the Academy of German Law (2, 1941, p. 25):

> We desire to achieve a well balanced system of internal order in which penal law does not degenerate into the absolute authority of the prosecution over an accused person who is condemned in advance and deprived of any means of defence. . . . The law must offer the individual the legal opportunity of defending himself, of establishing the facts and thus securing himself against arbitrariness and injustice. Otherwise we had better speak not of penal law but of penal authority. . . . It is impossible to reconcile the fabric of law with a sentence pronounced without any defence. . . . It is our task to proclaim, no less loudly and with no less emphasis than others defend authority in every form, that we have courageously to assert the authority of the law as an essential element in any enduring power.

These are the words of Reichsminister Dr Hans Frank.

I am conscious that as a bishop, a promulgator and defender of the legal and moral order willed by God and granting to each individual rights and freedoms to which, by God's will, all human claims must give way, I am called upon, no less than Reichsminister Frank, courageously to assert the authority of the law and to denounce the condemnation of innocent men, who are without any defence, as an injustice crying out to heaven.

My Christians! The imprisonment of many blameless persons without any opportunity for defence or any judgment of a court, the deprivation of the liberty of the two canons, the closing of religious houses and the eviction of guiltless religious, our brothers and sisters, compel me today to publicly recall an old and unshakeable truth, "Justitia est fundamentum regno"—Justice is the only solid foundation of any state.

The right to life, to inviolability, to freedom is an indispensable part of any moral order of society. It is true that the state is entitled to restrict these rights as a penal measure against its citizens, but the state is only entitled to do so against those who have broken the law and whose guilt has been established in an impartial judicial process. A state which transgresses this boundary laid down by God and permits or causes innocent persons to be punished is undermining its own authority and the respect for its sovereignty in the conscience of its citizens.

Unfortunately, however, we have repeatedly seen in recent years how penalties of greater or lesser severity, usually involving terms of imprisonment, have been imposed and carried out without the victim's guilt having been proved in a regular court of law and without giving him any opportunity of asserting his right to prove his innocence. How many Germans are now languishing in police custody or in concentration camps, how many have been driven from home, who have never been sentenced by a regular court or how numerous are those who have been freed by the court or released after serving their sentence and have then been re-arrested and held in confinement by the Gestapo! How many have been expelled from their home town and the town where they worked! Here again I think of the venerable bishop of Rottenburg, Johann Baptist Sproll, an old man of 70, who not long ago had to celebrate his 25th jubilee as a bishop far away from his diocese, from which the Gestapo had banned him three years ago.

I mention again the names of our two canons, Vorwerk and Echelmeyer. And I commemorate our venerable teacher of religion Friedrichs, now in a concentration camp.

I will forbear to mention any other names today. The name of a Protestant minister who served Germany in the first world war as a German officer and submarine commander, who later worked as a Protestant clergyman in Münster and for some years now has been deprived of his liberty, is well known to you, and we all have the greatest respect for this noble German's courage and steadfastness in professing his faith.

From this example you will see, my Christians, that I am not talking about a matter of purely Catholic concern but about a matter of Christian concern, indeed of general human and national concern. "Justice is the foundation of all states!" We lament, we observe with the greatest anxiety that this foundation is nowadays shaken, that justice—the natural and Christian virtue which is indispensable for the ordered existence of any human community—is not maintained and held in honour for everybody in an unequivocally recognizable way. It is not only for the sake of the Church's rights but also out of love for our people and in grave concern for our country that we beg, we appeal, we demand: Justice! Who must not fear for the existence of a house when he sees that its foundations are being undermined?

"Justice is the foundation of all states!"

The state can take action with honesty and any prospect of enduring success, against the misuse of power by those whom chance has made stronger, against the oppression of the weak and their debasement to the mean employments of a slave, only if those who hold the powers of the state submit in reverence to the royal majesty of Justice and wield the sword of punishment in the service of Justice alone.

No holder of authority can expect to command the loyalty and willing service of honourable men unless his actions and penal decisions prove in an impartial judgment to be free from any element of arbitrariness and weighed on the incorruptible scales of Justice.

Accordingly the practice of condemning and punishing men who are given no chance of defence and without any judicial sentence—in Reichsminister Dr Frank's words: the prosecution of an accused person who is condemned in advance and deprived of any means of defence—engenders a feeling of legal defencelessness and an attitude of apprehensive timidity and subservient cowardice, which must in the long run deprave the national character and destroy the national community.

That is the conviction and anxiety of all honest Germans. It was given open and courageous expression by a high legal officer in the "National Administration Paper" in 1937: "The greater the power of a public authority, the more necessary is a guarantee of the impeccable use of that power; for the more deeply felt are the mistakes that are made, and the greater is the danger of arbitrariness and abuse of power. If there is no possibility of redress by an administrative tribunal there must be in each case some regular means of providing a form of control which is as impartial as possible, so as to leave no room for a feeling of legal defencelessness, which in the course of time must gravely jeopardise the national community" (Herbert Schelcher, President of the Supreme Administrative Court of Saxony, Dresden: "National Administration Paper" (i.e., *Reichsverwaltungsblatt*), 1937, p. 572).

The orders and penal decisions of the Gestapo are not open to redress by any administrative tribunal. Since none of us know of any means of achieving impartial control over the actions and persecutions of the Gestapo, the restrictions they impose on men's freedom, their banishment and arrest and their imprisonment of German men and women in concentration camps, there is by now among our people a widespread feeling of defencelessness, even of cowardly apprehension, which does grave harm to the national community. The duty imposed on me by my Episcopal office to speak up for the moral order, by the oath which I swore before God and the representative of the government to "ward off," to the best of my ability, "any harm which might threaten the German people," this duty compels me, in the face of the Gestapo's actions, to state this fact and pronounce this public warning.

My Christians! It will perhaps be held against me that by this frank statement I am weakening the home front of the German people during this war.

I, on the contrary, say this: It is not I who am responsible for a possible weakening of the home front, but those who regardless of the war, regardless of this fearful week of terrible air-raids, impose heavy punishments on innocent people without the judgment of a court or any possibility of defence, who evict our religious orders, our brothers and sisters, from their property, throw them on to the street, drive them out of their own country. They destroy men's security under the law, they undermine trust in law, they destroy men's confidence in our government. And therefore I raise my voice in the name of the upright German people, in the name of the majesty of Justice, in the interests of peace and the solidarity of the home front; therefore as a German, an honourable citizen, a representative of the Christian religion, a Catholic bishop, I exclaim: we demand justice! If this call remains unheard and unanswered, if the reign of Justice is not restored, then our German people and our country—in spite of the heroism of our soldiers and the glorious victories they have won—will perish through an inner rottenness and decay.

Let us pray for all who are in trouble, particularly for our religious orders, for our city of Münster, that God may preserve us from further trials; for our German people and fatherland and for its leader.

Sermon by the Bishop of Münster, Clemens August Count von Galen, on Sunday, July 20, 1941, in the Liebfrauenkirche, Münster

Today the collection which I ordered for the inhabitants of the city of Münster is held in all the parishes in the diocese of Münster which have not themselves suffered war damage. I hope that through the efforts of the state and municipal authorities responsible and the brotherly help of the Catholics of this diocese, whose contributions will be administered and distributed by the offices of the Caritas, much need will be alleviated.

Thanks be to God, for several days our city has not suffered any new enemy attacks from without. But I am distressed to have to inform you that the attacks by our opponents within the country, of the beginning of which I spoke last Sunday in St Lambert's, that these attacks have continued, regardless of our protests, regardless of the anguish this causes to the victims of the attacks and those connected with them.

Last Sunday I lamented, and branded as an injustice crying out to heaven, the action of the Gestapo in closing the convent in Wilkinghege and the Jesuit residences in Münster, confiscating their property and possessions, putting the occupants into the street and expelling them from their home area. The convent of Our Lady of Lourdes in Frauenstrasse was also seized by the Gau authorities. I did not then know that on the same day, Sunday 13th July, the Gestapo had occupied the Kamillus-kolleg in Sudmühle and the Benedictine abbey of Gerleve and expelled the fathers and lay brothers. They were forced to leave Westphalia that very day. On 15th July the Benedictine Sisters of Perpetual Adoration in Vinnenberg, near Warendorf, were expelled from their convent and from the province. On 17th July the Sisters of the Cross were driven out of their convent, Haus Aspel in Rees, and forced to leave the district of Rees. Had not Christian love shown compassion for all these homeless ones, these men and women would have been exposed to hunger and the rigours of the weather.

Then a few hours ago I learned the sad news that yesterday, 19th July, at the end of this second terrible week in our region of Münster, the Gestapo occupied, confiscated and expropriated the administrative centre of the German province of the Holy Cross, the great missionary house at Hiltrup which is well known to you all. The fathers and lay brothers still living there were given until 8 o'clock yesterday evening to leave their residence and their possessions. They too are expelled from Westphalia and the province of Rhineland.

The fathers and lay brothers still living there: I do emphasise these words, for, as I happened to learn recently, 161 men from the ranks of the Hiltrup missionaries are serving as German soldiers in the field, some of them directly in face of the enemy; 53 fathers are caring for the wounded as medical orderlies, and 42 theologians and 66 lay brothers are serving their country as soldiers, some having been decorated with the

Iron Cross and other distinctions. The same can be said of the fathers of Sudmühle, the Jesuits of Sentmaring and the Benedictines of Gerleve. While these German men are fighting for their country in accordance with their duty and in loyal comradeship with other German brothers, at the risk of their lives, they are being deprived, ruthlessly and without any basis in law, of their home, their parent monastery is being destroyed. When, as we hope, they return victorious they will find their monastic family driven from house and home and their home occupied by strangers, by enemies!

How is this going to end? It is not a question of providing temporary accommodation for homeless inhabitants of Münster. The religious orders were very ready to reduce their own accommodation requirements to the minimum in order to take in and care immediately for those made homeless. No: that was not the reason. I have heard that the convent of the Immaculate Conception in Wilkinghege is occupied by the Gau film unit. I am told that a maternity home for unmarried mothers is installed in the Benedictine abbey. I have not yet learned what is happening to Sentmaring, Sudmühle and Vinnenberg. And no newspaper has so far carried any account of the safe victories won by the Gestapo in recent days over defenceless men and unprotected women, of the conquests made at home by the Gau authorities of the property of fellow Germans.

On Monday 14th July I called on the President of the Regional Council and asked for protection for the freedom and property of innocent German citizens. He told me that the Gestapo was a completely independent authority with whose actions he could not interfere. He promised, however, that he would at once convey my complaints and my requests to the Senior President and Gauleiter, Dr Meyer. To no avail.

On the same day I sent a telegram to the Führer's Chancellery of the Reich in Berlin, in the following terms:

> After a series of terrible nightly air attacks from 6th July onwards in which the enemy have sought to destroy the city of Münster, the Gestapo began on 12th July to seize religious houses in the city and surrounding area and to make them over, along with their contents, to the Gau authorities. The occupants, innocent men and women, honourable members of German families, whose relatives are fighting for Germany as soldiers, are robbed of their homes and possessions, thrown into the street, driven out of the province. I ask the Führer and Reichskanzler, in the interest of justice and the solidarity of the home front, for the protection of the

freedom and property of German men and women against the arbitrary actions of the Gestapo.

I addressed similar requests by telegram to the Governor of Prussia, Marshal Göring, the Minister of the Interior, the Minister for Ecclesiastical Affairs and the Supreme Command of the Wehrmacht. I hoped that, if not considerations of justice, at any rate a recognition of the consequences for the solidarity of the home front in wartime would move these authorities to put a stop to the action taken by the Gestapo against our brothers and sisters, and that innocent German women would not be refused chivalrous protection. It was a vain hope. The action continued, and the situation which I had long foreseen and of which I spoke last Sunday has now come to pass: we are faced with the ruins of the inner national community of our people, which in the last few days has been ruthlessly shattered.

I urgently pointed out to the President of the Regional Council, the ministers and the Supreme Command of the Wehrmacht that these acts of violence against blameless German men and this brutal treatment of defenceless German women, which make a mockery of all chivalry and can arise only from deep-seated hatred of the Christian religion and the Catholic Church, that these machinations are sabotaging and destroying the national community of our people. For how can there be any feeling of community with the men who are driving our religious, our brothers and sisters, as easy victims out of the country, without any basis in law, without any investigation, without any possibility of defence and without any judgment by a court?

No! With them and with all those responsible for these actions I cannot possibly have any community of thought or feeling. I shall not hate them; I wish from my heart that they may gain a new insight and mend their ways.

In this spirit I also at once said a prayer for the soul of Ministerialdirigent (i.e., Assistant Secretary) Roth, who died suddenly on 5th July. He was a Catholic priest, originally in the archdiocese of Munich, who worked for years, without the permission and against the will of the bishop, as an official in the Ministry of Ecclesiastical Affairs, composing and signing many documents which encroached on the Church's rights and injured the Church's dignity. And now he has been drowned during a boat trip on the river Inn. May God have mercy upon his poor soul!

Thus, in accordance with our Saviour's command, we will pray for all who persecute us and slander us. But as long as they do not change, as long as they continue to rob and banish and imprison innocent people, so long do I refuse any community with them.

No: the community of convictions and aspirations in our people has been irreparably destroyed, against our will and regardless of our warnings. I cannot believe that our long-established citizenry and farmers, craftsmen and workers, that our fathers and brothers and sons, who even now are risking their lives for Germany at the front, can have any community of convictions with those who have persecuted and turned out our religious orders.

We shall obey them in so far as they are entitled to give us orders as representatives of the lawful authorities. But a community of convictions, a sense of inner solidarity, with these persecutors of the Church, these invaders of religious houses, who expel defenceless women from their convents, the children of our best families, our sisters, many of whom have lived there for decades in work and prayer, doing nothing but good for our people. I should feel ashamed before God and before you, I should feel ashamed before our noble forefathers, before my own late father, who was a chivalrous man and brought up, admonished and taught my brothers and me sternly to show the most delicate respect to every woman or girl, to afford chivalrous protection to all the unjustly oppressed, particularly to women as the images of our own mothers, and of the beloved Mother of God herself in heaven, if I had any community with those who drive innocent and defenceless women out of house and home and drive them out of their country without shelter and without resources! Moreover, as I showed last Sunday in St Lambert's church and as I must repeat today with great solemnity, in a warning inspired by love for my people and my country, that these punitive actions by the Gestapo against innocent people, without any judgment by a court or judicial proceedings or opportunity for defence—the "prosecution of accused persons who are condemned in advance and deprived of any means of defence," in Reichsminster Dr Frank's words—destroy men's security under the law, undermine faith in law and destroy confidence in the government of our country.

We Christians, of course, are not aiming at revolution. We shall continue loyally to do our duty in obedience to God and in love of our people and fatherland. Our soldiers will fight and die for Germany, but not for those men who by their cruel actions against our religious, against their brothers and sisters, wound our hearts and shame the German name before God and men. We shall continue to fight against the external enemy; but against the enemy within, who strikes us and torments us, we cannot fight with arms. Against him we have only one weapon: endurance—strong, tough, hard endurance.

Become hard! Remain firm! We see and experience clearly what lies behind the new doctrines which have for years been forced on us, for the sake of which religion has been banned from the schools, our organisations have been suppressed and now Catholic kindergartens are about to be abolished—there is a deep-seated hatred of Christianity, which they are determined to destroy. If I am correctly informed, the Schulungsleiter (i.e. head of indoctrination), Herr Schmidt, before an audience which had been invited by force and which included schoolboys and schoolgirls, expressed quite frankly his intention to exert himself for the execution of such plans.

Become hard! Remain firm! At this moment we are the anvil rather than the hammer. Other men, strangers and renegades, are hammering us, seeking by violent means to bend our nation, ourselves and our young people aside from their straight relationship with God. But ask the blacksmith and hear what he says: the object which is forged on the anvil receives its shape not alone from the hammer but also from the anvil. The anvil cannot and need not strike back: it must only be firm, only hard! If it is sufficiently tough and firm and hard the anvil usually lasts longer than the hammer. However hard the hammer strikes, the anvil stands quietly and firmly in place and will long continue to shape the objects forged upon it.

The anvil represents those who are injustly imprisoned, those who are driven out and banished for no fault of their own. God will support them, that they may not lose the form and attitude of Christian firmness when the hammer of persecution strikes its harsh blows and inflicts unmerited wounds on them.

It is our religious, the fathers, lay brothers and the sisters, who are now forged on the anvil. The day before yesterday I was able to visit some of those who had been driven out in their temporary accommodation and to speak with them. I was greatly edified and encouraged by the valiant bearing of the good men and the weak and defenceless women, who had been so ruthlessly torn from their convent, from the chapel, from the vicinity of the tabernacle, and who are now going into unjust banishment with their heads held high, in the consciousness of their innocence, trusting in Him who feeds the birds of the air and clothes the lilies of the field and even joyous in the joy which the Saviour en-joins on His disciples: "Blessed are ye, when men shall revile you, and persecute you, for my sake. Rejoice and be exceeding glad, for great is your reward in heaven." Verily, these men and women are masterpieces of God's forging.

What is being forged in these days between the hammer and the anvil is our young people—the new generation, which is still unformed, still capable of being shaped, still malleable.

We cannot shield them from the hammer-blows of unbelief, of hos-tility to Christianity, of false doctrines and ethics. What is instilled into them at the meetings of those youth organisations, which we are told they joined voluntarily and with the agreement of their parents? What do they hear in the schools which the children are compelled to attend with-out regard to the wishes of their parents? What do they read in the new school-books? Christian parents, ask your children to show you these books, particularly the history books used in the secondary schools. You will be appalled to see how these books, in complete disregard of his-torical truth, seek to fill inexperienced children with mistrust of Chris-tianity and the Church, indeed with hatred of the Christian faith. In the favoured state educational establishments, the Hitler schools, the new teachers' training schools, all Christian influence and even all religious activity are excluded as a matter of principle. And what is happening to the children who were sent last spring to remote parts of the country to escape the air-raids? What religious instruction are they getting? How far can they practise their religion? Christian parents, you must concern yourselves with all this. If you do not, you are neglecting your sacred duties; if you do not, you cannot face your own conscience, nor Him who entrusted the children to you that you might lead them on the way to heaven.

We are the anvil, not the hammer! You cannot shield your children from the hammer-blows of hostility to the faith and hostility to the Church. But the anvil also plays a part in forging. Let your family home, your parental love and devotion, your exemplary Christian life be the strong, tough, firm and unbreakable anvil which absorbs the force of the hostile blows, which continually strengthens and fortifies the still weak powers of the young in the sacred resolve not to let themselves be di-verted from the direction that leads to God.

It is we, almost without exception, who are forged in this present time. How many people are dependent—on an occupational pension, on a state pension, on children's allowances and so on! Who nowadays is still independent, unrestricted master in his own property or business? It may be that, particularly in time of war, strict control and guidance, even the concentration and compulsory direction of products, of production and consumption, is necessary, and who will not readily bear this out of love for his people and his country? But through this follows dependence on many persons and authorities, who not only restrict freedom of action but also bring free independence of sentiments and convictions into grave danger and temptation, as soon as, at the same time, these persons and authorities represent an ideology hostile to Christianity, which they seek to impose on those who are dependent on them. Dependence of this kind is most evident in officials; and what courage, what heroic courage is required of those officials who in spite of all pressure maintain and publicly confess their faith as Christians, as true Catholics!

At this present time we are the anvil receiving all the blows that rain down on us, in loyal service to our people and country, but also ready at any time to act, in the spirit of supreme sacrifice, in accordance with the precept: "Men must obey God more than men." Through a conscience formed by faith God speaks to each one of us. Obey always without any doubt the voice of conscience. Take as your model the old Prussian minister of justice—I have spoken of him before—who was ordered by King Frederick the Great to overturn and alter in accordance with the monarch's wishes a judgment which he had pronounced in accordance with the law. Then this true nobleman, a certain Herr von Münchhausen, gave his king this magnificent answer: "My head is at your majesty's disposal, but not my conscience. I am ready to die for my king; indeed I am obedient to him and shall even accept death at the hands of the hangman. My life belongs to the king, not my conscience!" Is the race of such noblemen, who have this attitude and act in accordance with it, are Prussian officials of this stamp now extinct? Are there no longer any citizens or country people, craftsmen or workers of similar mind? Of similar conscientiousness and nobility of mind? That I cannot and will not believe. And so I say once again: become hard, remain firm, remain steadfast! Like the anvil under the blows of the hammer! It may be that obedience to our God and faithfulness to our conscience may cost me or any of you life, freedom or home. But better to die than to sin! May the grace of God, without which we can do nothing, grant this unshakeable firmness to you and to me and keep us in it!

My dear Catholics of Münster! After a bomb had crashed through the aisle of the Cathedral during the night of 7th–8th July another bomb hit the outer wall and destroyed St Ludger's Fountain, the monument to the return from banishment of Bishop Johann Bernhard in 1884. The statues of Bishops Suitger and Erpho flanking the monument were badly damaged, but the figure of St Ludger, apostle of the Münster region and first Bishop of Münster, remained almost unscathed. The undamaged right hand is raised in blessing and pointing to heaven, as if to convey to us through the almost miraculous preservation of the statue this admonition: Whatever may befall, hold firm to the Catholic faith that was revealed by God and handed down by our forefathers! In all the destruction of the works of man, in all trouble and sorrow I address to you the words which the first Pope addressed to the oppressed Christians of his day: "Humble yourselves therefore under the mighty hand of God, that He may exalt you in due time: Casting all your care upon Him; for He careth for you. Be sober, be vigilant; because your adversary, the devil, as a roaring lion, walketh about, . . . Whom resist stedfast in the faith . . . But the God of all grace, who hath called us unto His eternal glory by Christ Jesus, after that ye have suffered a while, make you perfect, stablish, strengthen, settle you. To Him be glory and dominion for ever and ever" (1 Peter 5:6–11).

Let us pray for our relatives, for the religious orders, for all who must suffer unjustly, for all in trouble, for our soldiers, for Münster and its inhabitants, for our people and country and for its leader.

Sermon by the Bishop of Münster, Clemens August Count von Galen, on Sunday, August 3, 1941, in St. Lambert's Church, Münster

To my regret I have to inform you that during the past week the Gestapo has continued its campaign of annihilation against the Catholic orders. On Wednesday 30th July they occupied the administrative centre of the province of the Sisters of Our Lady in Mühlhausen (Kempen district), which formerly belonged to the diocese of Münster, and declared the convent to be dissolved. Most of the nuns, many of whom come from our diocese, were evicted and required to leave the district that very day. On Thursday 31st July, according to reliable accounts, the monastery of the missionary brothers of Hiltrup in Hamm was also occupied and confiscated by the Gestapo and the monks were evicted.

Already on 13th July, referring to the expulsion of the Jesuits and the missionary sisters of St Clare from Münster, did I publicly make the following statement in this same church: None of the occupants of these convents is accused of any offence or crime, none has been brought before a court, none has been found guilty. I hear that rumours are now being spread in Münster that after all these religious, in particular the Jesuits, have been accused, or even convicted, of criminal offences, and indeed of treason. I declare: These are base slanders of German citizens, our brothers and sisters, which we will not tolerate. I have already lodged a criminal charge with the Chief Prosecutor against a fellow who went so far as to make such allegations in front of witnesses. I express the expectation that the man will be brought swiftly to account and to punish slanderers who seek to destroy the honour of innocent German citizens whose property has already been taken from them. I call on all my listeners, indeed on all decent fellow-citizens, who in future hear accusations made against the religious expelled from Münster to get the name and address of the person making the accusations and of any witnesses. I hope that there are still men in Münster who have the courage to play their part in securing the judicial examination of such accusations, which poison the national community of our people, by coming forward with their person, their name and if necessary their oath. I ask them, if such accusations against the religious are made in their presence, to report them at once to their parish priest or to the Episcopal Vicariate-General and have them recorded. I owe it to the honour of our religious orders, the honour of our Catholic Church and also the honour of our German people and our city of Münster to report such cases to the state prosecution service so that the facts may be established by a court and base slanderers of our religious punished.

(After the Gospel reading for the 9th Sunday after Pentecost: "And when He was come near, He beheld the city, and wept over it . . . ," Luke 19:41-47):

My dear diocesans!

It is a deeply moving event that we read of in the Gospel for today. Jesus weeps! The Son of God weeps! A man who weeps is suffering pain—pain either of the body or of the heart. Jesus did not suffer in the body; and yet he wept. How great must have been the sorrow of soul, the heart-felt pain of this most courageous of men to make him weep! Why did he weep? He wept for Jerusalem, for God's holy city that was so dear to him, the capital of his people. He wept for its inhabitants, his fellows-countrymen, because they refused to recognise the only thing that could avert the judgment foreseen by his omniscience and determined in advance by his divine justice: "If thou hadst known the things which belong unto thy peace!" Why do the inhabitants of Jerusalem not know it? Not long before Jesus had given voice to it: "O Jerusalem, Jerusalem . . . how often would I have gathered thy children together, as a hen doth gather her brood under her wings, and ye would not!" (Luke 13:34).

Ye would not. I, your King, your God, I would. But ye would not! How safe, how sheltered is the chicken under the hen's wing: she warms it, she feeds it, she defends it. In the same way I desired to protect you, to keep you, to defend you against any ill. I would, but ye would not!

That is why Jesus weeps; that is why that strong man weeps; that is why God weeps. For the folly, the injustice, the crime of not being willing. And for the evil to which that gives rise—which his omniscience sees coming, which his justice must impose—if man sets his unwillingness against God's commands, in opposition to the admonitions of conscience, and all the loving invitations of the divine Friend, the best of Fathers: "If thou hadst known, in this thy day, the things which belong unto thy peace! But thou wouldst not!" It is something terrible, something incredibly wrong and fatal, when man sets his will against God's will. I would! Thou wouldst not! It is therefore that Jesus weeps for Jerusalem.

Dearly beloved Christians! The joint pastoral letter of the German bishops, which was read in all Catholic churches in Germany on 26 June 1941, includes the following words: "It is true that in Catholic ethics there are certain positive commandments which cease to be obligatory if their observance would be attended by unduly great difficulties; but there are also sacred obligations of conscience from which no one can release us, which we must carry out even if it should cost us our life. Never, under any circumstances, may a man, save in war or in legitimate self-defence, kill an innocent person."

I had occasion on 6th July to add the following comments on this passage in the joint pastoral letter:

> For some months we have been hearing reports that inmates of establishments for the care of the mentally ill who have been ill for a long period and perhaps appear incurable have been forcibly removed from these establishments on orders from Berlin. Regularly the relatives receive soon afterwards an intimation that the

patient's body has been cremated and that they can collect the ashes. There is a general suspicion, verging on certainty, that these numerous unexpected deaths of the mentally ill do not occur naturally but are intentionally brought about, in accordance with the doctrine that it is legitimate to destroy a so-called "worthless life"—in other words to kill innocent men and women, if it is thought that their lives are of no further value to the people and the state. A terrible doctrine which seeks to justify the murder of innocent people, which legitimises the violent killing of disabled persons who are no longer capable of work, of cripples, the incurably ill and the aged and infirm!

I am reliably informed that in hospitals and homes in the province of Westphalia lists are being prepared of inmates who are classified as "unproductive members of the national community" and are to be removed from these establishments and shortly thereafter killed. The first party of patients left the mental hospital at Marienthal, near Münster, in the course of this week.

German men and women! Article 211 of the German Penal Code is still in force, in these terms: "Whoever kills a man of deliberate intent is guilty of murder and punishable with death." No doubt in order to protect those who kill with intent these poor men and women, members of our families, from this punishment laid down by law, the patients who have been selected for killing are removed from their home area to some distant place. Some illness or other is then given as the cause of death. Since the body is immediately cremated, the relatives and the criminal police are unable to establish whether the patient had in fact been ill or what the cause of death actually was. I have been assured, however, that in the Ministry of the Interior and the office of the Chief Medical Officer, Dr Conti, no secret is made of the fact that a large number of mentally ill persons in Germany have already been killed with intent and that this will continue.

Article 139 of the Penal Code provides that "anyone who has knowledge of an intention to commit a crime against the life of any person . . . and fails to inform the authorities or the person whose life is threatened in due time . . . commits a punishable offence." When I learned of the intention to remove patients from Marienthal I reported the matter on 28th July to the State Prosecutor of Münster Provincial Court and to the Münster chief of police by registered letter, in the following terms:

According to information I have received it is planned in the course of this week (the date has been mentioned as 31st July) to move a large number of inmates of the provincial hospital at Marienthal, classified as "unproductive members of the national community," to the mental hospital at Eichberg, where, as is generally believed to have happened in the case of patients removed from other establishments, they are to be killed with intent. Since such action is not only contrary to the divine and the natural moral law but under article 211 of the German Penal Code ranks as murder and attracts the death penalty, I hereby report the matter in accordance with my obligation under article 139 of the Penal Code and request that steps should at once be taken to protect the patients concerned by proceedings against the authorities planning their removal and murder, and that I may be informed of the action taken.

I have received no information of any action by the State Prosecutor or the police. I had already written on 26th July to the Westphalian provincial authorities, who are responsible for the running of the mental hospital and for the patients entrusted to them for care and for cure, protesting in the strongest terms. It had no effect. And I am now told that 800 patients have already been removed from the hospital at Warstein.

We must expect, therefore, that the poor defenceless patients are, sooner or later, going to be killed. Why? Not because they have committed any offence justifying their death; not because, for example, they have attacked a nurse or attendant, who would be entitled in legitimate self-defence to meet violence with violence. In such a case the use of violence leading to death is permitted and may be called for, as it is in the case of killing an armed enemy.

No: these unfortunate patients are to die, not for some such reason as this but because in the judgment of some official body, on the decision of some committee, they have become "unworthy to live," because they are classed as "unproductive members of the national community." The judgment is that they can no longer produce any goods: they are like an old piece of machinery which no longer works, like an old horse which has become incurably lame, like a cow which no longer gives any milk. What happens to an old piece of machinery? It is thrown on the scrapheap. What happens to a lame horse, an unproductive cow?

I will not pursue the comparison to the end—so fearful is its appropriateness and its illuminating power.

But we are not here concerned with pieces of machinery; we are not dealing with horses and cows, whose sole function is to serve mankind, to produce goods for mankind. They may be broken up, they may be slaughtered when they no longer perform this function.

No: We are concerned with men and women, our fellow-creatures, our brothers and sisters! Poor human beings, ill human beings, they are unproductive, if you will. But does that mean that they have lost the right to live? Have you, have I, the right to live only so long as we are productive, so long as we are recognised by others as productive?

If the principle that man is entitled to kill his unproductive fellow-man is established and applied, then woe betide all of us when we become aged and infirm! If it is legitimate to kill unproductive members of the community, woe betide the disabled who have sacrificed their health or their limbs in the productive process! If unproductive men and women can be disposed of by violent means, woe betide our brave soldiers who return home with major disabilities, as cripples, as invalids!

If it is once admitted that men have the right to kill "unproductive" fellow-men—even though it is at present applied only to poor and defenceless mentally ill patients—then the way is open for the murder of all unproductive men and women: the incurably ill, those disabled in industry or war. The way is open, indeed, for the murder of all of us when we become old and infirm and therefore unproductive. Then it will require only a secret order to be issued that the procedure which has been tried and tested with the mentally ill should be extended to other "unproductive" persons, that it should also be applied to those suffering from incurable tuberculosis, the aged and infirm, persons disabled in industry, soldiers with disabling injuries! Then no man will be safe: some committee or other will be able to put him on the list of "unproductive" persons, who in their judgment have become "unworthy to live." And there will be no police to protect him, no court to avenge his murder and bring his murderers to justice. Who could then have any confidence in a doctor? He might report a patient as unproductive and then be given instructions to kill him! It does not bear thinking of, the moral depravity, the universal mistrust which will spread even in the bosom of the family, if this terrible doctrine is tolerated, accepted and put into practice. Woe betide mankind, woe betide our German people, if the divine commandment, "Thou shalt not kill," which the Lord proclaimed on Sinai amid thunder and lightning, which God our Creator wrote into man's conscience from the beginning, if this commandment is not merely violated but the violation is tolerated and remains unpunished!

I will give you an example of what is happening. One of the patients in Marienthal was a man of 55, a farmer from a country parish in the Münster region—I could give you his name—who has suffered for some years from mental disturbance and was therefore admitted to Marien-

thal hospital. He was not mentally ill in the full sense: he could receive
visits and was always happy when his relatives came to see him. Only a
fortnight ago he was visited by his wife and one of his sons, a soldier on
home leave from the front. The son is much attached to his father, and
the parting was a sad one: no one can tell, whether the soldier will return and see his father again, since he may fall in battle for his country.
The son, the soldier, will certainly never again see his father on earth,
for he has since then been put on the list of the "unproductive." A rela-
tive, who wanted to visit the father this week in Marienthal, was turned
away with the information that the patient had been transferred else-
where on the instructions of the Council of State for National Defence.
No information could be given about where he had been sent, but the
relatives would be informed within a few days. What information will
they be given? The same as in other cases of the kind? That the man has
died, that his body has been cremated, that the ashes will be handed over
on payment of a fee? Then the soldier, risking his life in the field for
his fellow-countrymen, will not see his father again on earth, because
fellow-countrymen at home have killed him.

The facts I have stated are firmly established. I can give the names
of the patient, his wife and his son the soldier, and the place where they
live.

"Thou shalt not kill!" God wrote this commandment in the conscience of man long before any penal code laid down the penalty for
murder, long before there was any prosecutor or any court to investigate
and avenge a murder. Cain, who killed his brother Abel, was a murderer,
long before there were any states or any courts of law. And he confessed
his deed, driven by his accusing conscience: "My punishment is greater
than I can bear . . . and it shall come to pass, that every one that findeth
me the murderer shall slay me" (Genesis 4:13–14).

"Thou shalt not kill!" This commandment from God, who alone has
power to decide on life or death, was written in the hearts of men from
the beginning, long before God gave the children of Israel on Mount
Sinai his moral code in those lapidary sentences inscribed on stone which
are recorded for us in Holy Scripture and which as children we learned
by heart in the catechism.

"I am the Lord thy God!" Thus begins this immutable law. "Thou
shalt have not [sic] other gods before me." God—the only God, transcendent, almighty, omniscient, infinitely holy and just, our Creator and
future Judge—has given us these commandments. Out of love for us he

wrote these commandments in our heart and proclaimed them to us. For they meet the needs of our God-created nature; they are the indispensable norms for all rational, godly, redeeming and holy individual and community life. With these commandments God, our Father, seeks to gather us, His children, as the hen gathers her chickens under her wings. If we follow these commands, these invitations, this call from God, then we shall be guarded and protected and preserved from harm, defended against threatening death and destruction like the chickens under the hen's wings.

"O Jerusalem, Jerusalem . . . how often would I have gathered thy children together, even as a hen gathereth her chickens under her wings, and ye would not!" Is this to come about again in our country of Germany, in our province of Westphalia, in our city of Münster? How far are the divine commandments now obeyed in Germany, how far are they obeyed here in our community?

The eighth commandment: "Thou shalt not bear false witness, thou shalt not lie." How often is it shamelessly and publicly broken!

The seventh commandment: "Thou shalt not steal." Whose possessions are now secure since the arbitrary and ruthless confiscation of the property of our brothers and sisters, members of Catholic orders? Whose property is protected, if this illegally confiscated property is not returned?

The sixth commandment: "Thou shalt not commit adultery." Think of the instructions and assurances on free sexual intercourse and unmarried motherhood in the notorious Open Letter by Rudolf Hess, who has disappeared since, which was published in all the newspapers. And how much shameless and disreputable conduct of this kind do we read about and observe and experience in our city of Münster! To what shamelessness in dress have our young people been forced to get accustomed to—the preparation for future adultery! For modesty, the bulwark of chastity, is about to be destroyed.

And now the fifth commandment: "Thou shalt not kill," is set aside and broken under the eyes of the authorities whose function it should be to protect the rule of law and human life, when men presume to kill innocent fellow-men with intent merely because they are "unproductive," because they can no longer produce any goods.

And how do matters stand with the observance of the fourth commandment, which enjoins us to honour and obey our parents and those in authority over us? The status and authority of parents is already much undermined and is increasingly shaken by all the obligations imposed on children against the will of their parents. Can anyone believe that sincere respect and conscientious obedience to the state authorities can be maintained when men continue to violate the commandments of the supreme authority, the Commandments of God, when they even combat and seek to stamp out faith in the only true transcendent God, the Lord of heaven and earth?

The observance of the first three commandments has in reality for many years been largely suspended among the public in Germany and in Münster. By how many people are Sundays and feast days profaned and withheld from the service of God! How the name of God is abused, dishonoured and blasphemed!

And the first commandment: "Thou shalt have no other gods before me." In place of the only true eternal God men set up their own idols at will and worship them: nature, or the state, or the people, or the race. And how many are there whose God, in Paul's words, "is their belly" (Philippians 3:19)—their own wellbeing, to which they sacrifice all else, even honour and conscience—the pleasures of the senses, the lust for money, the lust for power! In accordance with all this men may indeed seek to arrogate to themselves divine attributes, to make themselves lords over the life and death of their fellow-men.

When Jesus came near to Jerusalem and beheld the city he wept over it, saying: "If thou hadst known, even thou, at least in this thy day, the things which belong unto thy peace! But now they are hid from thine eyes. For the day shall come upon thee, that thine enemies . . . shall lay thee even with the ground, and thy children within thee; and they shall not leave in thee one stone upon another; because thou knewest not the time of thy visitation." Looking with his bodily eyes, Jesus saw only the walls and towers of the city of Jerusalem, but the divine omniscience looked deeper and saw how matters stood within the city and its inhabitants: "O Jerusalem, Jerusalem how often would I have gathered thy children together, as a hen doth gather her brood under her wings—and ye would not!" That is the great sorrow that oppresses Jesus's heart, that brings tears to his eyes. I wanted to act for your good; but ye would not!

Jesus saw how sinful, how terrible, how criminal, how disastrous this unwillingness is. Little man, that frail creature, sets his created will against the will of God! Jerusalem and its inhabitants, his chosen and favoured people, set their will against God's will! Foolishly and criminally, they defy the will of God! And so Jesus weeps over the heinous sin and the inevitable punishment. God is not mocked!

Christians of Münster! Did the Son of God in his omniscience in that day see only Jerusalem and its people? Did he weep only over Jerusalem? Is the people of Israel the only people whom God has encompassed and protected with a father's care and a mother's love, has drawn to Himself? Is it the only people that would not? The only one that rejected God's truth, that threw off God's law and so condemned itself to ruin?

Did Jesus, the omniscient God, also see in that day our German people, our Land of Westphalia, our region of Münster, the Lower Rhineland? Did he also weep over us? Over Münster?

For a thousand years he has instructed our forefathers and us in his truth, guided us with his law, nourished us with his grace, gathered us together as the hen gathers her chickens under her wings. Did the omniscient Son of God see in that day that in our time he must also pronounce this judgment on us: "Ye would not: see, your house will be laid waste!" How terrible that would be!

My Christians! I hope there is still time; but then indeed it is high time: That we may realise, in this our day, the things that belong unto our peace! That we may realise what alone can save us, can preserve us from the divine judgment: that we should take the divine commandments as the guiding rule of our lives and act in sober earnest according to the words, "Rather die than sin."

That in prayer and sincere penitence we should beg that God's forgiveness and mercy may descend upon us, upon our city, our country and our beloved German people.

But with those who continue to provoke God's judgment, who blaspheme our faith, who scorn God's commandments, who make common cause with those who alienate our young people from Christianity, who rob and banish our religious, who bring about the death of innocent men and women, our brothers and sisters—with all those we will avoid any confidential relationship, we will keep ourselves and our families out of reach of their influence, lest we become infected with their godless ways of thinking and acting, lest we become partakers in their guilt and thus liable to the judgment which a just God must and will inflict on all those who, like the ungrateful city of Jerusalem, do not will what God wills.

O God, make us all know, in this our day, before it is too late, the things which belong to our peace!

O most sacred heart of Jesus, grieved to tears at the blindness and iniquities of men, help us through Thy grace, that we may always strive after that which is pleasing to Thee and renounce that which displeases Thee, that we may remain in Thy love and find peace for our souls! Amen

Source: In the St. Lambert's Cathedral, at the time of my visit in 1994, copies of von Galen's summer 1941 sermons, both German and English versions, were made available. The English version from that source is reproduced here.

Notes

Introduction

1. According to Cornwell's account in *Hitler's Pope,* 83, the sheer act of publishing *Mit brennender Sorge* served as an example of the possibilities of resistance. It was printed in twelve different plants and delivered by young couriers by foot or bicycle, often given to parish priests in the confessional. It was read from German pulpits on March 21, 1937. For an in-depth examination of the language used in the encyclical, see Zuccotti, *Under His Very Windows,* 21–23.

2. Dietrich, *Catholic Citizens in the Third Reich,* 158.

3. The closest thing to an admission that Catholics should have done more to help ease the persecution of the Jews would be the document released by the Vatican in March 1998, "We Remember: A Reflection on the Shoah." Von Galen was elevated to the rank of cardinal along with two other "anti-Nazi" bishops, Archbishop Joseph Frings of Cologne and Bishop Konrad, Count von Preysing of Berlin.

4. See works such as Corsten, *Kölner Aktenstücke;* Mariaux, *The Persecution of the Catholic Church in Germany;* Micklem, *National Socialism and the Roman Catholic Church;* Neuhäusler, *Kreuz und Hakenkreuz;* and Rothfels, *German Opposition to Hitler.* Neuhäusler collected Nazi antichurch information until he was arrested and imprisoned for the remainder of the war. His evidence was incorporated into Micklem's work *National Socialism and the Roman Catholic Church.* In 1946 Neuhäusler published *Kreuz und Hakenkreuz.* There were also works by German opponents of Nazism such as Gisevius, *Bis zum bitteren Ende;* Hassell, *The Other Germany;* and Pechel, *Deutscher Widerstand.*

5. The two essays appeared in Schmitthenner and Buchheim, *Der deutsche Widerstand gegen Hitler.* I refer specifically to Conway, *The Nazi Persecution of the Churches, 1933–45;* Lewy, *The Catholic Church and Nazi Germany;* Müller, *Katholische Kirche und Nationalsozialismus;* and Zahn, *German Catholics and Hitler's Wars.*

6. See Nowak, *"Euthanasie" und Sterilisierung im "Dritten Reich".* For other more recent works that address the euthanasia project, see Burleigh, *Death and Deliverance;* Bock,

"Racism and Sexism in Nazi Germany,"271–296; Klee, *"Euthanasie" im NS-Staat;* and Proctor, *Racial Hygiene.*

7. Helmreich, *The German Churches under Hitler.* Helmreich's work addressed the specific role of the churches in resistance. For a more general work on the nature of resistance that was published at about the same time as Helmreich's, see Hoffmann, *The History of the German Resistance.* Hoffmann's definition evaluated resistance according to armed uprising, networks of secret organizations, and the extent to which individuals were ideologically committed to ending National Socialism. Dietrich, *Catholic Citizens in the Third Reich,* 285.

8. See works such as Mason, *Arbeiterklasse und Volksgemeinschaft;* or Detlev Peukert, *Volksgenossen und Gemeinschaftsfremde* (Cologne, 1982).

9. For the definition of resistance, see Peter Hüttenberger's "Vorüberlegungen zum 'Widerstandsbegriff,'" in *Theorien in der Praxis des Historikers,* ed. Kocka; Broszat, *Bayern in der NS-Zeit.* For one of the most critical views of Broszat, questioning the concept of resistance, see Walter Hofer's essay in *Der Widerstand gegen den Nationalsozialismus,* ed. Schmädeke and Steinbach. For a more elaborate account of the historiography of resistance, see Kershaw, *The Nazi Dictatorship,* chap. 8.

10. For Kuropka's discussion of Hehl's work, see "Widerstand gegen den Nationalsozialismus in Münster." I have written a review of this book; see Griech-Polelle, review of *Clemens August Graf von Galen.*

11. Geyer and Boyer, *Resistance against the Third Reich,* 325–350.

12. See Claudia Koonz, "Ethical Dilemmas and Nazi Eugenics: Single-Issue Dissent in Religious Contexts," in *Resistance against the Third Reich,* ed. Geyer and Boyer, 15–38.

13. Here I am referring to the following works: Mussinghoff, *Rassenwahn in Münster;* Kuropka, *Clemens August Graf von Galen;* Sandstede-Auzelle and Sandstede, *Clemens August Graf von Galen;* and Rahner et al., *Treu deutsch sind wir.*

14. See Werner Teuber and Gertrud Seelhorst's essay, "'Die christliche Frohbotschaft ist die von Gott den Menschen aller Rassen geschenkte unveränderliche Wahrheit,' die deutsche Episkopat, der Bischof von Münster und die Juden," in *Clemens August Graf von Galen,* ed. Kuropka, 221–244.

Chapter One: Von Galen's Early Life

1. Portmann, *Kardinal von Galen* (1953), 24. Except for the sermons in the appendix, all quotations from French and German works are my own.

2. Beaugrand, *Kardinal Graf von Galen,* 14.

3. Portmann, *Kardinal von Galen: Ein Gottesmann,* 31.

4. O'Meara, *Church and Culture,* 178.

5. Maria Anna Zumholz, "'Die Tradition meines Hauses': Zur Prägung Clemens August Graf von Galen in Schule und Universität," in *Clemens August Graf von Galen,* ed. Kuropka, 14, 63.

6. Smith, *German Nationalism and Religious Conflict*, 62, 174. The following quotations are from 63 and 75, respectively.

7. Von Galen's text is cited in Portmann, *Kardinal von Galen: Ein Gottesmann*, 76–77.

8. Portmann, *Bischof Graf von Galen spricht!* 20.

9. For the appeal of Nazism in Protestant Prussia, see Baranowski's work *The Sanctity of Rural Life*, where she argues that Pomeranian nobles allowed their resentment of and revulsion for Nazism to be held in check because of the many other areas in which Nazism and their conservatism overlapped.

10. Dietrich, *Catholic Citizens in the Third Reich*, 153.

11. Portmann, *Kardinal von Galen: Ein Gottesmann*, 45–46.

12. Zumholz, "'Die Tradition meines Hauses,'" 14–15; Portmann, *Kardinal von Galen: Ein Gottesmann*, 33.

13. Zumholz, "'Die Tradition meines Hauses,'" 16.

14. Portmann, *Kardinal von Galen: Ein Gottesmann*, 27.

15. Zumholz, "'Die Tradition meines Hauses,'" 20.

16. Friedrich had gone to Rome to study to become a priest. Instead he married Paula von Wendt. Wendt's family was imbued with a sense of "fighting Catholicism," because her father, during the Kulturkampf, had delivered Pope Pius IX's bull in the Prussian Parliament despite Bismarck's outlawing of its reading on German soil.

17. Zumholz, "'Die Tradition meines Hauses,'" 20–21.

18. Portmann, *Kardinal von Galen: Ein Gottesmann*, 45, 43.

19. Zumholz, "'Die Tradition meines Hauses,'" 22.

20. Galen to Franz, June 13, 1900, cited in Zumholz, "'Die Tradition meines Hauses,'" 24.

21. Zumholz, "'Die Tradition meines Hauses,'" 26.

22. Portmann, *Kardinal von Galen: Ein Gottesmann*, 52; McLeod, *Piety and Poverty*, 26.

23. For a detailed description of the rapid modernization of the city of Berlin, see Large, *Berlin*, chaps. 2 and 3. For descriptions of the nightlife of post–World War I Berlin, see Gordon, *Voluptuous Panic*.

24. McLeod, *Piety and Poverty*, 3, 28.

25. For examples of religious strife at the turn of the century in Baden, see Smith's article "Religion and Conflict." Smith argues that anti-Semitism coexisted with confessional antagonisms between Catholics and Protestants.

26. McLeod, *Piety and Poverty*, 86.

27 Ibid., 23, quotation on 117. For Catholic feelings of inferiority and the desire for parity with Protestants, see Baumeister, *Parität und katholische Inferiorität*.

28. Ibid., 53, 54.

29. Galen to his mother, August 3, 1914, quoted in Barbara Imbusch's "'Nicht partei-

politische, sondern katholische Interessen': Clemens August Graf von Galen als Seelsorger in Berlin 1906 bis 1929," in *Clemens August Graf von Galen,* ed. Kuropka, 38.

30. Imbusch, "'Nicht parteipolitische, sondern katholische Interessen," 38.

31. Galen to his mother, September 5, 1917, cited ibid.

32. Report of von Galen about the situation in the East after the war, 1917, cited ibid., 39; quoted phrase in "Erinnerungsbericht Sedgwicks," January 30, 1946, in *Bischof Clemens August Graf von Galen,* ed. Löffler, no. 544, 1290.

33. Cited in Imbusch, "'Nicht parteipolitische, sondern katholische Interessen,'" 39.

34. Portmann, *Kardinal von Galen: Ein Gottesmann,* 71, 73; Imbusch, "'Nicht parteipolitische, sondern katholische Interessen,'" 40.

35. Portmann, *Kardinal von Galen: Ein Gottesmann,* 68; Beaugrand, *Kardinal Graf von Galen,* 20–21.

36. Portmann, *Cardinal von Galen,* 53.

37. McLeod, *Piety and Poverty,* 28.

38. Portmann, *Kardinal von Galen: Ein Gottesmann,* 67.

39. Ibid., 68; Portmann, *Cardinal von Galen,* 53.

40. Portmann, *Kardinal von Galen: Ein Gottesmann,* 66.

41. Quotation in "Gesprächsnotizen v. Galens," June 21, 1945, in *Bischof Clemens August Graf von Galen,* ed. Löffler, no. 483, 1171; Portmann, *Cardinal von Galen,* 53–54.

42. *Dictionnaire d'histoire et de géographie ecclésiastiques,* under the direction of Alfred Baudrillart (Paris, 1912–), s.v. "Galen, Clemens August, Card."; Klocke, *Kardinal von Galen,* 12–13.

43. *Dictionnaire d'histoire et de géographie ecclésiastiques,* s.v. "Galen, Clemens August, Card."

44. Jones, "Catholic Conservatives in the Weimar Republic," 61–65.

45. Ibid., 70–71, 74, quotation on 71.

46. Ibid., 79.

47. Ibid., 80.

48. Ibid., 81.

49. "Katholische Korrespondenz," no. 106, May 2, 1922, cited in Imbusch, "'Nicht parteipolitische, sondern katholische Interessen,'" 41.

50. Here I am referring to portrayals of von Galen contained in the works of Bierbaum, *Nicht lob, nicht furcht;* Hünermann, *Clemens August;* Klocke, *Kardinal von Galen;* Morsey, *Clemens August Kardinal von Galen zum Gedachtnis;* Portmann, *Der Bischof von Münster;* and Portmann, *Kardinal von Galen: Ein Gottesmann.*

Chapter Two: The Legacy of the Kulturkampf

1. Quotation in Stern, *Dreams and Delusions,* 97; See Baumeister, *Parität und katholische Inferiorität, 1890–1914,* for an account of the Catholic search for equality with Protestants.

2. Smith, *German Nationalism and Religious Conflict,* 237, quotation on 113.

3. See Herzog's work *Intimacy and Exclusion* for a revealing examination of the pre-Kulturkampf struggles between Catholics and Protestants to define Germanness.

4. Quotation in O'Meara, *Church and Culture,* 19; see Blackbourn, *Class, Religion and Local Politics in Wilhelmine Germany;* Blackbourn and Eley, *The Peculiarities of German History;* and Levy, *The Downfall of the Anti-Semitic Liberal Parties in Imperial Germany.*

5. O'Meara, *Church and Culture,* 20.

6. The literature on the official Kulturkampf is immense. For a detailed account, see Weber, *Kirchliche Politik zwischen Rom, Berlin, und Trier.* For a concise chronological summary and a detailed bibliography, see Rudolf Lill, "Der Kulturkampf in Preussen und im Deutschen Reich (bis 1878)," in *Handbuch der Kirchengeschichte,* no. 2, ed. Jedin, 28–47. See also studies by Evans, *The German Center Party,* and Sperber, *Popular Catholicism in Nineteenth-Century Germany.*

7. Carroll, *Constantine's Sword,* 487.

8. Ibid., 491; quotation in O'Meara, *Church and Culture,* 24.

9. Stolz, "Schreibende Hand auf Wand und Sand."

10. See Heilbronner, "From Ghetto to Ghetto," for a presentation of the place of German Catholic historians, arguing that many are still mentally imprisoned in a ghetto.

11. Treitschke, *History of Germany in the Nineteenth Century,* 20.

12. Smith, *German Nationalism and Religious Conflict,* 208.

13. Heinrich von Sybel, "Klerikale Politik im 19. Jahrhundert," in *Kleine Schriften,* 450; Heinrich von Treitschke, "Osterreich und das deutsche Reich," in *Zehn Jahr deutscher Kämpfe* (Berlin, 1879), 367.

14. Smith, *German Nationalism and Religious Conflict,* 37.

15. Pulzer, *The Rise of Political Anti-Semitism in Germany and Austria,* 274.

16. Cited in Dietrich, *Catholic Citizens in the Third Reich,* 14.

17. Rohling, *Der Talmudjude;* Rebbert, *Blicke in's Talmudische Judentum,* 8, 13–14, 81, 88–89.

18. Cited in Tal, *Christians and Jews in Germany,* 92–93.

19. This is not to imply that Catholics and conservative Protestants were completely willing to overlook their confessional animosities. For assertions that anti-Semitism did not always work to unify Catholics and Protestants, see Bergen, "Catholics, Protestants, and Christian anti-Semitism in Nazi Germany"; and Smith, "The Learned and the Popular Discourse of Anti-Semitism in the Catholic Milieu of the Kaiserreich."

20. Marvin Perry, "Racial Nationalism and the Rise of Modern Anti-Semitism," in *Jewish-Christian Encounters over the Centuries,* ed. Perry and Schweitzer, 261.

21. Stern, *Dreams and Delusions,* 108.

22. Ibid., 111.

23. Smith, *German Nationalism and Religious Conflict,* 92; Helmreich, *The German Churches under Hitler,* 57.

24. Sperber, *Popular Catholicism in Nineteenth-Century Germany,* 227–228; quotation in Smith, *German Nationalism and Religious Conflict,* 44.

25. Smith, *German Nationalism and Religious Conflict,* 123, quotation on 127.

26. Ibid., 200–201.

27. Rector Matchewsky, chairman of the Union of German Catholics, in *Katholische Rundschau.*

28. A pamphlet, *Der Mauscheljude,* was published in 1879 in Paderborn; there the anonymous author asserted that the Poles of Posen and West Prussia were no more German than the Jews were. Smith, "The Learned and the Popular Discourse of Anti-Semitism in the Catholic Milieu of the Kaiserreich," 317.

29. Dietrich, *Catholic Citizens in the Third Reich,* 40.

30. Ibid., 52.

31. Gallin, *German Resistance to Hitler,* 216; Helmreich, *The German Churches under Hitler,* 366.

32. Helmreich, *The German Churches under Hitler,* 256.

33. National Archives, T-175, roll 270, frame 2766403; quotation in Helmreich, *The German Churches under Hitler,* 240.

34. Müller, *Katholische Kirche und Nationalsozialismus,* 79; Clergymen's fears of Catholics abandoning the church in the event of an all-out, open confrontation with the government are discussed in Pawlikowski's "Catholic Leadership and the Holocaust."

35. Cited in Tinnemann's "Attitudes of the German Catholic Hierarchy toward the Nazi Regime," 340ff. The Dolchstosslegende, or the stab-in-the-back myth, argued that Germany's military would never have lost the First World War had it not been for internal enemies (German civilians) who agreed to the November 11, 1918, armistice.

36. Stern, *Dreams and Delusions,* 189.

37. "Vorwort v. Galens zum Hirtenbrief der deutschen Bischöfe," August 25, 1935, *Bischof Clemens August Graf von Galen,* ed. Löffler, no. 127, 281.

38. All of my biblical quotations are taken from the Jerusalem Bible.

39. "Entwurf v. Galens zu einem gemeinsam Hirtenwort der deutschen Bishöfe," end of December 1935, *Bischof Clemens August Graf von Galen,* ed. Löffler, no. 146, 325–326.

40. Lüninck was the Oberpresident of the province of Westphalia. See chapter 1 for more information about him. He was replaced by Dr. Alfred Meyer on July 21, 1938, and

he later joined resistance circles. He was arrested after the July 20, 1944, plot failed, tried November 13, 1944, found guilty of treason, and killed in Berlin-Plötzensee; Lüninck to Frick, June 3, 1935, *Bischof Clemens August Graf von Galen,* ed. Löffler, no. 101, 226, 227; June 14, 1935, no. 109, 241–242.

41. "Anlage v. Galen an Gestapo Münster," August 9, 1935, *Bischof Clemens August Graf von Galen,* ed. Löffler, no. 123/III, 272.

42. Ibid.

43. Article 31 of the Concordat promised to keep Catholic Unions open.

44. "Ansprache v. Galens auf der Dechantenkonferenz," October 28, 1935, *Bischof Clemens August Graf von Galen,* ed. Löffler, no. 139, 301–309.

45. Ibid., 310.

46. Ibid., 310–312.

47. "Fastenhirtenbrief v. Galens," January 12, 1941, *Bischof Clemens August Graf von Galen,* ed. Löffler, no. 325, 816, 817, 822, quotation on 816.

48. Ibid., 826, 827.

49. Portmann, *Cardinal von Galen,* 66–67.

50. Klemm to Frick, July 13, 1935, *Bischof Clemens August Graf von Galen,* ed. Löffler, no. 118, 260, 261.

51. Portmann, *Cardinal von Galen,* 67, 68, quotations on 67.

52. Ibid., 68.

53. "Ansprache v. Galens," January 20, 1935, *Bischof Clemens August Graf von Galen,* ed. Löffler, no. 83, 166.

54. Ibid., 167.

55. Bishop Sproll was one of the few German Roman Catholic bishops to be imprisoned by the Nazis in a concentration camp. "Hirtenbrief v. Galens," July 27, 1938, *Bischof Clemens August Graf von Galen,* ed. Löffler, no. 256, 651.

56. Article 23 of the Concordat guaranteed the continued existence of confessional schools on German soil. Gestapo agents made note of this sermon, but no action was taken against von Galen. Löffler, *Bischof Clemens August Graf von Galen,* 653.

57. For a detailed report on the fate of all Jewish families in Telgte, see the study by Rüter and Westhoff, *Geschichte und Schicksal der Telgter Juden.* Ironically, the two men who did the study were students at the Kardinal-von-Galen-Realschule. Portmann, *Cardinal von Galen,* 88.

58. Rüter and Westhoff, *Geschichte und Schicksal der Telgter Juden,* 18; quotation in Portmann, *Cardinal von Galen,* 84.

59. Husen, "The 20th of July and the German Catholics," 4.

60. Ibid., 5. Niemöller himself drew on scriptural traditions of anti-Semitism explaining the centuries of Jewish persecution, "Dearly beloved, the answer is evident, the Jews

have caused the crucifixion of God's Christ. . . . They bear the curse. . . . They drag with them as a fearsome burden the unforgiven blood-guilt of their fathers." Quoted in Bergen, "Catholics, Protestants, and Christian Antisemitism in Nazi Germany," 332.

61. Helmreich, *The German Churches under Hitler*, 277.

62. Oberländer, "My God, They Just Have Other Interests."

63. Ibid., 39, 40–48, quotation on 48.

Chapter Three: Von Galen and Church-State Relations

1. Gallin, *German Resistance to Hitler*, 28.

2. Ibid.

3. Helmreich, *The German Churches under Hitler*, 366.

4. Gallin, *German Resistance to Hitler*, 32.

5. O'Meara, *Church and Culture*, 34–43.

6. Koch, *A Handbook of Moral Theology*, 168.

7. Gallin, *German Resistance to Hitler*, 30, 32, quotation on 32.

8. Husen, "The 20th of July and the German Catholics," 7. The Kreisau Circle was an opposition group named after Kreisau, the home of Count Helmuth von Moltke. The group met to discuss and to plan for the restructuring of Germany after the war.

9. Gallin, *German Resistance to Hitler*, 229.

10. Helmreich, *The German Churches under Hitler*, 239.

11. Ibid.

12. Portmann, *Kardinal von Galen: Ein Gottesmann*, 82.

13. Portmann, *Cardinal von Galen*, 60. SA is the abbreviation for Sturmabteilung (storm troopers). Also known as the Brownshirts, they served as a paramilitary organization of the Nazi Party. The SA was disbanded after a purge in the summer of 1934. SS is the abbreviation for Schutzstaffeln (defense [protection] squads). Originally an elite group of bodyguards for Hitler, they became the chief information gatherers for Heinrich Himmler. The SS eventually ran the concentration camp system.

14. Ibid., 59; Pieper, *No One Could Have Known*, 93.

15. "Erlass v. Galens," July 9, 1934, *Bischof Clemens August Graf von Galen*, ed. Löffler, no. 54, 101–103.

16. Pieper, *No One Could Have Known*, 95.

17. Helmreich, *The German Churches under Hitler*, 241.

18. "Fastenhirtenbrief v. Galens," January 12, 1941, *Bischof Clemens August Graf von Galen*, ed. Löffler, no. 325, 816–827.

19. Helmreich, *The German Churches under Hitler*, 296, 240.

20. "Predigt v. Galens," September 6, 1936, *Bischof Clemens August Graf von Galen*, ed. Löffler, no. 189, 439.

21. Ibid., 439–447.

22. Pieper, *No One Could Have Known*, 190.

23. Portmann, *Cardinal von Galen*, 85.

24. Helmreich, *The German Churches under Hitler*, 347.

25. Sermon reproduced in the appendix; also in *Clemens August Kardinal von Galen: Predigten in dunkler Zeit* (Münster, 1994), 27. See chap. 4 of this volume for an in-depth examination of all three sermons.

26. Dietrich, *Catholic Citizens in the Third Reich*, 227–228.

27. "Ansprache v. Galens auf der Dechantenkonferenz," October 28, 1935, *Bischof Clemens August Graf von Galen*, ed. Löffler, no. 139, 301–313.

28. Dietrich, *Catholic Citizens in the Third Reich*, 84.

29. Werner Jeanrond, "From Resistance to Liberation Theology: German Theologians and the Non/Resistance to the National Socialist Regime," in *Resistance against the Third Reich, 1933–90*, ed. Geyer and Boyer, 298, 299; Dietrich, *Catholic Citizens in the Third Reich*, 51; Ward, "Guilt and Innocence," 421. The Enabling Act, passed March 23, 1933, abolished the basic principles of democracy in Germany. It allowed the Reich government the right to pass laws that deviated from the Weimar Constitution. It also allowed Hitler, as chancellor, to draw up laws bypassing the president. Most people felt that the Enabling Act made Hitler a legal dictator in Germany.

30. Dietrich, *Catholic Citizens in the Third Reich*, 137–138.

31. Ibid., 112.

32. "Vorwort v. Galens zum Hirtenbrief der deutschen Bischöfe," August 25, 1935, *Bischof Clemens August Graf von Galen*, ed. Löffler, no. 127, 281.

33. Helmreich, *The German Churches under Hitler*, 255, 256, quotation on 255.

34. Details cited in Helmreich, *The German Churches under Hitler*, 253–254, quotation on 254.

35. Ibid., 276.

36. Ibid., 277.

37. Ibid., 277, 361–362, quotation on 361–362.

38. See Zuccotti, *Under His Very Windows*, 33–35, for the distinctions made by clergymen between racism and anti-Semitism.

39. Mussinghoff, *Rassenwahn in Münster*.

40. Portmann, *Kardinal von Galen: Ein Gottesmann*, 88.

41. Ibid., 216.

42. See Heilbronner, *Catholicism, Political Culture, and the Countryside*. Heilbronner's study of Baden-Württemburg reveals that anticlerical Catholics tended to imitate Protestant behavioral patterns in their attempts to break free of what they viewed as a Catholic ghetto. Their tremendous fears regarding Communism and socialism influenced them to choose the Nazi Party over the Catholic Center Party.

43. Portmann, *Kardinal von Galen: Ein Gottesmann,* 10–11.

44. As Helmut Walser Smith's research has shown, anti-Semitism had permeated Catholic almanacs, pamphlets, and newspapers as well as theological treatises. It was different from racial anti-Semitism, but myths regarding Jews had been effectively disseminated into Catholic popular culture. See Smith, "The Learned and Popular Discourse of Anti-Semitism in the Catholic Milieu of the Kaiserreich."

45. Portmann, *Cardinal von Galen,* 63; Dietrich, *Catholic Citizens in the Third Reich,* 242.

46. Dietrich, *Catholic Citizens in the Third Reich,* 186.

47. Cited in Portmann, *Bischof Graf von Galen Spricht!* 41.

48. Dietrich, *Catholic Citizens in the Third Reich,* 14; Smith, *German Nationalism and Religious Conflict,* 155, 160, 144.

49. Portmann, *Cardinal von Galen,* 166.

50. Dietrich, *Catholic Citizens in the Third Reich,* 185; Przywara, "Judentum und Christentum: Zwischen Orient und Okzident," 83, 98–99.

51. Dietrich, *Catholic Citizens in the Third Reich,* 71.

52. Ibid., 193; Fuchs, "Ein Bischofswort über das Alte Testament," 471–472.

53. Fuchs, "Ein Bischofswort über das Alte Testament," 184.

54. Dietrich, *Catholic Citizens in the Third Reich,* 207, 209.

55. Gallin, *German Resistance to Hitler,* 37, 187.

56. Zuccotti, *Under His Very Windows,* 35.

Chapter Four: Von Galen, Eugenics, and the Nazis

1. Here I am referring specifically to the presentation of von Galen as a "symbolic resister" in the recent essay of Kuropka, "Leistete Clemens August Graf von Galen Widerstand gegen den Nationalsozialismus?" in *Clemens August Graf von Galen,* ed. Kuropka, 371–390.

2. Gallin, *German Resistance to Hitler,* 139; Portmann, *Cardinal von Galen,* 64; the oath quoted in Gallin, *German Resistance to Hitler,* 141.

3. Gallin, *German Resistance to Hitler,* 141; quotation in Dietrich, *Catholic Citizens in the Third Reich,* 153.

4. Helmreich, *The German Churches under Hitler,* 287; Ethel Mary Tinnemann, "Attitudes of the German Catholic Hierarchy toward the Nazi Regime," 335–340.

5. Harcourt, *The German Catholics,* 190–191.

6. Lehr, *Germans against Hitler.*

7. Gallin, *German Resistance to Hitler,* 225.

8. Dietrich, *Catholic Citizens in the Third Reich,* 154.

9. Lehr, *Germans against Hitler.*

10. See in particular Hehl and Repgen's *Priester unter Hitlers Terror.*

11. "Aus den Meldungen aus dem Reich," August 14, 1942, *Meldungen aus Münster,* ed. Kuropka, no. 156, 566, 586, quotation on 566.

12. Portmann, *Cardinal von Galen,* 102, emphasis mine.

13. Helmreich, *The German Churches under Hitler,* 357.

14. Göring to Galen, March 5, 1942, no. 364, 938-939; Galen to Göring, March 16, 1942, no. 368, 947-948, *Bischof Clemens August Graf von Galen,* ed. Löffler.

15. Proctor, *Racial Hygiene,* 177.

16. For the most recent literature discussing euthanasia in German society, see Burleigh, *Death and Deliverance;* Friedlander, *The Origins of Nazi Genocide;* and Proctor, *Racial Hygiene.* For a historical discussion on the principle of euthanasia in German society prior to 1933, see Klaus Dörner, "Nationalsozialismus und Lebensvernichtung," 121-137. See also Neuhäusler, *Kreuz und Hakenkreuz,* 2:307-308, 354-356. The quotation is in Proctor, *Racial Hygiene,* 177.

17. According to Proctor's research, half of Germany's institutionalized mentally ill had died during World War I from starvation and disease. The patients were ranked very low on the rations list. Proctor, *Racial Hygiene,* 178.

18. Cited in Noakes and Pridham, *Nazism 1919-1945,* 998.

19. Ibid., no. 718, 1000, 1001.

20. Cited in Proctor, *Racial Hygiene,* 179.

21. For a good description of the movie *Ich klage an!* see Adolph, *Kardinal Preysing und zwei Diktaturen,* 167-68. For an in-depth examination of how the movie came about, see Burleigh, *Death and Deliverance,* chap. 6, 183-219.

22. *Hitlerschnitt* (Hitler's cut) was the popular vernacular for forced sterilization, one of Hitler's other solutions. Proctor, *Racial Hygiene,* 102, 95. See Bock, "Racism and Sexism in Nazi Germany," 271.

23. Proctor, *Racial Hygiene,* 95. The following countries legalized sterilization of the mentally ill and the criminally insane on the dates indicated: Norway, 1934; Sweden, 1935; Finland, 1935; Estonia, 1936; Iceland, 1938. Later Cuba, Czechoslovakia, Yugoslavia, Lithuania, Latvia, Hungary, and Turkey also joined this list (97-98).

24. Bock, "Racism and Sexism in Nazi Germany," 273; Burleigh, *Death and Deliverance,* 36.

25. Burleigh, *Death and Deliverance,* 36, 37.

26. Ibid., 38, quotation on 40. As prescient as Bumke was, he ignored his own warnings and by the 1940s had become an advocate for the National Socialist eugenics legislation.

27. Ibid., 38.

28. Ibid., 41.

29. Proctor, *Racial Hygiene,* 102.

30. Phayer, *Protestant and Catholic German Women in Nazi Germany,* 84.

31. Ibid., 85, 86, quotations on 85.

32. Burleigh, *Death and Deliverance*, 43, 45, quotation on 43; for a description of the films, see 187–191.

33. *Reichsgesetzblatt* I (1933): 529–531; Helmreich, *The German Churches under Hitler*, 253–254; quotation in Claudia Koonz, "Ethical Dilemmas and Nazi Eugenics: Single-Issue Dissent in Religious Contexts," in *Resistance against the Third Reich*, ed. Geyer and Boyer, 29.

34. "Protokoll der Verhandlungen der Plenar-Konferenz der deutschen Bischofe vom 29. bis 31. August 1933," photocopy of a manuscript, 12 (this title cited in Lewy, *The Catholic Church and Nazi Germany*); Koonz, "Ethical Dilemmas and Nazi Eugenics," 33.

35. Freemantle, *The Papal Encyclicals in Their Historical Context*, 235–243; Mayer, *Gesetzliche Unfruchtbarmachung Geisteskranker*, 113, 121, 124–125, 128, 352, 373–386, 422, 434; *Ecclesiastica* 14 (1934): 345–346 (incidentally, both Eschweiler and Barion joined the Nazi Party in May 1933); Walther, *Die Euthanasie und die Heiligkeit des Lebens*, 22; Schilling, "Richtiges und Falsches bei der sog. Eugenik," 570–572, 597–598.

36. For discussions about the role that priests and nuns played in the involuntary sterilization and euthanasia processes, see Burleigh, *Death and Deliverance*, chap. 5; Ernst Klee, *"Euthanasia" im NS-Staat*, 49; and Koonz, "Ethical Dilemmas and Nazi Eugenics," 15–38.

37. Dietrich, *Catholic Citizens in the Third Reich*, 223; quotation in Lewy, *The Catholic Church and Nazi Germany*, 262.

38. Koonz, "Ethical Dilemmas and Nazi Eugenics," 24–25, 19. Frick's speech was given in Münster, July 7, 1935. In it he stated that the sterilization law was binding on Catholics. He attempted to force Catholic compliance. Rome protested state intervention in church teaching. Hitler intervened on July 16, 1935, by replacing Frick with Hans Kerrl, in the newly created Ministry of Church Affairs. See Helmreich, *The German Churches under Hitler*, 272–273.

39. Bock, "Racism and Sexism in Nazi Germany," 277.

40. Proctor, *Racial Hygiene*, 102–104, quotation on 104.

41. Ibid., 106, 107; Bock, "Racism and Sexism in Nazi Germany," 280–281, 282.

42. Burleigh estimates 400,000; Proctor's figures are 300,000–350,000, and Bock's are 350,000–400,000. Burleigh, *Death and Deliverance*, 56; Proctor, *Racial Hygiene*, 108; Bock, "Racism and Sexism in Nazi Germany," 282.

43. Proctor, *Racial Hygiene*, 114–115.

44. Bock, "Racism and Sexism in Nazi Germany," 282.

45. Burleigh, *Death and Deliverance*, 53; Phayer, *Protestant and Catholic German Women in Nazi Germany*, 118.

46. Quotation in Proctor, *Racial Hygiene*, 182; Gruchmann, "Euthanasie und Justiz im Dritten Reich," 238; Helmreich, *The German Churches under Hitler*, 311.

47. Proctor, *Racial Hygiene*, 186; Noakes and Pridham, *Nazism 1919–1945*, 1009.

48. Burleigh and Wippermann, *The Racial State*, 152; Burleigh, *Death and Deliverance*, 172.

49. Noakes and Pridham, *Nazism 1919–1945*, no. 755, 1034; Burleigh, *Death and Deliverance*, 173.

50. Quotation in Dietrich, *Catholic Citizens in the Third Reich*, 215; Freemantle, *The Papal Encyclicals in their Historical Context*, 263-270; Galen to Bertram, July 28, 1940, *Bischof Clemens August Graf von Galen*, ed. Löffler, no. 310, 794, 796.

51. "Aufzeichnungen Kolbows," July 25, 1939, *Bischof Clemens August Graf von Galen*, ed. Löffler, no. 286, 737; Helmreich, *The German Churches under Hitler*, 311.

52. Brandt, *Friedrich von Bodelschwingh*, 209.

53. Ehrhardt, *Euthanasie und Vernichtung "lebensunwerten" Lebens*, 37.

54. Brandt, *Friedrich von Bodelschwingh*, 186-187, 208.

55. Gruchmann, "Euthanasie und Justiz im Dritten Reich," 242.

56. Helmreich, *The German Churches under Hitler*, 311, 312; quotation in Noakes and Pridham, *Nazism 1919–1945*, no. 756, 1035.l.

57. Quotation in Schäfer, *Landesbischof D. Wurm und der Nationalsozialistische Staat*, 119-124; Wurm, *Erinnerungen aus meinem Leben*, 155.

58. Here I am referring to a large body of work ranging from the earliest biographies of von Galen to more recent studies. Because most of these works focus exclusively on von Galen and Catholicism, they have neglected the connections between Protestants and the bishop. See works such as Bierbaum, *Nicht lob, nicht furcht*; Portmann, *Kardinal von Galen* (1953); Kuropka, *Clemens August Graf von Galen*; Kuropka, "Widerstand gegen den Nationalsozialismus in Münster"; and Sandstede-Auzelle and Sandstede, *Clemens August Graf von Galen.*

59. See the research of Aly, *"Final Solution,"* 243-244, for proof that in some cases parents of handicapped children did not object to the murder of their own children, so long as they were not informed of the true cause of death. Burleigh, *Death and Deliverance.*

60. Dietrich, *Catholic Citizens in the Third Reich*, 231.

61. For more information on Wienken, see Höllen, *Heinrich Wienken, der "unpolitische" Kirchenpolitiker;* and Heinrich Missalla, *Für Volk und Vaterland: Die Kirchliche Kriegshilfe im Zweiten Weltkrieg* (Königstein, 1978). Quotation in Dietrich, *Catholic Citizens in the Third Reich*, 232.

62. Burleigh, *Death and Deliverance*, 174, quotation on 175. See Wienken to Galen, October 20, 1943, no. 394, 1010-1011; December 15, 1943, no. 402, 1025-1027; December 20, 1943, no. 403, 1027-1029; January 7, 1944, no. 405, 1031; May 23, 1945, no. 471, 1145-1146, *Bischof Clemens August Graf von Galen*, ed. Löffler.

63. Burleigh, *Death and Deliverance*, 175; Neuhäusler, *Kreuz und Hakenkreuz*, 2:357-363; quotation in Noakes and Pridham, *Nazism 1919–1945*, no. 757, 1035; Blet et al., *Actes et documents du Saint Siege relatifs à la Seconde Guerre Mondiale*, 2:208-209. Whether a co-

incidence or not, Konrad von Preysing, bishop of Berlin, gave an anti-euthanasia sermon on March 9, 1941. See Rahner et al., *Treu deutsch sind wir*, 45.

64. Cited in Dietrich, *Catholic Citizens in the Third Reich*, 226.

65. Blet et al., *Actes et documents du Saint Siege relatifs à la Seconde Guerre Mondiale*, 2:224.

66. Helmreich, *The German Churches under Hitler*, 360.

67. Ibid. See Aly, *"Final Solution,"* 203, where he asserts that the RAF specifically targeted cities with Catholic populations in northwestern Germany, including Münster, because they believed that Catholics were not as deeply committed to National Socialism. See also Schwartz's research on voting statistics for Münster: "Widerstand und Verweigerung im Münsterland."

68. Portmann, *Cardinal von Galen*, 100–102, quotations on 102.

69. Ibid., 103.

70. Ibid., 104.

71. Von Galen's sermon of July 13, 1941, in the appendix to this volume (hereafter Sermon of July 13, 1941).

72. Ibid., 16, 17.

73. In the summer of 1943, the bishop of Canterbury complained that both von Galen's and Bishop Wurm's protests were motivated by self-protection rather than a sense of lost justice. He also noted their silence concerning the mass murders of Poles and Jews; see Rahner et al., *Treu deutsch sind wir*, 46.

74. Sermon of July 13, 1941.

75. Portmann, *Cardinal von Galen*, 105; Helmreich, *The German Churches under Hitler*, 359.

76. Portmann, *Cardinal von Galen*, 106.

77. Ibid., 106–107.

78. Sermon of July 20, 1941 (see appendix).

79. Ibid., 27.

80. Ibid., 28.

81. Ibid., 31.

82. See Aly, *"Final Solution,"* 204–205, where he argues that Hitler viewed von Galen's sermon as defeatist but attempted to react flexibly to the already strained public mood. Burleigh, *Death and Deliverance*, 178.

83. Sermon of August 3, 1941 (see appendix).

84. Ibid., 36–37, 38–41. Article 211 stated that an individual was guilty of murder if convicted of killing another person.

85. Ibid., 41–45.

86. Ibid., 45, emphasis mine.

87. Bauer, *A History of the Holocaust*, 9.

88. Dietrich, *Catholic Citizens in the Third Reich*, 241.

89. R. L. Sedgwick, in the introduction to Portmann's *Cardinal von Galen*, 12.

90. Ibid., 13.

91. "Predigt v. Galens," July 20, 1941, *Bischof Clemens August Graf von Galen*, ed. Löffler, no. 336, 863; Neuhäusler, *Kreuz und Hakenkreuz*, 2:371–373. Rahner et al., *Treu deutsch sind wir*, assert that not only did von Galen remain silent over the murder of Jews in the East; in 1943, when the euthanasia project resumed in areas such as Essen, the bishop, although informed, maintained his silence (45).

92. Löffler, *Bischof Clemens August Graf von Galen*, no. 340, 870, 871. Father Mucker-mann died in Switzerland, April 2, 1946; Father Maring died in Sachsenhausen on April 7, 1943.

93. Ibid., 871, 872, 873.

94. Ibid., no. 342, 884.

95. Ibid., 890–892, quotations on 890 and 891.

96. Ibid., no. 343, 894, 895, quotation on 895.

97. Ibid., 895; "Aus dem Lagebericht der NSDAP-Gauleitung Westfalen-Nord für Ok-tober," *Meldungen aus Münster*, ed. Kuropka, no. 135, 551–552, quotation on 552. There is a hint that T-4 personnel were actually involved in the murder of wounded German soldiers on the Eastern Front. See Burleigh, *Death and Deliverance*, 160.

98. Meyer to Bormann, August 13, 1941, *Bischof Clemens August Graf von Galen*, ed. Löffler, no. 343, 895, 896, 897.

99. Portmann, *Bischof Graf von Galen Spricht!* 103, 105, 106, 107, quotation on 106.

100. Ibid., 104, 105; quotation in entry of July 4, 1942, *Hitlers Tischgespräche im Führer-hauptquartier*, ed. Picker, 372–373.

101. Portmann, *Cardinal von Galen*, 145.

102. Burleigh, *Death and Deliverance*, 178.

103. Ibid., 179, 180. Paula S. was interviewed by Michael Burleigh in 1991.

104. Portmann, *Cardinal von Galen*, 108–109; quoted phrase in "Aus den Meldungen aus dem Reich," November 19, 1941, no. 141, 557; January 19, 1942, no. 146, 558; March 20, 1942, no. 149, 560; April 10, 1942, no. 152, 561, *Meldungen aus Münster*, ed. Kuropka; remaining quotations in Portmann, *Cardinal von Galen*, 109. Franz himself was arrested and liberated from Sachsenhausen at the end of the war.

105. "Aus dem Bericht des Inspekteurs der Sicherheitspolizei und des SD," August 20, 1941, no. 123, 542–543; September 25, 1941, no. 128, 545, *Meldungen aus Münster*, ed. Kuropka.

106. "Aus dem Bericht des Abteilungsleiters für Propananda an den Reichspropagan-daminister Dr. Goebbels," August 12, 1941, *Meldungen aus Münster*, ed. Kuropka, no. 117, 537.

107. "Aus dem Schreiben eines Rüstungbetriebes an die Staatspolizeileitstelle Münster

und die NSDAP-Gauleitung Westfalen-Nord," August 15, 1941, *Meldungen aus Münster,* ed. Kuropka, no. 122, 541.

108. "Meis an Oberstaatsanwalt in Kleve," September 27, 1941, no. 352, 913; "Meis an Oberstaatsanwalt in Kleve," October 3, 1941, no. 353, 914; Stosch to Galen, December 18, 1942, no. 374, 965, *Bischof Clemens August Graf von Galen,* ed. Löffler.

109. "Erklärung des Generalvikariats Münster," November 19, 1941, *Bischof Clemens August Graf von Galen,* ed. Löffler, no. 356, 919-920.

110. Ibid., 919.

111. Ibid.

112. "Aus den Meldungen der Staatspolizeileitstellen im Bereich des Inspekteurs der Sicherheitspolizei," August 8-13, 1941, *Meldungen aus Münster,* ed. Kuropka, no. 119, 539-540.

113. "Aus dem Lagebericht des Generalstaatsanwalts in Hamm an den Reichsminister der Justiz," November 30, 1941, no. 137, 556; "Aus dem Bericht des Inspekteurs der Sicherheitspolizei und des SD," October 6, 1941, no. 134, 550; September 30, 1941, no. 130, 547, *Meldungen aus Münster,* ed. Kuropka.

114. Burleigh and Wipperman, *The Racial State,* 156, 157.

115. Gruchmann, "Euthanasie und Justiz im Dritten Reich," 277-278; Helmreich, *The German Churches under Hitler,* 313. See also Burleigh, *Death and Deliverance,* 180; or Rahner et al., *Treu deutsch sind wir.* Rahner argues that von Galen had knowledge of a revived euthanasia project being carried out in Essen in 1943 and remained silent (45).

116. See Burleigh's work in particular.

117. Burleigh, *Death and Deliverance,* 180; Burleigh and Wippermann, *The Racial State,* 153.

118. Stoltzfus, "Dissent in Nazi Germany," 94, quotation on 92; Phayer, *The Catholic Church and the Holocaust,* 177-178.

119. Aly, *"Final Solution,"* 245.

120. "Hirtenbrief v. Galens," September 14, 1941, *Bischof Clemens August Graf von Galen,* ed. Löffler, no. 348, 901, 902-903, 907, 909, quotations on 902-903 and 907.

121. Helmreich, *The German Churches under Hitler,* 350.

122. Anonymous letter to Galen, September 19, 1941, *Bischof Clemens August Graf von Galen,* ed. Löffler, no. 350, 910-911.

123. Rahner et al., *Treu deutsch sind wir,* 42. Here I would like to point out a difference between my interpretation and Rahner's. Although Rahner reveals the evidence regarding the local NSDAP leadership, he still emphasizes throughout his work that von Galen's name came to represent symbolic Catholic resistance.

124. Helmreich, *The German Churches under Hitler,* 363.

125. Boberbach, *Berichte des SD und der Gestapo über Kirchen und Kirchenvolk in Deutschland,* 943-944.

126. Hofmann, *Zeugnis und Kampfe des deutschen Episkopats,* 72; Neuhaüsler, *Kreuz und Hakenkreuz,* 2:70.

Chapter Five: Von Galen and the Jews

1. "Erinnerungsbericht Sedgwick," January 30, 1946, *Bischof Clemens August Graf von Galen,* ed. Löffler, no. 544, 1290.

2. Rahner et al., *Treu deutsch sind wir,* 41.

3. "Lagebericht-Münster," October 1934, *Meldungen aus Münster,* ed. Kuropka, no. 4, 282.

4. "Entwurf v. Galens für eine Denkschrift an Hitler," May 1935, *Bischof Clemens August Graf von Galen,* ed. Löffler, no. 97, 206, 208–211, 218–221, quotation on 206.

5. Galen to Meyer, June 3, 1935, *Bischof Clemens August Graf von Galen,* ed. Löffler, no. 102, 228, 229.

6. Rahner et al., *Treu deutsch sind wir,* 48.

7. Neville Laski, "Report on Journey to Austria, Poland and Danzig. August 15 to 31, 1934," quoted in Hagen, "Before the 'Final Solution,'" 357.

8. Dietrich, *Catholic Citizens in the Third Reich,* 233; Dawidowicz, *A Holocaust Reader.*

9. Rohling's *Talmud-Jew,* published in Münster, was a standard reference work on Jewish religious practices. Münster's Bonifacius Verein distributed 38,000 copies of it gratis. Smith, "The Learned and the Popular Discourse of Anti-Semitism," 321; Kuropka, "Vom Antisemitismus zum Holocaust," 187–188.

10. Kuropka, "Vom Antisemitismus zum Holocaust," 187–188.

11. Ibid., 190. See also "15 Jahre NSDAP Münster, Kreistreffen," October 15–17, 1937, 6, 8, Stadtarchiv Münster.

12. Hans-Joachim Bieber, "Anti-Semitism as a Reflection of Social, Economic and Political Tensions in Germany: 1880–1933," in *Jews and Germans from 1860 to 1933: The Problematic Symbiosis,* ed. David Bronson (Heidelberg, 1979), 46.

13. Gundlach, "Antisemitismus," 1:504; see also Lewy, *The Catholic Church and Nazi Germany,* 80, 271.

14. Cited in Dietrich, *Catholic Citizens in the Third Reich,* 234.

15. Ibid., 234; Hagen, "Before the 'Final Solution,'" 358.

16. Erb, *Bernhard Lichtenberg,* 43; Dietrich, *Catholic Citizens in the Third Reich,* 235; quoted phrase in "Entwurf v. Galens für ein Hirtenwort der Westdeutschen Bischöfe," February 1946, *Bischof Clemens August Graf von Galen,* ed. Löffler, no. 549, 1306.

17. Quotation in *Handbuch der religiösen Gegenwarts-fragen,* ed. Gröber, s.v. "Bolschewismus," 86–87; "Presseberich," October 28, 1933, *Bischof Clemens August Graf von Galen,* ed. Löffler, no. 21, 43–44.

18. Kuropka, "Vom Antisemitismus zum Holocaust," 192.

19. See Kershaw, "The Persecution of the Jews and German Popular Opinion in the Third Reich," which emphasizes the regime's success in convincing a majority of the public of the importance of the Jewish Question. Quotation in Hagen, "Before the 'Final Solution,'" 366.

20. For further treatment on the issue of levels of anti-Semitism in German society and their implications for Jews living under National Socialism, see works such as Friedländer, *Nazi Germany and the Jews;* Gordon, *Hitler, Germans and the "Jewish Question";* and Kaplan, *Between Dignity and Despair.*

21. Aschoff, *Geschichte original—am Beispiel der Stadt Münster,* 2.

22. Ibid., 3, 13.

23. Ibid., 5–6.

24. Ibid., 6, 13.

25. Ibid., 14, 9.

26. Ibid., 9; Brilling and Dieckmann, *Juden in Münster,* 12–31; Aschoff, *Geschichte original—am Beispiel der Stadt Münster,* 10. Brilling and Dieckmann provide a complete list of all 697 Jewish citizens of Münster, their dates of birth, and their fate under the Nazi regime.

27. Sandstede-Auzelle and Sandstede, *Clemens August Graf von Galen,* 76–77; Mussinghoff, *Rassenwahn in Münster,* 69; Kuropka, *Meldungen aus Münster,* 278.

28. Kuropka, *Meldungen aus Münster,* 278; Sandstede-Auzelle and Sandstede, *Clemens August Graf von Galen,* 52.

29. "Ansprache v. Galens," January 28, 1934, no. 31, 61–64; "Hirtenbrief v. Galens," March 26, 1934, no. 35, 67–72; Röver to the Reich Chancellery, April 6, 1934, no. 38, 74–75, *Bischof Clemens August Graf von Galen,* ed. Löffler.

30. Mussinghoff, *Rassenwahn in Münster,* 74.

31. Rahner et al., *Treu deutsch sind wir,* 29.

32. "Rundschreiben v. Galens," December 21, 1937, *Bischof Clemens August Graf von Galen,* ed. Löffler, no. 235, 589–590.

33. Rahner et al., *Treu deutsch sind wir,* 32.

34. See Bartov, "Defining Enemies, Making Victims."

35. "Hirtenbrief v. Galens," September 14, 1941, *Bischof Clemens August Graf von Galen,* ed. Löffler, no. 348, 902.

36. "Predigt v. Galens," June 23, 1935, *Bischof Clemens August Graf von Galen,* ed. Löffler, no. 113, 247.

37. Ibid., 249, 250, quotations on 249.

38. "Hirtenbrief v. Galens," April 7, 1940, *Bischof Clemens August Graf von Galen,* ed. Löffler, no. 293, 764.

39. Dietrich, *Catholic Citizens in the Third Reich,* 242.

40. Ibid., 236.

41. Lewy, *The Catholic Church and Nazi Germany*, 280.

42. Dietrich, *Catholic Citizens in the Third Reich*, 237; Privy Councillor, Münster, "Die Regelung des Rassenproblems durch die Nürnberger Gesetze," *Klerusblatt* 17 (1936): 47.

43. Aschoff, *Geschichte original—am Beispiel der Stadt Münster*, 9.

44. "Aus dem Lagebericht der Staatspolizeistelle für den Regierungsbezirk Münster für Juni 1935," *Meldungen aus Münster*, ed. Kuropka, no. 10, 286; Dieter Heuwing and Bärbel Sosna, "Die Verfolgung der Münsteraner Juden," in *Überwältigte Vergangenheit*, ed. Thien, Wienold, and Preuss, 91.

45. "Aus dem Tätigkeits—und Stimmungsbericht der NSDAP—Ortsgruppe Münster-Niedersachsen für März 1937," *Meldungen aus Münster*, ed. Kuropka, no. 23, 289.

46. Kuropka, *Meldungen aus Münster*, 278; "Aus dem Lagebericht der Staatspolizei-stelle für den Regierungsbezirk Münster für April 1935," no. 7, 283; no. 8, 283; "Aus dem Tätigkeits-und Stimungsbericht des Organisationsleiters der NSDAP-Ortsgruppe Münster-Rathaus für Dezember 1936," no. 15, 287; "Aus dem Tätigkeitsbericht des Organisations-leiters der NSDAP-Ortsgruppe Münster-Kreuztor für Februar 1937," no. 19, 288; "Aus dem Stimmungsbericht der NSDAP-Ortsgruppe Münster-Mitte für März 1937," no. 21, 288–289, *Meldungen aus Münster*, ed. Kuropka.

47. "Aus dem Lagebericht der Staatspolizeistelle für den Regierungsbezirk Münster für Mai 1935," no. 9, 283-285; "Aus dem Stimmungsbericht der NSDAP-Ortsgruppe Münster-Ost für April 1937," no. 25, 290; "Aus dem Bericht der NSDAP-Kreisleitung Münster-Stadt für Mai 1937," no. 28, 290; Aus dem Stimmungsbericht der NSDAP-Ortsgruppe Münster-Gutenberg für Dezember 1937, no. 29, 290, *Meldungen aus Münster*, ed. Kuropka.

48. "Aus dem Stimmungsbericht des Reichsbundes der deutschen Beamten, Kreis Mün-ster für März 1937," *Meldungen aus Münster*, ed. Kuropka, no. 22, 289.

49. "Aus dem Tätigkeits-und Stimmungsbericht des NSDAP-Stützpunktes Münster-Mecklenbeck für März 1937," no. 20, 288; no. 22, 289; "Aus dem Tätigkeits-und Stimmungs-bericht des Organisationsleiters der NSDAP-Ortsgruppe Münster-Rathaus für Dezember 1936," no. 15, 287; "Aus dem Stimmungsbericht der NSDAP-Ortsgruppe Münster-Ost für April 1937," no. 25, 290; "Aus dem Bericht der NSDAP-Kreisleitung Münster-Stadt für Mai 1937," no. 26, 290, *Meldungen aus Münster*, ed. Kuropka.

50. "Aus dem Lagebericht der Staatspolizeistelle für den Regierungsbezirk Münster für Mai 1935," *Meldungen aus Münster*, ed. Kuropka, no. 9, 283-285.

51. "Aus dem Lagebericht der Staatspolizeistelle für den Regierungsbezirk Münster für Januar 1936," *Meldungen aus Münster*, ed. Kuropka, no. 13, 287.

52. Galen to Fritsch, March 8, 1936, *Bischof Clemens August Graf von Galen*, ed. Löff-ler, no. 158, 357-358.

53. *Kirchliches Amtsblatt für die Diözese Münster*, March 7, 1936; Rahner et al., *Treu deutsch sind wir*, 30; "Predigt v. Galens," February 23, 1936, *Bischof Clemens August Graf von Galen*, ed. Löffler, no. 154, 350.

54. "Predigt v. Galens," March 22, 1936, *Bischof Clemens August Graf von Galen,* ed. Löffler, no. 164, 369.

55. Ibid., 375.

56. Ibid., 374, 376, quotation on 374. Reinhard Heydrich cynically suggested, in his article "Gibt es noch Staatsfeinde?" in *Westdeutscher Beobachter,* 1936, passim, that the bishop's sermons were just as dangerous as those of Communist traitors.

57. "Hirtenbrief v. Galens," October 1, 1936, *Bischof Clemens August Graf von Galen,* ed. Löffler, no. 191, 451.

58. Ibid., August 14, 1936, no. 185, 424. Von Galen was not the only clergyman who used the language of disease and damnation to describe Communism. Father Friedrich Muckermann, another priest from Münster, who was famous for fleeing the Nazis and living in exile, employed similar metaphors. See Doris Kaufmann's "Ein 'Warner gegen die Mächte der Finsternis': Pater Friedrich Muckermanns Kampf gegen Bolschewismus und National-sozialismus in Münster, 1924-1934," in *Überwältigte Vergangenheit,* ed. Thien, Wienold, and Preuss, 13-28.

59. "Hirtenbrief v. Galens," August 14, 1936, *Bischof Clemens August Graf von Galen,* ed. Löffler, no. 185, 425.

60. Scholder, *The Churches and the Third Reich,* 146-148.

61. "Predigt v. Galens," August 30, 1936, no. 188, 437, 436, 438; February 14, 1939, no. 272, 685-691, *Bischof Clemens August Graf von Galen,* ed. Löffler. Many of the Nazi publications that asserted a link between Catholicism and Communism came out after the appearance of *Mit brennender Sorge* in 1937. Once the encyclical revealed only conditional Catholic support for National Socialism ideology, Hitler turned away and announced that those who did not fight against his enemies, including Christians, must be contaminated by Judaism. This was followed by Hitler's authorization to Martin Bormann to move against church property in Germany. Scholder, *The Churches and the Third Reich,* 179.

62. "Predigt v. Galens," March 6, 1938, *Bischof Clemens August Graf von Galen,* ed. Löffler, no. 237, 609, 612.

63. "Hirtenbrief v. Galens," April 1, 1939, *Bischof Clemens August Graf von Galen,* ed. Löffler, no. 279, 713-714.

64. "Bericht des Rabbiners Dr. Steinthal zu den Ereignissen während und nach der Pogromnacht," in Mussinghoff, *Rassenwahn in Münster,* 11, 26, quotation on 11.

65. Ibid., 11-16.

66. Ibid., 17-21; Brilling and Dieckmann, *Juden in Münster, 1933-1945,* 30.

67. Mussinghoff, *Rassenwahn in Münster,* 35.

68. Ibid., 20-21.

69. Ibid., 50.

70. Father Maring worked with Friedrich Muckermann, an opponent of Nazism who lived in exile in Holland during the war. Maring remained in Germany, was arrested in 1941, and was sent to Dachau in 1942, where he died in April 1943. Because Mussinghoff's

study *Rassenwahn in Münster* is the only current publication exclusively devoted to the issue of anti-Semitism and the events surrounding Kristallnacht in Münster, I primarily address his interpretation of the actions and events involved throughout this section of the chapter. I also reference arguments put forth by Kuropka in his essay "Vom Antisemitismus zum Holocaust."

71. Mussinghoff, *Rassenwahn in Münster,* 52.

72. Ibid., 53, 52. Both men survived their internment.

73. Kuropka, "Vom Antisemitismus zum Holocaust," 199; quotation in Aschoff, *Geschichte original—am Beispiel der Stadt Münster,* 9.

74. Mussinghoff, *Rassenwahn in Münster,* 90.

75. Twenty-four priests and thirteen ordained persons were arrested and sent to concentration camps following the 1941 sermons. Six died in the camps.

76. Although von Galen did not officially endorse assisting persecuted Jews, there were individuals in Münster who were willing to offer minimal aid. One case of a family providing food to sick Jews is recorded in Maria Lucia Dunschen, "Von Hilfsbereitschaft und von Angst: Eine Münsteranerin berichtet über Leben und Deportation jüdischer Mitbürger," in *Überwältigte Vergangenheit,* ed. Thien, Wienold, and Preuss, 98–102.

77. Mussinghoff, *Rassenwahn in Münster,* 76. The second document, on racism, was sent only to clergy.

78. Sandstede-Auzelle and Sandstede, *Clemens August Graf von Galen,* 54.

79. Noakes and Pridham, *Nazism 1919–1945,* 1050. A brief survey of the contending positions of intentionalists, functionalists, and moderate functionalists can be found in works such as Browning, *The Path to Genocide;* Marrus, *The Holocaust in History;* Kershaw, *The Nazi Dictatorship;* Hans Mommsen, "Die Realisierung des Utopischen"; and Friedländer, "From Anti-Semitism to Extermination."

80. Noakes and Pridham, *Nazism 1919–1945,* no. 796, 1074.

81. Ibid., 1081. On December 3, 1940, Schirach was granted permission to send Jews to Kraków.

82. Ibid., no. 804, 1081.

83. Ibid., no. 809, 1084, quotation on 1085.

84. Morsey, *Clemens August, Kardinal von Galen zum Gedächtnis,* 18.

85. Noakes and Pridham, *Nazism 1919–1945,* no. 810, 1086; no. 813, 1090.

86. Ibid., 1090.

87. Boberbach, *Meldungen aus dem Reich,* no. 309, 286–288.

88. Cited in Mayer, *Why Did the Heavens Not Darken?* 216.

89. Ibid., 217.

90. Noakes and Pridham, *Nazism 1919–1945,* no. 770, 1049.

91. Ibid.

92. Boberbach, *Meldungen aus dem Reich,* no. 256, 217–218.

93. Hilberg, *The Destruction of the European Jews,* 294.

94. Noakes and Pridham, *Nazism 1919-1945,* no. 828, 1107.

95. "Hirtenbrief v. Galens," September 14, 1941, *Bischof Clemens August Graf von Galen,* ed. Löffler, no. 348, 902, 901, 908, 907, quotations on 902, 901, and 907.

96. "Ansprache v. Galens," January 28, 1934, *Bischof Clemens August Graf von Galen,* ed. Löffler, no. 31, 62.

97. Ibid., June 16, 1935, no. 110, 243-244.

98. "Schreiben v. Galens an den Klerus," August 15, 1935, *Bischof Clemens August Graf von Galen,* ed. Löffler, no. 124, 275, 276, quoted phrase on 275.

99. "Entwurf v. Galens zu einem gemeinsamen Hirtenwort der deutschen Bischöfe," December 1935, no. 146, 325; Galen to Hitler, June 9, 1939, no. 285, 731-734, *Bischof Clemens August Graf von Galen,* ed. Löffler.

100. Galen to Frick, November 18, 1939, no. 291, 751; "Predigt v. Galens," February 1, 1942, no. 362, 931-935, *Bischof Clemens August Graf von Galen,* ed. Löffler.

101. "Predigt v. Galens," February 1, 1942, *Bischof Clemens August Graf von Galen,* ed. Löffler, no. 362, 942-944.

102. Rahner et al., *Treu deutsch sind wir,* 34; Helmreich, *The German Churches under Hitler,* 237, 239.

103. Ibid., 238.

104. Quotation in Rahner et al., *Treu deutsch sind wir,* 36; Sandstede-Auzelle and Sandstede, *Clemens August Graf von Galen,* 39.

105. "Entwurf v. Galens zu einem Hirtenwort der deutschen Bischöfe," March 15, 1942, no. 367, 941-946; "Hirtenwort v. Galens," February 25, 1943, no. 377, 970; "Fastenhirtenbrief v. Galens," February 1, 1944, no. 407, 1033, *Bischof Clemens August Graf von Galen,* ed. Löffler. See Bartov, *Hitler's Army,* for a study of the changing nature of morality on Germany's Eastern Front.

106. Hilberg, *The Destruction of the European Jews,* 164; 226-227; quotation in Noakes and Pridham, *Nazism 1919-1945,* 1114.

107. Noakes and Pridham, *Nazism 1919-1945,* 1114; Mussinghoff, *Rassenwahn in Münster,* 33.

108. Hilberg, *The Destruction of the European Jews,* 175; Noakes and Pridham, *Nazism 1919-1945,* 1114.

109. Aschoff, *Geschichte original—am Beispiel der Stadt Münster,* 10; Heuwing and Sosna, "Die Verfolgung der Münsteraner Juden," 85; Kuropka, "Vom Antisemitismus zum Holocaust," 203.

110. Aschoff, *Geschichte original—am Beispiel der Stadt Münster;* Kuropka, "Vom Antisemitismus zum Holocaust," 203.

111. Mussinghoff, *Rassenwahn in Münster,* 33-34; Brilling and Dieckmann, *Juden in Münster,* 13. Most of Münster's Jewish citizens were placed in the Marks-Haindorf Stiftung,

but originally in 1941 there were numerous homes designated as *Judenhäuser,* including addresses such as Hermannstrasse 44 and Viktoriastrasse 4. For more information on housing, see Heuwing and Sosna's essay "Die Verfolgung der Münsteraner Juden," 84–85. Following the September 15, 1935, Nuremberg Laws, the Nazis created the concept of *Mischling,* which argued that each person was the product of blood mixing. Mischling specifically referred to a person with both German and Jewish ancestry.

112. "Bericht des Siegfried Weinberg aus Münster vom 9.10.1944 über seine Deportation," *Meldungen aus Münster,* ed. Kuropka, no. 32, 291–294.

113. Ibid., 294–298, quotation on 298.

114. Phayer, *The Catholic Church and the Holocaust,* 69; Heuwing and Sosna, "Die Verfolgung der Münsteraner Juden," 93.

115. Noakes and Pridham, *Nazism 1919–1945,* 1120, 1123, 1135.

116. Quotation in Sandstede-Auzelle and Sandstede, *Clemens August Graf von Galen,* 54; Morsey, *Clemens August, Kardinal von Galen zum Gedächtnis,* 19. Here Morsey is using this as part of a larger explanation arguing that von Galen could not have been expected to believe all the various reports and rumors to which he was exposed.

117. Phayer, *The Catholic Church and the Holocaust,* 70, 54–55, 71.

118. Neuss to Galen, September 26, 1944, *Bischof Clemens August Graf von Galen,* ed. Löffler, no. 422, 1066, 1067, 1068.

119. Mussinghoff, *Rassenwahn in Münster,* 94.

120. Helmreich, *The German Churches under Hitler,* 362, 363.

121. Phayer, *The Catholic Church and the Holocaust,* 81; Lewy, *The Catholic Church and Nazi Germany,* 288–289.

122. "Predigt v. Galens," July 4, 1943, *Bischof Clemens August Graf von Galen,* ed. Löffler, no. 382, 984; Helmreich, *The German Churches under Hitler,* 364.

123. National Archives, Washington, D.C., T-580, roll 42, file 245; Dietrich, *Catholic Citizens in the Third Reich,* 240.

124. See my discussion of the Vatican and Pius XII in chapter 6 for an examination of those who advocated silence to avoid the unknown.

125. "Entwurf v. Galens für ein Hirtenwort der Westdeutschen Bischöfe," February 1946, *Bischof Clemens August Graf von Galen,* ed. Löffler, no. 549, 1305, 1312, quotation on 1305.

126. "Presseerklärung v. Galens," April 9, 1945, *Bischof Clemens August Graf von Galen,* ed. Löffler, no. 448, 1104.

127. "Vortragsnotizen v. Galens," April 13, 1945, *Bischof Clemens August Graf von Galen,* ed. Löffler, no. 449, 1105.

128. Ibid., 1106.

129. Galen to Ledingham, May 17, 1945, no. 466, 1137; Galen to McAlister, June 12, 1945, no. 479, 1165–1166, *Bischof Clemens August Graf von Galen,* ed. Löffler.

130. Galen to Ledingham, May 17, 1945, no. 466, 1138; Spottiswoode to Galen, June 14, 1945, no. 480, 1167, *Bischof Clemens August Graf von Galen,* ed. Löffler. See Phayer, *The Catholic Church and the Holocaust,* 138–144, for shameful examples of the German Catholic episcopacy working to free convicted killers.

131. "Gesprächsnotizen v. Galens," June 21, 1945, *Bischof Clemens August Graf von Galen,* ed. Löffler, no. 483, 1171.

132. "Aufzeichnung Portmanns," July 24, 1945, *Bischof Clemens August Graf von Galen,* ed. Löffler, no. 490, 1190, 1191, 1192, quotation on 1190.

133. Spottiswoode to Galen, July 25, 1945, *Bischof Clemens August Graf von Galen,* ed. Löffler, no. 491, 1193, 1194, quotations on 1194.

134. "Anlage. Erklärung v. Galens," July 25, 1945, *Bischof Clemens August Graf von Galen,* ed. Löffler, no. 492/I, 1197.

135. Phayer, *The Catholic Church and the Holocaust,* 139. See Phayer's argument that von Galen's statement, issued from Rome, altered the German Catholic clergy's position on the Nuremberg Trials, inspiring them to actively campaign for the release of imprisoned war criminals (139–140).

136. Galen to Pius XII, August 20, 1945, *Bischof Clemens August Graf von Galen,* ed. Löffler, no. 497, 1209.

137. Ibid., 1211.

138. Anonymous letter to Galen, September 23, 1945, *Bischof Clemens August Graf von Galen,* ed. Löffler, no. 504, 1224, quotations on 1225.

139. Ibid., 1226.

140. Quotation ibid., 1226; See Bartov, "Defining Enemies, Making Victims."

Chapter Six: The Construction of an Image: Von Galen in Retrospect

1. This reason for Münster's acceptance of von Galen seems correct particularly when one considers that the citizens renamed streets for Hitler, Göring, and Horst Wessel; held an exhibit to pillory Jewish literature; and participated in forced sterilization and euthanasia. One former university professor from Münster, Dr. Kremer, helped kill inmates in Auschwitz. These examples can be found in Rahner et al., *Treu deutsch sind wir,* 64.

2. Upon his election as Bishop of Münster, von Galen chose *Nec laudibus, Nec timore* (Neither praise nor fear) as his motto.

3. "Hirtenbrief v. Galens," October 28, 1933, *Bischof Clemens August Graf von Galen,* ed. Löffler, no. 20, 29–30.

4. Ibid., 30.

5. Ibid., 31.

6. Ibid., 32–35.

7. Ibid., 37.

8. Ibid., 29.

9. Hochhuth's work was by no means the first to raise these issues. See, e.g., Lehmann, *Vatican Politics in the Second World War;* Reitlinger, *The Final Solution;* and Scheinmann, *Der Vatikan in Zweiten Weltkrieg.* More recent works still exploring the role that Pius XII played include Morley, *Vatican Diplomacy and the Jews during the Holocaust;* Marrus, "The Vatican and the Holocaust"; Fein, *Accounting for Genocide;* Gotto and Repgen, *Kirche, Katholiken und Nationalsozialismus;* Pawlikowski, "The Catholic Response to the Holocaust"; Phayer, *The Catholic Church and the Holocaust;* and Braham, *The Vatican and the Holocaust.* For a controversial examination of Pius XII, see Cornwell, *Hitler's Pope.* For a more balanced analysis, see Zuccotti, *Under His Very Windows.* For recent works that strongly seek to defend Pius XII, see Graham, *Pius XII's Defense of Jews and Others;* and Holmes, *The Papacy in the Modern World.*

10. For a full discussion of the relationship between Pius XII and Great Britain, see Conway, "The Vatican, Great Britain, and Relations with Germany"; quoted phrase in Conway, "The Silence of Pope Pius XII," 109.

11. Friedländer, *Pius XII and the Third Reich,* 10, 12.

12. Ibid., 16; quotation in Conway, "The Vatican, Great Britain, and Relations with Germany," 151.

13. Quotation in Falconi, *The Silence of Pius XII,* 18-19; Freemantle, *The Papal Encyclicals in their Historical Context,* 263-269.

14. Cited in Falconi, *The Silence of Pius XII,* 17.

15. See Scholder's argument, *Die Kirchen zwischen Republik und Gewaltherrschaft.*

16. Falconi, *The Silence of Pius XII,* 22.

17. Conway, "The Silence of Pope Pius XII," 115.

18. This account is related in Falconi, *The Silence of Pius XII,* 86. See Kulka and Mendes-Flohr, *Judaism and Christianity under the Impact of National Socialism,* for essays addressing the connections between Bolshevism and the "subversive" influence of the Jews and how that suspicion might have influenced Pius XII.

19. Cited in Langer and Gleason, *The Undeclared War,* 547.

20. Friedländer, *Pius XII and the Third Reich,* 192, 191.

21. Friedländer, *Pius XII and the Third Reich,* 173. See Phayer, *The Catholic Church and the Holocaust,* chap. 3, for information about Pius XII and his relationship with profascist Catholic leaders.

22. Friedländer, *Pius XII and the Third Reich,* 207. For details regarding the roundup and deportations, and the pope's knowledge of the situation, see Zuccotti, *Under His Very Windows,* chaps. 11-13.

23. Friedländer, *Pius XII and the Third Reich,* 55-56.

24. Scholder, *The Churches and the Third Reich,* 134, 132, quotation on 134.

25. Kirchmann, *St. Ambrosius und die deutschen Bischöfe;* also cited by Scholder, *The Churches and the Third Reich,* 132.

26. Friedländer, *Pius XII and the Third Reich,* 132.

27. Ibid., 131.

28. Pius XII demonstrated the level of reserve he intended to follow by stating, "Every Man Will be Answerable to God for His Own Actions," when he was criticized by Mussolini for sending telegrams to the recently invaded Benelux nations. Saul Friedländer, *Pius XII and the Third Reich: A Documentation* (New York, 1966), 51.

29. Cited in Falconi, *The Silence of Pius XII*, 63.

30. Letter quoted in Rhodes, *The Vatican in the Age of the Dictators*, 348; Falconi, *The Silence of Pius XII*, 75.

31. Conway, "The Vatican, Great Britain, and Relations with Germany," 167.

32. Conway, "The Silence of Pope Pius XII," 123.

33. Ibid., 124–125.

34. Phayer, *The Catholic Church and the Holocaust*, 109, quotations on 127 and 130.

35. Falconi, *The Silence of Pius XII*, 72; Zuccotti, *Under His Very Windows*, 319.

36. Scholder, *The Churches and the Third Reich*, 131.

37. Adenauer to Pastor Bernhard Custodis, February 23, 1946, in Adenauer, *Briefe, 1945–1947*, 172–173; also quoted in Scholder, *The Churches and the Third Reich*, 39.

38. Galen to Pius XII, November 4, 1943, *Bischof Clemens August Graf von Galen*, ed. Löffler, no. 396, 1014.

39. Pius XII to Galen, June 12, 1940, *Bischof Clemens August Graf von Galen*, ed. Löffler, no. 306, 788. This letter can also be found in *Actes et documents du Saint Siège relatifs à la Seconde Guerre Mondiale*, vol. 2, *Lettres de Pie XII aux évêques allemands, 1939–1944*, ed. Blet et al. (1966), no. 47, 144; Pius XII to Galen, February 16, 1941, *Bischof Clemens August Graf von Galen*, ed. Löffler, no. 328, 195, 832; also in *Lettres de Pie XII*, no. 63; Pius XII to Galen, February 24, 1943, *Bischof Clemens August Graf von Galen*, ed. Löffler, no. 376, 310, 968; also in *Lettres de Pie XII*, no. 124.

40. Pius XII to Galen, June 12, 1940, no. 306, 788–789; Pius XII to Galen, February 16, 1941, no. 328, 832, *Bischof Clemens August Graf von Galen*, ed. Löffler; Scholder, *The Churches and the Third Reich*, 113–114.

41. Galen to Pius XII, November 4, 1943, no. 396, 1012–1016; September 25, 1945, no. 505, 1226; November 4, 1943, no. 396, 1014; February 20, 1944, no. 408, 1047, *Bischof Clemens August Graf von Galen*, ed. Löffler.

42. Galen to Pius XII, February 20, 1944, *Bischof Clemens August Graf von Galen*, ed. Löffler, no. 408, 1045–1046; quotation in Hochhuth, "'Eine ungeheure Lüge.'"

43. "A l'Evêque de Berlin," September 30, 1941, in *Lettres de Pie XII*, no. 76, 230, emphasis mine.

44. Cited in Damberg, *Veröffentlichungen der Kommission für Zeitgeschichte*, 10.

45. Van Elten, "Drei Deutsche Kardinäle!" 152; quotation in Bierbaum, *Nicht lob nicht furcht*, 181.

46. Galen to Pius XII, January 6, 1946, *Bischof Clemens August Graf von Galen*, ed. Löffler, no. 528, 1262–1263; Portmann, *Cardinal von Galen*, 178.

47. Van Elten, "Drei Deutsche Kardinäle!" 153.

48. See accounts in Portmann, *Kardinal von Galen: Ein Gottesmann,* 274-316; and Bier-baum, *Die letze Romfahrt des Kardinal von Galen,* 17-100.

49. Kuropka, "Eine diplomatische Aktion aus dem Jahre 1945," 209.

50. Ibid., 208. The British were not totally incorrect in the belief that von Galen might be interested in political life after the war. He worked to begin a new political party based on Christian principles and sent his proposals to Konrad Adenauer. See Susanne Leschinski's work "Clemens August Kardinal von Galen in der Nachkriegszeit 1945/46," in *Clemens August Graf von Galen,* ed. Kuropka, 245-272. For Adenauer's response to von Galen's proposal, see Adenauer, *Briefe, 1945-47,* no. 535, 486.

51. Kuropka, "Eine diplomatische Aktion aus dem Jahre 1945," 209.

52. Ibid., 209, 210.

53. Ibid., 210.

54. Portmann, *Kardinal von Galen: Ein Gottesmann,* 197.

55. The pope and the diplomat quoted ibid., 204; Frings quoted in van Elten, "Drei Deutsche Kardinäle!" 158.

56. Portmann, *Kardinal von Galen: Ein Gottesmann,* 207. See also Hasenkamp, *Heim-kehr und Heimgang des Kardinals,* for further details of von Galen's travel-related troubles.

57. Leschinski, "Clemens August Kardinal von Galen in der Nachkriegszeit 1945/46," 246; the description of Münster's destruction was included in an article, "Münster: Cultural Center of Westphalia," in the *British Zone Review* from November 24, 1945 (246); Portmann, *Kardinal von Galen: Ein Gottesmann,* 217-219.

58. "Ansprache v. Galens," March 16, 1946, *Bischof Clemens August Graf von Galen,* ed. Löffler, no. 557, 1324-1325.

59. Ibid., 1326-1327.

60. Spottiswoode to Galen, December 27, 1945, no. 521, 1256; "Ehrenbürgerbrief v. Galens," March 15, 1946, no. 555, 1321, *Bischof Clemens August Graf von Galen,* ed. Löffler.

61. "Vertreter von Flüchtlingsverbänden an v. Galen," March 15, 1946, *Bischof Clemens August Graf von Galen,* ed. Löffler, no. 554, 1320. Ernst W. Stählin called von Galen a "Fearless Witness to Earthly and Spiritual Truth," in a letter to Franz Meis, doctor of theology. *Bischof Clemens August Graf von Galen,* ed. Löffler, no. 561, 1332.

62. "Todesanziege v. Galens," March 23, 1946, no. 558, 1328; Zuhorn to Franz von Galen, March 23, 1946, no. 559, 1329; Spottiswoode to Kapitularvikar in Münster, after March 23, 1946, no. 560, 1331, *Bischof Clemens August Graf von Galen,* ed. Löffler.

63. Stählin to Meis, March 25, 1946, *Bischof Clemens August Graf von Galen,* ed. Löffler, no. 561, 1331-1332.

64. Auerbach to Kapitularvikar in Münster, March 27, 1946, no. 563, 1334; "Synagogen-gemeinde Köln an Frings," March 27, 1946, no. 564, 1335, *Bischof Clemens August Graf von Galen,* ed. Löffler; Brilling and Dieckmann refer to Steinthal's letters in *Juden in Münster,* 10. Zuccotti, speaking of the Jewish response to Pius XII in the postwar world, argues that

Jews did not want to spoil the atmosphere by pointing out Pius's inaction, that many Jews were interested in having the church aid the remnants of European Jews, and that some had misplaced gratitude at best. Zucotti, *Under His Very Windows,* 300–304. The feelings expressed by Jews about von Galen may have been motivated similarly.

65. Huch to Galen, September 4, 1941, *Bischof Clemens August Graf von Galen,* ed. Löffler, no. 347, 900; Gallin, *German Resistance to Hitler,* 194.

66. "Trauerpredigt Frings," March 28, 1946, *Bischof Clemens August Graf von Galen,* ed. Löffler, no. 565, 1336–1337.

67. Cited in Stehle, "Widerstand mit Widersprüchen."

68. R. L. Sedgwick wrote this in his introduction to Portmann's *Cardinal von Galen,* 15.

69. Portmann, *Cardinal von Galen,* 170.

70. *New York Times,* August 6, 1942. The article examined various church leaders. See Rahner et al., *Treu deutsch sind wir,* 59; Gestapo story in "Presserklärung v. Galens," April 9, 1945, *Bischof Clemens August Graf von Galen,* ed. Löffler, no. 448, 1104–1105.

71. Portmann, *Cardinal von Galen,* 16.

72. Ibid., 16, 17, quotation on 16.

73. "Presserklärung v. Galens," April 9, 1945, *Bischof Clemens August Graf von Galen,* ed. Löffler, no. 448, 1104–1105.

74. Allemann, "Deutsche Bilanz 1945." This article was reprinted on January 4, 1946, by the *Glasgow Observer* under the title "Der Neue Kardinal von Münster." For clarity I will cite page numbers from Rahner et al., *Treu deutsch sind wir,* where a reprint of the article appears. The quotation here is on 102.

75. Rahner et al., *Treu deutsch sind wir,* 103.

76. Ibid., 103–104.

77. "Münster, Cultural Center of Westphalia." Also quoted in Kuropka, "Eine diplomatische Aktion aus dem Jahre 1945," 211.

78. Cited in Portmann, *Cardinal von Galen,* 17.

79. They were not the only early biographers of von Galen. For similar presentations of him, see also Deimel, *Clemens August Graf von Galen als Bischof von Münster;* Hünermann, *Clemens August;* and Neuss, *Kampf gegen den Mythus des 20. Jahrhunderts.*

80. Fleischer, "Der Mythos vom heiligen Widerstandskämpfer," 2–4.

81. Böckenförde, "Der deutsche Katholizismus im Jahre 1933."

82. For a recent discussion of the changing nature of historiographical coverage of both the Catholic and the Protestant churches, see Ward, "Guilt and Innocence."

83. Deschner, *Mit Gott und den Faschisten.*

84. Here I am mainly referring to works by Morsey, such as *Clemens August Kardinal von Galen zum Gedachtnis* or "Clemens August Kardinal von Galen: Bischöfliches Wirken

in der Zeit der Hitler-Diktatur." Morsey's works continued the traditional depiction seen in Bierbaum and Portmann.

85. *Westfälische Nachrichten,* October 18, 1975, quoted by Schmidt, *Der Kardinal und das Dritte Reich,* 3rd ed., 3; "Ein Vorkämpfer für menschliche Freiheit, Feier zum 100. Geburtstag von Kardinal von Galen," in *Münstersche Zeitung* (Münster), April 10, 1978, also quoted by Rahner et al., *Treu deutsch sind wir,* 52; See Schmidt, *Der Kardinal und das Dritte Reich.*

86. For a summary of the ceremony, see Rahner et al., *Treu deutsch sind wir,* 53.

87. Ibid., 61 (citation of Vennenbernd's research), 66–69, 70.

Conclusion

1. I am referring to the following works: Mussinghoff, *Rassenwahn in Münster;* Sandstede-Auzelle and Sandstede, *Clemens August Graf von Galen;* Rahner et al., *Treu deutsch sind wir;* Kuropka, *Clemens August Graf von Galen;* and Kuropka, "Widerstand gegen den Nationalsozialismus in Münster."

2. Rahner et al., *Treu deutsch sind wir,* 45; Kershaw, *The Nazi Dictatorship,* chap. 8, "Resistance without People?" 184; See my explanation of the Bavaria Project in the introduction to this volume.

3. Michael Geyer, "Resistance as Ongoing Project: Visions of Order, Obligations to Strangers, and Struggles for Civil Society, 1933–1990," in *Resistance against the Third Reich,* ed. Geyer and Boyer, 325–350.

4. Geyer and Boyer, *Resistance against the Third Reich.*

5. The most recent works that include a discussion of von Galen's views regarding the Jews do not include an analysis of his opinions on Bolshevism or his ability to use other ciphers such as liberalism or materialism. See, specifically, Werner Teuber and Gertrud Seelhorst's essay, "'Die christliche Frohbotschaft ist die von Gott den Menschen aller Rassen geschenkte unveränderliche Wahrheit' die deutsche Episkopat, der Bischof von Münster und die Juden," in *Clemens August Graf von Galen,* ed. Kuropka, 221–244. See also Sandstede-Auzelle and Sandstede, *Clemens August Graf von Galen,* 49–56.

6. Zuccotti, *Under His Very Windows,* 321.

7. Claudia Koonz, "Ethical Dilemmas and Nazi Eugenics: Single-Issue Dissent in Religious Contexts," in *Resistance against the Third Reich,* ed. Geyer and Boyer, 38.

8. Cited in the Vatican document about the Holocaust, "We Remember: A Reflection on the Shoah," 1. This document was issued in March 1998 by the Holy See's Commission for Religious Relations with Jews.

Bibliography

Archival Materials

Bistumsarchiv Münster

Bundesarchiv Koblenz

National Archives, Washington, D.C.

Nordrhein-Westfälisches Staatsarchiv Münster

Newspapers and Diocesan Gazettes

Amtsblatt (specific dioceses are identified in note citations)

British Zone Review

Ecclesiastica

Germania

Katholische Rundschau

Klerusblatt

Münstersche Zeitung

New York Times

L'Osservatore Romano

Reichsgesetzblatt

Das Schwarze Korps

Stars and Stripes

Die Tat

Times (London)

Vierteljahrshefte für Zeitgeschichte

Völkischer Beobachter

Die Zeit

Published Primary Sources

Aschoff, Diethard, ed. *Geschichte original—am Beispiel der Stadt Münster: Die Juden in Münster von den Anfängen bis zur Gegenwart.* Münster, 1981.

Blet, Pierre, Robert A. Graham, Angelo Martini, and Burkhart Schneider, eds. *Actes et documents du Saint Siège relatifs à la Seconde Guerre Mondiale.* 12 vols. Vatican City, 1965-81.

Boberbach, Heinz, ed. *Berichte des SD und der Gestapo über Kirchen und Kirchenvolk in Deutschland, 1934-1944.* Mainz, 1971.

———. *Meldungen aus dem Reich: Auswahl aus den geheimen Lageberichten des Sicherheitsdienstes der SS, 1939-1944.* 17 vols. Neuwied, Germany, 1965.

Buchberger, Michael. *Lexikon für Theologie und Kirche.* 9 vols. Freiburg, 1930.

Cassidy, Edward Idris, Pierre Duprey, and Remi Hoeckman. "We Remember: A

Reflection on the Shoah." Distributed by John S. Conway in connection
with his E-mail newsletter for the Association of Contemporary Church
Historians, March 16, 1998.

Corsten, Wilhelm, ed. *Kölner Aktenstücke: Zur Lage der katholischen Kirche in
Deutschland, 1933–1945.* Cologne, 1949.

Dawidowicz, Lucy, ed. *A Holocaust Reader.* New York, 1976.

Friedländer, Saul. *Pius XII and the Third Reich: A Documentation.* Translated by
Charles Fullman. London, 1966.

Hitler, Adolf. *Mein Kampf.* Munich, 1935.

———. *Mein Kampf.* Translated by Ralph Manheim. Boston, 1970.

Hofer, Walter, ed. *Der Nationalsozialismus: Dokumente, 1933–1945.* Frankfurt,
1957.

Kuropka, Joachim, ed. *Meldungen aus Münster, 1924–1944: Geheime und vertrau-
liche Berichte von Polizei, Gestapo, NSDAP und ihren Gliederungen, staat-
licher Verwaltung, Gerichtsbarkeit und Wehrmacht über die politische und
gesellschaftliche Situation in Münster.* Münster, 1992.

Löffler, Peter, ed. *Bischof Clemens August Graf von Galen: Akten, Briefe und
Predigten, 1933–1946.* Vols. 1–2. Mainz, 1988.

Müller, Hans. *Katholische Kirche und Nationalsozialismus: Dokumente, 1930–1935.*
Munich, 1963.

Neuhäusler, Johann. *Kreuz und Hakenkreuz: Der Kampf des Nationalsozialismus
gegen die katholische Kirche und der kirchliche Widerstand.* Munich, 1946.

Noakes, Jeremy, and Geoffrey Pridham, eds. *Nazism 1919–1945: A History in
Documents and Eyewitness Accounts.* New York, 1988.

Picker, Henry, ed. *Hitlers Tischgespräche im Führerhauptquartier, 1941–42.* Bonn,
1951.

Remak, Joachim, ed. *The Nazi Years: A Documentary History.* New York, 1969.

Sagebiel, Herta, ed. *Geschichte original—am Beispiel der Stadt Münster: Der Kulturkampf im Bismarckreich.* Münster, 1983.

Stasiewski, Bernhard. *Akten Deutscher Bischöfe über die Lage der Kirche, 1933–
1945.* Vol. 1, *1933–1934.* Mainz, 1968.

———. *Akten Deutscher Bischöfe über die Lage der Kirche, 1933–1945.* Vol. 2, *1934–
1935.* Mainz, 1976.

Volk, Ludwig. *Akten Deutscher Bischöfe über die Lage der Kirche, 1936–1939.*
Mainz, 1981.

———. *Akten Kardinal Michael von Faulhabers, 1917–1945.* Vol. 1, *1917–1934.*
Mainz, 1975.

Books and Articles

Adam, Uwe Dietrich. *Die Judenpolitik im Dritten Reich.* Dusseldorf, 1972.

Adenauer, Konrad. *Briefe, 1945–1947.* Edited by Hans Peter Mensing. Berlin, 1983.

Adolph, Walter. *Kardinal Preysing und zwei Diktaturen: Sein Widerstand gegen die totalitäre Macht.* Berlin, 1971.

———. *Die katholische Kirche im Deutschland Adolf Hitlers.* Berlin, 1965.

Albert, Walter, Joachim Haas, and Bernhard Scwhank. "Ein Anderer Weg zum Ziel der Erkenntnis? Inhaltsanalyse über das Systemabweichende Verhalten Deutscher Christen im Nationalsozialismus, 1933–45." *Zeitgeschichte* (Austria) 11, no. 4 (1984): 121–133.

Albrecht, Dieter, ed. *Katholische Kirche im Dritten Reich: Eine Aufsatzsammlung.* Mainz, 1976.

Alexander, Edgar. *Church and Society in Germany: Social and Political Movements and Ideas in German and Austrian Catholicism, 1789–1950.* New York, 1953.

Algermissen, Konrad. "Christentum und Germanentum." *Theologie und Glaube* 26 (1934): 302–330.

Allemann, Fritz R. "Deutsche Bilanz 1945: Eine Rundfahrt durch die britische Zone in Deutschland." *Die Tat* 294 (October 26, 1945).

Allen, William Sheridan. *The Nazi Seizure of Power: The Experience of a Single German Town, 1930–1935.* Chicago, 1965.

Almond, Gabriel A. "The German Resistance Movement." *Current History* 10 (1946): 409–419.

Alvarez, David, and Robert A. Graham, S.J. *Nothing Sacred: Nazi Espionage against the Vatican, 1939–1945.* Portland, Oreg., 1997.

Aly, Götz. *"Final Solution": Nazi Population Policy and the Murder of the European Jews.* Translated by Belinda Cooper and Allison Brown. New York, 1999.

Aly, Götz, Christian Pross, and Peter Chroust, eds. *Cleansing the Fatherland: Nazi Medicine and Racial Hygiene.* Translated by Belinda Cooper. Baltimore, 1994.

Amery, Carl. *Die Kapitulation oder Deutscher Katholizismus heute.* Hamburg, 1963.

Anderson, Margaret Lavinia. "Piety and Politics: Recent Work on German Catholicism." *Journal of Modern History* 63 (December 1991): 681–716.

———. *Windthorst: A Political Biography.* Oxford, 1981.

Aretin, Karl Otmar. *Die Kirchen zwischen Republik und Gewaltherrschaft: Gesammelte Aufsatze.* Berlin, 1988.

Baerwald, Friedrich. "Catholic Resistance in Nazi Germany." *Thought* 20 (1945): 217–234.

Balfour, Michael. *Four-Power Control in Germany and Austria, 1945–46.* London, 1956.

Ballhorn, F. *Die Kelter Gottes: Tagebuch eines jungen Christen, 1940–45.* Münster, 1946.

Baranowski, Shelley. *The Sanctity of Rural Life: Protestantism, Agrarian Politics and Nazism in Pomerania.* Oxford, 1996.

Barth, Karl. *The German Church Conflict.* Richmond, Va., 1965.

Bartov, Omer. "Defining Enemies, Making Victims: Germans, Jews, and the Holocaust." *American Historical Review* 103 (June 3, 1998): 771–816.

———. *Hitler's Army: Soldiers, Nazis, and War in the Third Reich.* New York, 1991.

———, ed. *The Holocaust: Origins, Implementation, Aftermath.* New York, 2000.

Bauer, Yehuda. *A History of the Holocaust.* New York, 1982.

Baumeister, Martin. *Parität und katholische Inferiorität: Untersuchung zur Stellung des Katholizismus im Deutschen Kaiserreich.* Paderborn, Germany, 1987.

Baumgartner, Raimund. *Weltanschauungskampf im Dritten Reich: Die Auseinandersetzung der Kirchen mit Alfred Rosenberg.* Mainz, 1977.

Beaugrand, Günter. *Kardinal Graf von Galen.* Pattloch, Germany, 1985.

Bergen, Doris. "Catholics, Protestants, and Christian Antisemitism in Nazi Germany." *Central European History* 3 (1994): 329–348.

———. *Twisted Cross: The German Christian Movement in the Third Reich.* Chapel Hill, N.C., 1996.

Besier, Gerhard. "Anti-Bolshevism and Anti-Semitism: The Catholic Church in Germany and National Socialist Ideology, 1936–1937." *Journal of Ecclesiastical History* 43 (July 1992): 447–456.

Bessel, Richard, ed. *Life in the Third Reich.* New York, 1987.

Beyreuther, Erich. *Die Geschichte des Kirchenkampfes in Dokumenten, 1933–1945.* Wuppertal, Germany, 1966.

Bierbaum, Max. *Kardinal von Galen, Bischof von Münster.* Münster, 1947.

———. *Die letzte Romfahrt des Kardinal von Galen.* Münster, 1946.

———. *Nicht lob, nicht furcht: Das Leben des Kardinals von Galen nach unveröffentlichten Briefen und Dokumenten.* 4th enlarged ed. Münster, 1960.

Bindung, Karl, and Alfred Hoche. *Die Freigabe der Vernichtung lebensunwerten Lebens: Ihr Mass und ihre Form.* Leipzig, 1920.

Black, Peter. *Ernst Kaltenbrunner: Ideological Soldier of the Third Reich.* Princeton, N.J., 1984.

Blackbourn, David. "The Catholic Church in Europe since the French Revolution." *Comparative Studies in Society and History* 33 (October 1991): 778–790.

———. "Class and Politics in Wilhelmine Germany: The Center Party and the Social Democrats in Württemberg." *Central European History* 9 (1976): 220–249.

———. *Class, Religion and Local Politics in Wilhelmine Germany: The Centre Party in Württemberg before 1914.* New Haven, Conn., 1980.

Blackbourn, David, and Geoff Eley. *The Peculiarities of German History: Bourgeois Society and Politics in 19th Century Germany.* Oxford, 1984.

Blet, Pierre. *Pius XII and the Second World War: According to the Archives of the Vatican.* Translated by Lawrence J. Johnson. New York, 1999.

Bock, Gisela. "Racism and Sexism in Nazi Germany: Motherhood, Compulsory

Sterilization, and the State." In *When Biology Became Destiny: Women in Weimar and Nazi Germany,* edited by Renate Bridenthal, Atina Grossman, and Marion Kaplan, 271–296.

———. *Zwangsterilisation im Nationalsozialismus: Studien zur Rassenpolitik und Frauenpolitik.* Opladen, Germany, 1986.

Böckenförde, Ernst-Wolfgang. "Der deutsche Katholizismus im Jahre 1933: Eine kritische Betrachtung." *Hochland* 53 (1961): 215–239.

———. "Der deutsche Katholizismus im Jahre 1933: Stellungnahme zu einer Diskussion." *Hochland* 54 (1962): 217–245.

Boehm, Eric H., ed. *We Survived.* Santa Barbara, Calif., 1966.

Boyens, Armin. *Kirchenkampf und Okumene, 1933–1939: Darstellung und Dokumentation.* Munich, 1969.

Bracher, Karl Dietrich. *The German Dictatorship.* Translated by Jean Steinberg. New York, 1970.

Braham, Randolph L. *The Vatican and the Holocaust: The Catholic Church and the Jews during the Nazi Era.* New York, 2000.

Brandt, Wilhelm. *Friedrich von Bodelschwingh, 1877–1946: Nachfolger und Gestalter.* Bethel, Germany, 1967.

Bridenthal, Renate, Atina Grossman, and Marion Kaplan, eds. *When Biology Became Destiny: Women in Weimar and Nazi Germany.* New York, 1984.

Brilling, Bernhard, and Ulrich Dieckmann. *Juden in Münster, 1933–1945: Eine Gedenkschrift.* Münster, 1960.

Broszat, Martin, ed. *Bayern in der NS-Zeit.* 6 vols. Munich, 1977–83.

Browning, Christopher. *The Path to Genocide: Essays on Launching the Final Solution.* Cambridge, 1992.

Buchheim, Hans. *Glaubenskrise im Dritten Reich: Drei Kapitel nationalsozialistischer Religionspolitik.* Stuttgart, 1953.

———. *War die katholische Kirche eine vom nationalsozialistischen Regime verfolgte Organisation?* Munich, 1958.

Burleigh, Michael. *Death and Deliverance: "Euthanasia" in Germany c. 1900–1945.* Cambridge, England, 1994.

———. "Euthanasia and the Third Reich." *History Today* (February 1990).

———. *The Third Reich: A New History.* New York, 2000.

Burleigh, Michael, and Wolfgang Wippermann. *The Racial State: Germany, 1933–1945.* Cambridge, 1991; reprint, Cambridge, 1992. Page citations are to the reprint edition.

Carroll, James. *Constantine's Sword: The Church and the Jews.* New York, 2001.

Cary, Noel Demetri. "Political Catholicism and the Reform of the German Party System, 1900–1957." Ph.D. diss., University of Calif., Berkeley, 1988.

Ciano, Galeazzo. *Diaries, 1939–1943.* New York, 1946.

Cochrane, Arthur C. *The Churches' Confession under Hitler.* Philadelphia, 1962.

Cohn, E. J., and Martin Wolff. *Manual of German Law.* London, 1968.

Conrad, Walter. *Der Kampf um die Kanzeln: Erinnerungun und Dokumente aus der Hitlerzeit.* Berlin, 1957.

Conway, John S. "Der deutsche Kirchenkampf." *Vierteljahrshefte für Zeitgeschichte* 17 (October 1969): 423–449.

———. "The Holocaust and the Historians." *Annals of the American Academy of Political and Social Science* 450 (July 1980): 153–164.

———. *The Nazi Persecution of the Churches, 1933–45.* New York, 1968.

———. "Pius XII and the German Church: An Unpublished Gestapo Report." *Canadian Journal of History* 1, no. 1 (1966).

———. "The Silence of Pope Pius XII." *Review of Politics* 27 (1965): 105–131.

———. "Staatliche Akten zum Kirchenkampf, Archive und Bestande." In *Zur Geschichte des Kirchenkampfes,* edited by Heinze Brunotte, 25–34. Göttingen, 1971.

———. "The Vatican, Great Britain and Relations with Germany, 1938–1940." *Historical Journal* 16 (1973): 147–67.

Conzemius, Victor. *Eglises chrétiennes et totalitarisme national-socialiste: Un bilan historiographique.* Louvain, 1969.

———. "German Catholics and the Nazi Regime in 1933." *Irish Ecclesiastical Record* 103 (1967): 326–335.

Cornwell, John. *Hitler's Pope: The Secret History of Pius XII.* New York, 1999.

Damberg, Wilhelm. "Der Kampf um die Schulen in Westfalen, 1933–45." In *Veröffentlichungen der Kommission für Zeitgeschichte.* Series B, Research, vol. 43. Mainz, 1986.

Davis, Belinda. *Home Fires Burning: Food, Politics, and Everyday Life in World War I Berlin.* Chapel Hill, N.C., 2000.

Dawidowicz, Lucy. *The Holocaust and the Historians.* Cambridge, Mass., 1981.

Deimel, Ludwig. *Clemens-August Graf von Galen als Bischof von Münster.* Münster, 1948.

Denscher, Guenther. *Heydrich: The Pursuit of Total Power.* London, 1981.

Deschner, Karl-Heinz. *Mit Gott und den Faschisten: Der Vatikan im Bunde mit Mussolini, Franco, Hitler und Pavelic.* Stuttgart, 1965.

Deuerlein, Ernst. *Der Deutsche Katholizismus, 1933.* Osnabrück, Germany, 1963.

Diehn, Otto. *Bibliographie zur Geschicht des Kirchenkampfes, 1933–1945.* Göttingen, 1958.

Dietrich, Donald J. *Catholic Citizens in the Third Reich: Psycho-Social Principles and Moral Reasoning.* New Brunswick, N.J., 1988.

———. "Catholic Theologians in Hitler's Reich: Adaptation and Critique." *Journal of Church and State* 29 (winter 1987): 19–45.

Diner, Dan. "Rassistisches Volkerrecht: Elemente einer nationalsozialistischen Weltordnung." *Vierteljahrshefte für Zeitgeschichte* 37 (January 1989): 23–56.

Dörner, Klaus. "Nationalsozialismus und Lebensvernichtung." *Vierteljahrshefte für Zeitgeschichte* 15 (April 1967): 121–153.

Donohoe, James. *Hitler's Conservative Opponents in Bavaria, 1930–1945: A Study of Catholic, Monarchist and Separatist Anti-Nazi Activities.* Leiden, 1961.

Dreier, Ralf, and Wolfgang Sellert, eds. *Recht und Justiz im "Dritten Reich."* Munich, 1989.

Dulles, Allen. *Germany's Underground.* New York, 1947.

Duncan-Jones, A. S. *The Struggle for Religious Freedom in Germany.* London, 1938.

Ehrenfried, Matthias. "The Nazi War against the Catholic Church," National Catholic Welfare conference, Washington D.C., 1942.

Ehrhardt, Helmut. *Euthanasie und Vernichtung "lebensunwerten" Lebens.* Stuttgart, 1965.

Elten, Josef van. "Drei deutschen Kardinale: Die Erhebung der Bischöfe Frings (Köln), von Galen (Münster), und von Preysing (Berlin) zu Kardinälen der Hl. Römischen Kirche im Konsistorium des Jahres 1946." *Geschichte in Köln* 21 (1987): 149–166.

Erb, Alfons. *Bernhard Lichtenberg: Domprobst von St. Hedwig zu Berlin.* Berlin, 1949.

Eschweiler, Karl. "Die Kirche im neuen Reich." *Deutsches Volkstum* 15 (1933): 451–458.

Esposito, R. F. *Clemens August Graf von Galen, un vescovo indesirerabile: Le grandi prediche di sfida al nazismo.* Padova, 1985.

Evans, Ellen L. *The German Center Party, 1870–1933: A Study in Political Catholicism.* Carbondale, Ill., 1981.

Falconi, Carlo. *The Silence of Pius XII.* Translated by Bernard Wall. Boston, 1970.

Fein, Helen. *Accounting for Genocide: National Responses and Jewish Victimization during the Holocaust.* Chicago, 1984.

Fleischer, Johannes. "Adolf Hitler, sein Krieg und die Bischöfe: Wo bleibt das Schuldbekenntnis der katholischen Kirche?" *Die Andere Zeitung,* October 8, 1964.

———. "Der Mythos vom heiligen Widerstandskämpfer: Die 'Generallinie' des Kardinals von Galen." *Die Andere Zeitung,* December 13, 1956.

Ford, Caroline. "Religion and Popular Culture in Modern Europe." *Journal of Modern History* 65 (March 1993): 152–175.

Freemantle, Anne, ed. *The Papal Encyclicals in Their Historical Context.* New York, 1956.

Friedlander, Henry. *The Origins of Nazi Genocide: From Euthanasia to the Final Solution.* Chapel Hill, N.C., 1995.

Friedländer, Saul. "From Anti-Semitism to Extermination: A Historiographical Study of Nazi Policies toward the Jews and an Essay of Interpretation." *Yad Vashem Studies* 16 (1984): 1–50.

———. *Memory, History, and the Extermination of the Jews of Europe.* Bloomington, Ind., 1993.

————. *Nazi Germany and the Jews.* Vol. 1. New York, 1997.

Fuchs, Friedrich. "Ein Bischofswort über das Alte Testament." *Hochland* 31 (1933–1934): 469–483.

————. "Der totale Staat und seine Grenze." *Hochland* 30 (1932–1933): 558–560.

Galen, Clemens August von. *Die Pest des Laizismus und ihre Erscheinungsformen.* Münster, 1932.

Gallin, Mary Alice. *The Ethical and Religious Factors in the German Resistance to Hitler.* Washington, D.C., 1955.

————. *German Resistance to Hitler: Ethical and Religious Factors.* Washington, D.C., 1961.

Gamm, Hans-Jochen. *Der Braun Kult.* Hamburg, 1962.

Gellately, Robert. "Enforcing Racial Policy in Nazi Germany." In *Re-Evaluating the Third Reich: Interpretations and Debates,* edited by Thomas Childers and Jane Caplan, 42–65. New York, 1993.

————. *The Gestapo and German Society: Enforcing Racial Policy, 1933–1945.* Oxford, 1990.

Gericke, Fritz. *Der neue Glaube.* Stuttgart, 1943.

The German Resistance to Hitler. Translated by Ross, Peter, and Betty Ross. London, 1970.

Geyer, Michael, and John W. Boyer, eds. *Resistance against the Third Reich, 1933–1990.* Chicago, 1994.

Gisevius, Hans Bernd. *Bis zum bitteren Ende.* Zurich, 1946.

Gordon, Mel. *Voluptuous Panic: The Erotic World of Weimar Berlin.* Venice, Calif., 2000.

Gordon, Sarah. *Hitler, Germans, and the "Jewish Question."* Princeton, N.J., 1984.

Gotto, Klaus. *Die Katholiken und das Dritte Reich.* Mainz, 1983.

Gotto, Klaus, and Konrad Repgen, eds. *Kirche, Katholiken und Nationalsozialismus.* Mainz, 1980.

Graham, Robert A. "How Justify Resistance to Tyranny?" *America* 15 (1954): 355–357.

————. *Pius XII's Defense of Jews and Others: 1944–1945.* Milwaukee, 1982.

————. "The 'Right to Kill' in the Third Reich: Prelude to Genocide." *Catholic Historical Review* 62 (1976): 56–76.

Graml, Hermann. *Antisemitism and Its Origins in the Third Reich.* Oxford, 1992.

————. *The German Resistance to Hitler.* Berkeley, Calif., 1970.

————, ed. *Widerstand im Dritten Reich: Probleme, Ereignisse, Gestalten.* Frankfurt, 1994.

Griech-Polelle, Beth. "Image of a Churchman-Resister: Bishop von Galen, the Euthanasia Project and the Sermons of Summer 1941." *Journal of Contemporary History* 36, no. 1 (January 2001): 41–57.

————. "A Pure Conscience Is Good Enough: Bishop von Galen and Resistance to Nazism." In *In God's Name: Genocide and Religion in the Twentieth Century,* edited by Omer Bartov and Phyllis Mack, 106–122. New York, 2000.

———. Review of *Clemens August Graf von Galen: Neue Forschungen zum Leben und Wirken des Bischofs von Münster,* edited by Joachim Kuropka. *Catholic Historical Review* 82 (April 1996): 281–282.

Grieve, Hermann. *Theologie und Ideologie: Katholizismus und Judentum in Deutschland und Österreich, 1918–1935.* Heidelberg, 1969.

Gröber, Conrad. *Kirche, Vaterland, und Vaterlandsliebe: Zeitgemässe Erwägungen und Erwiderungen.* Freiburg, 1935.

———, ed. *Handbuch der religiösen Gegenwartsfragen.* Freiburg, 1934.

Gruchmann, Lothar. "Euthanasie und Justiz im Dritten Reich." *Vierteljahrshefte für Zeitgeschichte* 20 (1972): 235–279.

Grunberger, Richard. *The 12-Year Reich: A Social History of the Third Reich.* New York, 1971.

Gundlach, Gustav. "Antisemitismus." In *Lexicon für Theologie und Kirche.* 10 vols. Freiburg, Switzerland, 1957–1961.

———. "Fragen um die berufsständische Ordnung." *Stimmen der Zeit* 125 (1933): 217–226.

———. *Zur Soziologie der katholischen Ideenwelt und des Jesuitenordens.* Freiburg, 1982.

Gurian, Waldemar. *Hitler and the Christians.* New York, 1982.

———. "Hitler's Undeclared War on the Catholic Church." *Foreign Affairs* 16 (1938): 260–271.

———. *Der Kampf um die Kirche im Dritten Reich.* Lucerne, 1936.

Haffner, Sebastian. *The Meaning of Hitler.* New York, 1979.

Hagen, William W. "Before the 'Final Solution': Toward a Comparative Analysis of Political Anti-Semitism in Interwar Germany and Poland." *Journal of Modern History* 68 (June 1996): 351–381.

Harcourt, Robert d'. "Dictature hitlerienne et Catholiques en Allemagne." *Revue des Deux Mondes,* June 15, 1933, 762–786.

———. "En Allemagne l'insurrection du spirituel." *Revue des Deux Mondes,* December 1, 1934, 528–556.

———. *The German Catholics.* Translated by Reginald Dingle. London, 1939.

———. "La guerre au Catholicisme en Allemagne." *Revue des Deux Mondes,* September 1, 1935, 66–84.

———. "L'offensive hitlerienne contre l'église: Une vague de boue." *Etudes* 231 (1937): 785–803.

———. "The Other Germany." *Dublin Review* 443 (1948): 75–90.

———. "La religion du sang." *Etudes* 235 (1938): 500–516.

———. "Roman Catholic Church and National Socialism." *Nineteenth-Century and After* 126 (1938–39): 64–72.

Harrigan, William M. "Nazi Germany and the Holy See, 1933–36: The Historical Background." *Catholic Historical Review* 47 (1961): 164–198.

———. "Pius XII's Efforts to Effect a Détente in German-Vatican Relations, 1939–40." *Catholic Historical Review* 49 (1963): 173–191.

Hasenkamp, Gottfried. *Heimkehr und Heimgang des Kardinals.* Münster, 1946.

————. *Der Kardinal: Taten und Tage des Bischofs von Münster, Clemens August Graf von Galen.* Münster, 1984.

Hassell, Ulrich von. *The Other Germany.* Zurich, 1948.

Hatfield, W. "Kulturkampf: The Relationship of Church and State and the Failure of German Political Reform." *Journal of Church and State* 23 (1981): 465–484.

Heer, Friedrich. *Challenge of Youth.* Translated from the German by Geoffrey Skelton. University, Ala., 1974.

Hehl, Ulrich von, and Konrad Repgen. *Der deutsche Katholizismus in der zeitgeschichtlichen Forschung.* Mainz, 1988.

————. *Priester unter Hitlers Terror: Eine Biographische und Statistische Erhebung.* In the series Auftrag der Deutschen Bischofskonferenz unter Mitwirkung der Diözesanarchive. Ser. A, Sources, vol. 37. Mainz, 1984.

Heilbronner, Oded. *Catholicism, Political Culture, and the Countryside: A Social History of the Nazi Party in South Germany.* Ann Arbor, Mich., 1998.

————. "From Ghetto to Ghetto: The Place of German Catholic Society in Recent Historiography." *Journal of Modern History* 72 (June 2000): 453–495.

Heitzer, Horst W. "Deutscher Katholizismus und 'Bolschewismusgefahr' bis 1933." *Historisches Jahrbuch* 113, no. 2 (1993): 355–387.

Helmreich, Ernst Christian. *The German Churches under Hitler: Background, Struggle, and Epilogue.* Detroit, 1979.

————. *Religious Education in German Schools.* Cambridge, Mass., 1959.

Herbermann, Nanda, Hester Baer, and Elizabeth Roberts Baer, eds. *The Blessed Abyss: Inmate #6582 in Ravensbruck Concentration Camp for Women.* Detroit, 2000.

Herzog, Dagmar. *Intimacy and Exclusion: Religious Politics in Pre-Revolutionary Baden.* Princeton, N.J., 1996.

Herzstein, Robert E. *The War That Hitler Won: Nazi Propaganda.* London, 1979.

Heschel, Susannah. *Abraham Geiger and the Jewish Jesus.* Chicago, 1998.

Heydrich, Reinhard. "Gibt es noch Staatsfeinde?" *Westdeutscher Beobachter* 199 (April 30, 1936).

Hilberg, Raul. *The Destruction of the European Jews.* Rev. ed. New York, 1985.

————. *Perpetrators, Victims, and Bystanders.* New York, 1992.

Hirsch, Martin, Diemut Majer, and Jurgen Meinck, eds. *Recht, Verwaltung und Justiz im Nationalsozialismus: Ausgewählte Schriften, Gesetze und Gerichtsentscheidungen von 1933 bis 1945.* Cologne, 1984.

Hochhuth, Rolf. *The Deputy.* New York, 1964.

————. "'Eine ungeheure Lüge': Hat der Vatikan hunderttausende Juden vor dem Holocaust gerettet?" *Die Zeit* 13 (March 1998).

————. *Der Stellvertreter.* Hamburg, 1963.

Hoffmann, Peter. *German Resistance to Hitler.* Cambridge, Mass., 1988.

————. *The History of the German Resistance, 1933–1945.* Translated by Richard Barry. London, 1977.

Hofmann, Konrad. *Zeugnis und Kämpfe des deutschen Episkopats: Gemeinsame Hirtenbriefe und Denkschreiben.* Freiburg, 1946.

Höllen, Martin. *Heinrich Wienken, der "unpolitische" Kirchenpolitiker: Eine Biographie aus drei Epochen des deutschen Katholizismus.* Mainz, 1981.

———. "Katholische Kirche und NS-'Euthanasie': Eine vergleichende Analyse neuer Quellen." *Zeitschrift für Kirchengeschichte* 91 (1980): 53–82.

Holmes, J. Derek. *The Papacy in the Modern World.* New York, 1981.

Horn, Daniel. "The Struggle for Catholic Youth in Hitler's Germany: An Assessment." *Catholic Historical Review* 65 (1979): 561–582.

Hünermann, Wilhelm. *Clemens August: Aus dem Lebensbuch des Kardinals Graf von Galen.* Bonn, 1947.

Hürten, Heinz. *Kurze Geschichte des deutschen Katholizismus, 1800–1960.* Mainz, 1986.

Husen, Paulus van. "The 20th of July and the German Catholics." *Dublin Review* 219, no. 438 (July 1946): 1–9.

International Military Tribunal. *Trials of the Major War Criminals before the International Military Tribunals.* Washington, D.C., 1951.

Iserloh, Erwin. "Bischof Clemens August von Galen (1878–1946)." In *Kirche, Ereignis und Institution: Aufsätze und Vorträge,* edited by Erwin Iserloh, 427–435. 2 vols. Münster, 1985.

———. "Vom Abschluss des Reichskonkordats bis zur Ratifikation." *Trier Theologische Zeitschrift* 72 (1963): 39–52.

Jedin, Hubert, ed. *Handbuch der Kirchengeschichte.* Vol. 6. Freiburg, 1973.

Johnson, Eric A. *Nazi Terror: The Gestapo, Jews, and Ordinary Germans.* New York, 1999.

Jones, Larry Eugene. *Between Reform, Reaction, and Resistance: Studies in the History of German Conservatism from 1789 to 1945.* Providence, R.I., 1993.

———. "Catholic Conservatives in the Weimar Republic: The Politics of the Rhenish-Westphalian Aristocracy, 1918–1933." *German History* 18, no. 1 (2000): 60–85.

Kaplan, Marion A. *Between Dignity and Despair: Jewish Life in Nazi Germany.* New York, 1998.

Kaufmann, Doris. *Katholisches Milieu in Münster, 1928–1933.* Düsseldorf, 1984.

Kent, George O. "Pope Pius XII and Germany: Some Aspects of German-Vatican Relations, 1933–1943." *American Historical Review* 70 (1964): 54–78.

Kershaw, Ian. "German Popular Opinion and the 'Jewish Question,' 1939–1943: Some Further Reflections." In *Hostages of Modernization: Studies on Modern Antisemitism, 1870–1939,* edited by Herbert A. Strauss, 269–279. New York, 1993.

———. *Hitler, 1889–1936: Hubris.* New York, 1999.

———. *Hitler, 1936–1945: Nemesis.* New York, 2000.

———. *The Nazi Dictatorship: Problems and Perspectives of Interpretation.* 4th ed. London, 2000.

————. "The Persecution of the Jews and German Popular Opinion in the Third Reich." *Leo Baeck Institute Yearbook* 26 (1981): 261–289.

————. *Popular Opinion and Political Dissent in the Third Reich: Bavaria, 1933–1945.* Oxford, 1983.

Kersten, Felix. *The Kersten Memoirs, 1940–45.* London, 1956.

Ketteler, Wilhelm. *Freiheit, Autorität und Kirche: Erörterungen über die grossen Probleme der Gegenwart.* Mainz, 1862.

Kirchmann, S. *St. Ambrosius und die deutschen Bischöfe.* Lucerne, 1934.

Klee, Ernst. *"Euthanasie" im NS-Staat: Die "Vernichtung Lebensunwerten Lebens."* Frankfurt, 1983.

Klocke, Irmgard. *Kardinal von Galen: Der Löwe von Münster zum 100 Geburtstag.* Pattloch, Germany, 1979.

Koch, Antony. *A Handbook of Moral Theology.* Adapted and edited by Arthur Preuss. 5 vols. London, 1918.

Koch, Hansjoachim Wolfgang. *The Hitler Youth: Origins and Development, 1922–1945.* London, 1975.

————, ed. *Aspects of the Third Reich.* London, 1985.

Kocka, Jürgen, ed. *Theorien in der Praxis des Historikers.* Göttingen, 1977.

Koonz, Claudia. *Mothers in the Fatherland: Women, the Family, and Nazi Politics.* New York, 1987.

Kulka, Otto Dov, and Paul R. Mendes-Flohr, eds. *Judaism and Christianity under the Impact of National Socialism.* Jerusalem, 1987.

Kulka, Otto Dov, and Aron Rodrique. "The German Population and the Jews in the Third Reich: Recent Publications and Trends in Research on German Society and the 'Jewish Question.'" *Yad Vashem Studies* 16 (1984).

Kuropka, Joachim. "Eine diplomatische Aktion aus dem Jahre 1945 um die Romreise des Bischofs Clemens August von Münster: Zur Problematik des Verhältnisses von Kirche und Besatzungsmacht in den ersten Monaten nach der Kapitulation." *Westfälische Forschungen* 28 (1976–1977): 206–211.

————. "Vom Antisemitismus zum Holocaust: Zu Vorgeschichte und Folgen des 9. November 1938 unter Berücksichtigung der Stadt Münster." *Westfälische Zeitschrift* 140 (1990): 185–205.

————. "Widerstand gegen den Nationalsozialismus in Münster: Neuere Forschungen zu einigen Problemfeldern." *Westfälische Zeitschrift* 137 (1987): 159–182.

————, ed. *Clemens August Graf von Galen: Neue Forschungen zum Leben und Wirken des Bischofs von Münster.* Münster, 1992.

Kuropka, Joachim, and Maria-Anna Zumholz, eds. *Clemens August Graf von Galen: Sein Leben und Wirken in Bildern und Dokumenten.* Cloppenburg, Germany, 1992.

Langer, William, and R. Gleason. *The Undeclared War.* New York, 1953.

Laqueur, Walter. *The Terrible Secret: An Investigation into the Suppression of Information about Hitler's "Final Solution."* London, 1980.

Large, David Clay. *Berlin.* New York, 2000.

———, ed. *Contending with Hitler: Varieties of German Resistance in the Third Reich.* Cambridge, Mass., 1991.

Lehmann, Leo. *Vatican Politics in the Second World War.* New York, 1945.

Lehr, Robert, ed. *Germans against Hitler: July 20, 1944.* Translated by Allan Yahraes and Liselotte Yahraes. Wiesbaden, Germany, 1969.

Leiber, Robert. "Pius XII." *Stimmen der Zeit* 163 (1958): 81–101.

Leufkens, Josef, ed. *Clemens August, Kardinal von Galen: Ein Gedenkblatt zur Ruckkehr des Bischofs von Münster aus Rom nach seiner Erhebung zum Kardinal.* Münster, 1946.

Levy, Richard. *Anti-Semitism in the Modern World: An Anthology of Texts.* Lexington, Mass., 1991.

———. *The Downfall of the Anti-Semitic Liberal Parties in Imperial Germany.* New Haven, Conn., 1975.

Lewy, Günther. *The Catholic Church and Nazi Germany.* New York, 1964.

Lifton, Robert. *Nazi Doctors: Medical Killing and the Psychology of Genocide.* New York, 1986.

Littell, Franklin H., and Hubert G. Locke, eds. *The German Church Struggle and the Holocaust.* Detroit, 1974.

Liulevicius, Vejas Gabriel. *War Land on the Eastern Front: Culture, National Identity and Germany Occupation in World War I.* Cambridge, 2000.

Löcher, Paul. *In Gottesfurcht wandeln: Texte des Kardinals von Münster.* Ostfildern, Germany, 1978.

Löwenstein, Karl. "Law in the Third Reich." *Yale Law Journal* (1948): 724–760, 994–1022.

Lowenthal, Richard, and Patrik von zur Muehlen, eds. *Widerstand und Verweigerung in Deutschland, 1933 bis 1945.* Berlin, 1982.

Lüdke, Alf, ed. *The History of Everyday Life: Reconstructing Historical Experiences and Ways of Life.* Translated by William Templer. Princeton, N.J., 1995.

Lukacs, John. *The Hitler of History.* New York, 1998.

Madden, Paul. "Some Social Characteristics of Early Nazi Party Members, 1919–1923." *Central European Quarterly* (1982): 34–56.

Margaliot, Abraham. "The Reaction of the Jewish Public in Germany to the Nuremberg Laws." *Yad Vashem Studies* 12 (1977).

Mariaux, Walter, ed. *The Persecution of the Catholic Church in Germany: Facts and Documents.* Translated from the German. London, 1942.

———. *Dokumente betreffend die Verhandlunger zwischen der Hl.Stuhl und der Reichsregierung über des Ausfruhung der Reichskonkordat.* 3 vols. N.p., n.d.

Maron, Gottfried. *Die romish-Katholische Kirche von 1870 bis 1970.* Göttingen, 1972.

Marrus, Michael. *The Holocaust in History.* New York, 1987.

———. "The Vatican and the Holocaust." *Congress Monthly,* January 1988.

Mason, Timothy. *Arbeiterklasse und Volksgemeinschaft.* Opladen, Germany, 1975.

———. "The Workers' Opposition in Nazi Germany." *History Workshop Journal* 11 (1981): 120–137.

Matchewsky, Rector. *Katholische Rundschau,* April 1, 1905.

Matheson, Peter, ed. *The Third Reich and the Christian Churches.* Grand Rapids, Mich., 1981.

Mayer, Arno. *Why Did the Heavens Not Darken? The "Final Solution of the Jewish Question" in the Third Reich.* New York, 1988.

Mayer, Joseph. *Gesetzliche Unfruchtbarmachung Geisteskranker.* Freiburg, 1927.

McKale, Donald. *The Nazi Party Courts.* Lawrence, Kans., 1974.

McLeod, Hugh. *Piety and Poverty: Working-Class Religion in Berlin, London, and New York, 1870–1914.* New York, 1996.

Meier, Kurt. "Kirche und Nationalsozialismus: Ein Beitrag zum Problem der nationalsozialistischen Religionspolitik." In *Zur Geschichte des Kirchenkampfes,* edited by Heinz Brunötte, 9–29. Göttingen, 1971.

Merkl, Peter. *Political Violence under the Swastika: 581 Early Nazis.* Princeton, N.J., 1975.

Merritt, Anna, and Richard Merritt. *Public Opinion in Occupied Germany: The OMGUS Surveys, 1945–1949.* Urbana, Ill., 1970.

Messner, Johannes. "Der deutsche Katholizismus nach dem Reichskonkordat." *Schönere Zukunft* 8 (1933): 1099–1101.

Micklem, Nathaniel. *National Socialism and the Roman Catholic Church.* London, 1939.

Mikat, Paul. "Zur Kundgebung der Fuldaer Bischofskonferenz über die nationalsozialistische Bewegung vom 28. Marz 1933." *Jahrbuch des Instituts für christliche Sozialwissenschaften der Universität Münster* 3 (1962): 209–235.

Minuth, Karl-Heinz, ed. *Die Regierung Hitler: Teil I, 1933–34.* 2 vols. Boppard am Rhein, Germany, 1983.

Mommsen, Hans. "Die Realisierung des Utopischen: Die 'Endlösung der Judenfrage' im Dritten Reich." *Geschichte und Gesellschaft* 9 (1983): 381–420.

Morley, John. *Vatican Diplomacy and the Jews during the Holocaust: 1939–1943.* New York, 1980.

Morsey, Rudolf. "Clemens August, Kardinal von Galen: Versuch einer historischen Würdigung." *Jahrbuch für Instituts für christliche Sozialwissenschaften der Westfälischen Wilhelms—Universität Münster* 7–8 (1966–1967): 367–382.

———. "Clemens August Kardinal von Galen: Bischöfliches Wirken in der Zeit der Hitler-Diktatur." *Internationale Katholische Zeitschrift "Communio"* 7 (1978): 429–442.

———. *Clemens August Kardinal von Galen zum Gedachtnis.* Münster, 1967.

———. "Clemens August von Galen." *Zeitgeschichte in Lebensbildern* 2 (1975): 37–47.

———. "Zur Problematik und Geschichte des Reichskonkordats." *Neue Politische Literatur* (1960): 1–30.

———, ed. *Zeitgeschichte in Lebensbildern: Aus dem deutschen Katholizismus des 20 Jahrhunderts*. Mainz, 1975.

Muckermann, Friedrich. "An den Pforten des Reiches." *Der Graal* 22 (1927–1928): 205–214.

———. "Wir Katholiken und der Nationalsozialismus." *Schönere Zukunft* 7 (1932): 927–928.

Müller, Hans. "Zur Behandlung des Kirchenkampfes in der Nachkriegsliteratur." *Politische Studien* 12 (1961): 474–481.

———. "Zur Interpretation der Kundegebung der Fuldaer Bischofskonferenz vom 28. Marz 1933." *Werkhefte Katholischer Laien* 16 (1962): 196–200.

———. "Zur Vorgeschichte der Kundgebung der Fuldaer Bischofskonferenz vom 28. Marz 1933." *Werkhefte Katholischer Laien* 15 (1961): 258–265.

———, ed. *Katholische Kirche und Nationalsozialismus: Dokumente 1930–35*. Munich, 1963.

Müller, Ingo. *Hitler's Justice: The Courts of the Third Reich*. Translated by Deborah Lucas Schneider. Cambridge, Mass., 1991.

Müller, Klaus-Jürgen, ed. *Der deutsche Widerstand 1933–1945*. Paderborn, Germany, 1986.

"Münster: Cultural Center of Westphalia." *British Zone Review*, November 24, 1945, 24.

Mussinghoff, Heinz. *Rassenwahn in Münster: Der Judenpogrom 1938 und Bischof Clemens August Graf von Galen*. Münster, 1989.

Muth, Karl. "Das Reich als Idee und Wirklichkeit—Einst und Jetzt." *Hochland* 30 (1932–1933): 481–492.

Neuhäusler, Johann. "Bertram and Faulhaber Letters." *Thought* 20 (December 1945): 752–759.

Neuss, Wilhelm. *Kampf gegen den Mythus des 20. Jahrhunderts: Ein Gedenkblatt an Clemens August Kardinal Graf Galen*. Cologne, 1947.

Neyer, Paschalis. *Mit Herzblut geschrieben*. Werl, Germany, 1951, 109–122 (reprint of von Galen's letter of January 10, 1928, to his nephew Bernhard).

Nicolai, Helmut. *Rassengesetzliche Rechtslehre: Grundzüge einer nationalsozialistichen Rechtsphilosophie*. Munich, 1932.

Nowak, Kurt. *"Euthanasie" und Sterilisierung im "Dritten Reich": Die Konfrontation der Evangelischen und Katholischen Kirche mit dem "Gesetz zur Verhütung erbkranken Nachwuches" und der "Euthanasie"—Aktion*. Göttingen, 1978.

Oberländer, Franklin A. "My God, They Just Have Other Interests." *Oral History Review* 24, no. 1 (summer 1997): 23–53.

O'Meara, Thomas Franklin. *Church and Culture: German Catholic Theology, 1860–1914*. London, 1991.

Padover, Saul K. *Experiment in Germany*. New York, 1946.

Pawlikowski, John T. "Catholic Leadership and the Holocaust: An Uneven Response." *Proceedings of the Second Biennial Conference on Christianity and the Holocaust "Voices: Institutional and Individual Responses to the Holocaust."* Rider College, Lawrenceville, N.J., April 5-7, 1992.

———. "The Catholic Response to the Holocaust: Institutional Perspectives." In *The Holocaust and History: The Known, the Unknown, the Disputed and the Re-examined,* edited by Michael Berenbaum and Abraham J. Peck, 551-566. Bloomington, Ind., 1998.

Pechel, Rudolf. *Deutscher Widerstand.* Zurich, 1947.

Pehle, Walter H., ed. *Der Judenpogrom 1938: Von der "Reichskristallnacht" zum Völkermord.* Frankfurt, 1988.

Perry, Marvin, and Frederick M. Schweitzer. *Jewish-Christian Encounters over the Centuries: Symbiosis, Prejudice, Holocaust, Dialogue.* New York, 1994.

Peukert, Detlev. *Inside Nazi Germany: Conformity, Opposition, and Racism in Everyday Life.* London, 1987.

———. "Young People: For or against the Nazis?" *History Today* (1985): 15-22.

Phayer, Michael. *The Catholic Church and the Holocaust, 1930-1965.* Bloomington, Ind., 2000.

———. *Protestant and Catholic Women in Nazi Germany.* Detroit, Mich., 1990.

Pieper, Josef. *No One Could Have Known: An Autobiography: The Early Years, 1904-1945.* Translated by Graham Harrison. San Francisco, 1987.

Portmann, Heinrich. *Bischof Graf von Galen spricht! Ein apostolischer Kampf und sein Widerhall.* Freiburg, Breisgau, 1946.

———. *Der Bischof von Münster.* Münster, 1946.

———. *Der Bischof von Münster: Das Echo eines Kampfes für Gottesrecht und Menschenrecht.* Münster, 1947.

———. *Cardinal von Galen.* Translated by R. L. Sedgwick. London, 1957.

———. *Kardinal von Galen.* Münster, 1953.

———. *Kardinal von Galen: Ein Gottesmann seiner Zeit: Mit einem Anhang "Die drei weltberühmten Predigten."* Münster, 1948, 1981, 1986. Page citations are to the 1948 edition.

———, ed. *Dokumente um den Bischof von Münster.* Münster, 1948.

Power, Michael. *Religion in the Reich.* New York, 1939.

Pribilla, Max. "Christliche Haltung." *Stimmen der Zeit* 135 (1939): 169-179.

———. *Deutsche Schicksalsfragen: Rückblick und Ausblick.* Frankfurt, 1950.

———. "Ehe und Familie." *Stimmen der Zeit* 134 (1938): 53-56.

———. "Der Kampf der Kirche." *Stimmen der Zeit* 129 (1935): 242-253.

———. "Nationale Revolution." *Stimmen der Zeit* 125 (1933): 156-168.

———. "Nationalsozialistische Weltanschauung." *Stimmen der Zeit* 126 (1933): 415-418.

———. "Das Schweigen des deutschen Volkes." *Stimmen der Zeit* 139 (1946): 15-33.

———. "Verfassungstreue." *Stimmen der Zeit* 125 (1933): 57-61.

Prittie, Terence. *Germans against Hitler.* London, 1964.

Proctor, Robert. *Racial Hygiene: Medicine under the Nazis.* Cambridge, Mass., 1988.

Przywara, Erich. *Analogia Entis, Metaphysik.* Munich, 1932.

———. "Judentum und Christentum." *Stimmen der Zeit* 110 (1926): 83–99.

———. "Judentum und Christentum: Zwischen Orient und Okzident." *Stimmen der Zeit* 110 (1925–1926): 81–99.

———. *Logos, Abendland, Reich, Commercium.* Düsseldorf, 1964.

———. "Nation, Staat, Kirche." *Stimmen der Zeit* 125 (1933): 370–379.

Pulzer, Peter G. J. *The Rise of Political Anti-Semitism in Germany and Austria.* New York, 1964.

Quinn, Edward. "Nazism and Spiritual Resistance." *Commonweal,* November 25, 1938, 121–122.

Rahner, Stefan, Franz-Helmut Richter, Stefan Riese, and Dirk Stelter. *Treu deutsch sind wir—wir sind auch treu katholisch: Kardinal von Galen und das Dritte Reich.* Münster, 1987.

Rebbert, Joseph. *Blicke in's Talmudische Judentum: Nach den Forschungen den Dr. Konrad Martin, Bischof von Paderborn, dem christlichen Volke enthüllt.* Paderborn, Germany, 1876.

Reitlinger, Gerald. *The Final Solution.* London, 1953.

Rensing, F. "Clemens August Graf von Galen als Kuratus von St. Clemens und Kolpingspräses in Berlin." In *Paulus und Ludiger: Ein Jahrbuch aus dem Bistum Münster* 2 (1948): 28–36.

Repgen, Konrad. "Zur vatikanischen Strategie beim Reichskonkordat." *Vierteljahreshefte für Zeitgeschichte* 31 (1983): 506–535.

Rhodes, Anthony. *The Vatican in the Age of the Dictators, 1922–45.* London, 1973.

Ritter, Gerhard. "The German Opposition to Hitler" *Contemporary Review* 177 (1950): 339–345.

Rohling, August. *Der Talmudjude: Zur Beherzigung für Juden und Christen aller Stände.* 4th ed. Münster, 1873.

Roth, Heinrich, ed. *Katholische Jugend in der NS-Zeit.* Düsseldorf, 1959.

Rothfels, Hans. *The German Opposition to Hitler.* London, 1961.

———. "International Aspects of German Oppostion to Hitler." *Measure* 2 (1951): 175–190.

Ruhm von Oppen, Beate. *Religion and Resistance to Nazism.* Research Monograph no. 35, Center for International Studies, Woodrow Wilson School of Public and International Affairs, Princeton University, March 1971.

Rüter, Gregor, and Rainer Westhoff. *Geschichte und Schicksal der Telgter Juden, 1933–1945.* Telgte, 1985.

Sandstede-Auzelle, Marie-Corentine, and Gerd Sandstede. *Clemens August Graf von Galen: Bischof von Galen im Dritten Reich.* Münster, 1986.

Schäfer, Gerhard, ed. *Landesbischof D. Wurm und der nationalsozialistische Staat, 1940–1945: Eine Dokumentation.* Stuttgart, 1968.

Scheinmann, Mikhail Markovich. *Der Vatikan in Zweiten Weltkrieg.* East Berlin,
    1954.
Schilling, Otto. "Das Prinzip der Moral." *Theologische Quartalschrift* (1938): 419–
    426.
———. "Quelle und Charakter des Völkerrechtes." *Theologische Quartalschrift*
    (1939): 289–295.
———. "Richtiges und Falsches bei der sog. Eugenik." *Schönere Zukunft* 7 (1932):
    570–598.
———. "Die sozial Gerechtigkeit." *Theologische Quartalschrift* (1933): 269–277.
———. "Von der sozialen Gerechtigkeit." *Theologische Quartalschrift* (1939): 197–
    205.
Schlabendorff, Fabian von. *Offiziere gegen Hitler.* Zurich, 1946.
Schlömer, Hans. "Die deutschen Bischöfe und der Nationalsozialismus: Zur Vor-
    geschichte der bischoflichen Erklärung vom 28. Marz 1933." *KNA-Informa-
    tionsdienst* 9, no. 34 (September 2, 1961).
Schmädeke, Jürgen, and Peter Steinbach, eds. *Der Widerstand gegen den National-
    sozialismus.* Munich, 1985.
Schmaus, Michael. *Begegnungen zwischen katholischem Christentum und national-
    sozialistischer Weltanschauung.* 2nd ed. Münster, 1934.
———. *Katholische Dogmatik.* 3 vols. Munich, 1937–1941.
———. *Katholische Dogmatik.* 5th ed. 5 vols. Munich, 1954–1958.
Schmidt, Reinhold. *Der Kardinal und das Dritte Reich: Legende und Wahrheit über
    Kardinal von Galen.* 1st ed., Münster, May 1978; 2nd ed., September 1978;
    3rd ed., 1980.
Schmitthenner, Walter, and Hans Buchheim, eds. *Der deutsche Widerstand gegen
    Hitler.* Berlin, 1966.
Scholder, Klaus. *The Churches and the Third Reich: Preliminary History and the
    Time of Illusions, 1918–1934.* Translated by John Bowden. Philadelphia, 1988.
———. *Die Kirchen und das Dritte Reich: Vorgeschichte und Zeit der Illusionen,
    1918–1934.* Frankfurt, 1977.
———. *Die Kirche zwischen Republik und Gewaltherrschaft.* Berlin, 1988.
———. *A Requiem for Hitler and Other New Perspectives on the German Church
    Struggle.* Translated by John Bowden. Philadelphia, 1989.
Schreiber, Georg. *Zwischen Demokratie und Diktatur: Personliche Erinnerungen
    an die Politik und Kultur des Reiches, 1919–1944.* Münster, 1949.
Schwartz, Gisela. "Widerstand und Verweigerung im Münsterland, 1933–1945:
    Eine Untersuchung zu Oppositionsformen gegen das NS-Regime in West-
    falen." *Westfälische Forschungen* 34 (1984): 207–219.
Seydewitz, Max. *Civil Life in Wartime Germany: The Story of the Home Front.*
    New York, 1945.
Sinsheimer, Hermann. "The German Resistance Movement" *Political Quarterly*
    19 (1948): 356–362.

Smith, Helmut Walser. *German Nationalism and Religious Conflict: Culture, Ideology, Politics, 1870–1914.* Princeton, N.J., 1995.

———. "The Learned and Popular Discourse of Anti-Semitism in the Catholic Milieu of the Kaiserreich." *Central European History* 3 (1994): 315–328.

———. "Religion and Conflict: Protestants, Catholics, and Anti-Semitism in the State of Baden in the Era of Wilhelm II." *Central European History* 3 (1994): 283–314.

Smith, Patrick. *The Bishop of Münster and the Nazis.* London, 1943.

Sperber, Jonathan. *Popular Catholicism in Nineteenth-Century Germany.* Princeton, N.J., 1984.

———. "Roman Catholic Religious Identity in Rhineland-Westphalia, 1800–70: Quantitative Examples and Some Political Implications." *Social History* 7 (1982): 305–318.

———. "The Transformation of Catholic Associations in the Northern Rhineland and Westphalia, 1830–1870." *Journal of Social History* 14 (1981): 253–263.

Spotts, Frederic. *The Churches and Politics in Germany.* Middleton, Conn., 1973.

Stachura, Peter D. *The German Youth Movement 1900–45: An Interpretative and Documentary History.* New York, 1981.

———, ed. *The Shaping of the Nazi State.* London, 1978.

Staff, Ilse, ed. *Justiz im Dritten Reich: Eine Dokumentation.* 2nd ed. Frankfurt, 1978.

Stehle, Hansjakob. "Widerstand mit Widersprüchen: Des Bischofs von Münster treudeutscher Löwenmut: Zum 50. Todestag des Grafen Galen." *Die Zeit* 13 (March 29, 1996): 24.

Steinert, Marlis. *Hitlers Krieg und die Deutschen: Stimmung und Haltung der deutschen Bevölkerung im zweiten Weltkrieg.* Düsseldorf, 1970.

Stern, Fritz. *Dreams and Delusions: The Drama of German History.* New York, 1989.

Steward, John, ed. *Sieg des Glaubens.* Zurich, 1946.

Stoltzfus, Nathan. "Dissent in Nazi Germany." *Atlantic Monthly,* September 1994.

Stolz, Alban. "Schreibende Hand auf Wand und Sand." In *Gesammelte Werke,* vol. 16. Freiburg, 1894.

Strang, William. *Home and Abroad.* London, 1956.

Streit, Christian. "Ostkrieg, Antibolschewismus und 'Endlösung.'" *Geschichte und Gesellschaft* 17 (1991): 242–255.

Strobel, Ferdinand. *Christliche Bewährung: Dokumente des Widerstandes der katholischen Kirche in Deutschland, 1933–1945.* Olten, Switzerland, 1946.

Sybel, Heinrich von. *Kleine Schriften.* Stuttgart, 1880.

Tal, Uriel. *Christians and Jews in Germany: Religion, Politics, and Ideology in the Second Reich, 1870–1914.* Translated by Noah Jonathan Jacobs. Ithaca, N.Y., 1975.

———. *Religious and Anti-Religious Roots of Modern Anti-Semitism.* New York, 1971.

Thien, Hans-Günter, Hans Wienold, and Sabine Preuss, eds. *Überwältigte Vergangenheit-Erinnerungsscherben: Faschismus und Nachkriegszeit.* Münster, 1985.

Thomas, Theodore N. *Women against Hitler: Christian Resistance in the Third Reich.* Westport, Conn., 1995.

Tinnemann, Ethel Mary. "Attitudes of the German Catholic Hierarchy toward the Nazi Regime: A Study in German Psycho-Political Culture." *Western Political Quarterly* 22 (1969): 333–349.

———. "The Silence of Pope Pius XII." *Journal of Church and State* 21 (1979): 265–285.

Treitschke, Heinrich von. *Deutsche Geschichte im Neunzehnten Jahrhundert.* 4th ed., 5 vols. Leipzig, 1890.

———. *History of Germany in the Nineteenth Century.* Selections from the translation by Eden and Cedar Paul, edited by Gordon A. Craig. Chicago, 1975.

Trommler, Frank. "'Between Normality and Resistance': Catastrophic Gradualism in Nazi Germany." *Journal of Modern History* 64 (1992): 82–101.

Vernekohl, Wilhelm. *Begegnungen, kleine Portrats.* Münster, 1959.

———. *Über das Unzerstorbäre.* Münster, 1952.

Volk, Ludwig. "Die Fuldaer Bischofskonferenz von der Enzyklika 'Mit brennender Sorge' bis zum Ende der N.S.-Herrschaft." *Stimmen der Zeit* 178 (1966): 241–267.

———. *Das Reichskonkordat vom 20. Juli 1933: Von den Ansatzen in der Weimarer Republik bis zur Ratifizierung am 10. September 1933.* Vol. 5. Mainz, 1972.

Vollmer, Bernhard. *Volksopposition im Polizeistaat.* Stuttgart, 1957.

Walker, Lawrence D. *Hitler Youth and Catholic Youth, 1933–36.* New York, 1979.

———. *Hitler Youth and Catholic Youth, 1933–36: A Study in Totalitarian Conquest.* Washington, D.C, 1970.

Wall, Donald D. "The Reports of the Sicherheitsdienst on the Church and Religious Affairs in Germany, 1933–1944." *Church History* 40 (1971): 437–456.

Walther, Franz. *Die Euthanasie und die Heiligkeit des Lebens: Die Lebensvernichtung im Dienste der Medizin und Eugenik nach christlichen und materialistischer Ethik.* Munich, 1935.

Ward, W. R. "Guilt and Innocence: The German Churches in the Twentieth Century." *Journal of Modern History* 68 (June 1996): 398–426.

Warholoski, Ronald Alfred. *Neudeutschland: German Catholic Youth, 1919–1939.* Pittsburgh, 1964.

Watt, D. C. "Les allies et la Resistance Allemande, 1939–44." *Revue de deuxieme Guerre Mondiale* 9 (1959): 65.

Weber, Christoph. *Kirchliche Politik zwischen Rom, Berlin, und Trier, 1876–1888.* Mainz, 1970.

Wurm, Theophil. *Erinnerungen aus meinem Leben.* Stuttgart, 1953.

Wust, Peter. *Briefe an Freunde.* Münster, 1955.

Zahn, Gordon. "Catholic Opposition to Hitler: The Perils of Ambiguity." *Journal of Church and State* 13 (1971): 413–425.

———. *German Catholics and Hitler's Wars: A Study in Social Control.* New York, 1962.

———. *In Solitary Witness: The Life and Death of Franz Jaegerstaetter.* New York, 1964.

Zipfel, Friedrich. *Kirchenkampf in Deutschland, 1933–45.* Berlin, 1965.

Zuccotti, Susan. *Under His Very Windows: The Vatican and the Holocaust in Italy.* New Haven, Conn., 2000.

Index